HOMEGIRLS in the Public Sphere

HOMEGIRLS

in the

Public

Sphere

Marie "Keta" Miranda

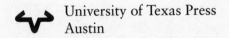
University of Texas Press
Austin

Requests for permission to reproduce material from this work
should be sent to Permissions, University of Texas Press,
Box 7819, Austin, TX 78713-7819.

♾ The paper used in this book meets the minimum
requirements of ANSI/NISO Z39.48-1992 (R1997)
(Permanence of Paper).

Library of Congress Cataloging-in-Publication Data

Miranda, Marie, 1950–
    Homegirls in the public sphere / Marie "Keta" Miranda.—
1st ed.
        p.   cm.
Includes bibliographical references and index.
    ISBN 0-292-70546-8 (cloth : alk. paper) —
ISBN 0-292-70192-6 (pbk. : alk. paper)
    1. Gangs—California—Oakland. 2. Female
gangs—California—Oakland. 3. Hispanic American
women—California—Oakland. 4. Female juvenile deliquents—
California—Oakland. 5. Teenage girls—California—Oakland.
I. Title.
HV6439.U7 0195 2003
364.1′06′608968079466—dc21

                                                    2003009778

To the young women of Oakland

CONTENTS

LIST OF ABBREVIATIONS

CDD   Community Development Districts
CFO   Coalition Forums of Oakland
DC   Da Crew
ESN   East Side Norteñas
FBI   Fresh Bitches In(effect)
FCC   Fruitvale Community Collaborative
FNL   Friday Night Live, events sponsored by Mothers Against
           Drunk Driving
LN   Las Norteñas
NACCS   National Association for Chicano/Chicana Studies
NEL   Narcotics Education League
NWA   Norteñas With Attitude
OCTF   Oakland Crack Task Force
PSA   Public service announcement
PUEBLO   People United for a Better Oakland
SFIFF   San Francisco International Film Festival
UC   University of California
WoC   Research Cluster for the Study of Women of Color in
           Conflict and Collaboration, at UC Santa Cruz

Initials used for the young women of Fruitvale

AD   Member of East Side Norteñas
DV   Member of second generation, Da Crew
FN   Former leader and member of Las Norteñas
GG   Founder and former member of East Side Norteñas
LK   Member of eighth generation, Da Crew; African American
MG   Founder and former leader of Da Crew, first and second
           generations
QG   Leader of fourth generation, Da Crew

SP   Leader of third generation, Da Crew
TC   Leader of fourth generation, Da Crew
TR   Former member of Las Norteñas
VR   Member of fifth generation, Da Crew

ACKNOWLEDGMENTS

I would like to thank the NEL Centro de Juventud for providing support and space to conduct my research, particularly Rosalinda Palacios, the Centro administrator who welcomed my research project in its early, nebulous stage, and peer counselors María and Beatriz, whose support enhanced my project. My thanks to the young women who participated in the discussion group at the Centro, especially Bibi, Claudia, Ruskie, Tere, and Angie, who shared their lives with me even though there were no guarantees about what I would write.

I want to thank the many graduate students and members of the Research Cluster for the Study of Women of Color in Conflict and Collaboration who offered their support in countless ways throughout the field research and through the difficult process of writing, particularly Kehaulani, Luz, Catriona, Maylei, Joanne, Charla, Annie Lorrie, Deb, and Michelle. Special thanks to the Women of Color Film and Video Festival Committee, from whom I ripped off the initial title of this work: *Subversive Geographies*. My thanks also to Phil, Chris, Peg, Max, and my *colegas* at the University of Texas, San Antonio, Josie Mendez-Negrete and Lisa de la Portilla. Special thanks to Michelle Zamora, Alice Sunshine, and Anne Boyd for all their help, and to my editor, Theresa May, for understanding my project.

With special appreciation for their enthusiastic and critical engagement with the various stages of this study as well as the many intriguing questions that critiqued my assumptions, I am grateful for the support and guidance of Olga Najera-Ramirez and Angela Y. Davis, who patiently considered my many paths in developing this project. My indebtedness to Rosa Linda Fregoso, whose work on representation and the public sphere emboldened me to frame my project. My appreciation to Herman Gray, who worked with me from the first stages of fieldwork to the production of the thesis, helping me to recognize and comprehend. And my deepest appreciation to Jim Clifford, who labored over my many drafts, offering great advice and through this process of revising and editing helped me discover the resonance of this project.

Finally, my love and prayers of thanks for my family, who sustain and nurture me through all of life's joys and sorrows.

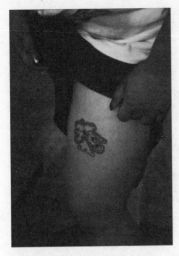

Body Speak/Smile now, cry later.
Photo by Anne Boyd.

New tat'/Red of the rose means
Norteña affiliation.
Photo by Anne Boyd.

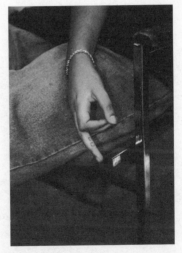

Homies/Best friends.
Photo by Anne Boyd.

Signin'/F*#@ off.
Photo by Anne Boyd.

Unity Council. Photo by Alice Sunshine.

Mercado. Photo by Alice Sunshine.

Looking toward Fruitvale. Photo by Alice Sunshine.

Fruitvale near 580. Photo by Alice Sunshine.

Church on Fruitvale. Photo by Alice Sunshine.

Fruitvale and 14th Street. Photo by Alice Sunshine.

La Clínica. Photo by Alice Sunshine.

12th Street and Fruitvale. Photo by Alice Sunshine.

Close-up view of mural on Fruitvale. Photo by Alice Sunshine.

HOMEGIRLS in the Public Sphere

REPRESENTATION AND
THE PUBLIC SPHERE

It was one thing to publish ethnographies about Trobrianders and Kwakiutls
half a century ago; it is another to study people who read what you write
and are more than willing to talk back.　　　　AMÉRICO PAREDES

In May 1994 I took ten Latina youth from Oakland to the San Francisco
International Film Festival (SFIFF) to see the screening of Allison Anders' *Mi Vida Loca*. They were excited about this film because it was
about girls in gangs—the first-ever such feature-length film! Moreover,
their excitement was stirred because a university professor, Rosa Linda
Fregoso, had talked about it at a conference they attended. The public
was finally interested in girls and gangs, finally talking, showing and
writing about the life these girls knew intimately. Before the film began,
a festival official announced that Anders and some of the actresses would
hold a question-and-answer session after the screening. When the discussion began, the teens from Fruitvale took over. More than half the
young women had their hands raised, and a few just stood up and spoke.
　　Anders' film captured the language of youth. The prominence of tattoo and graffiti art, and her use of music to render the story line, skill-
fully expressed the subcultural style of Chicana youth in gangs. Multiple
narrators illustrated different points of view and ways of seeing life in a
gang. But the girls in the audience felt Anders had gotten something
wrong—the reason for the fights. She had worked with gang members
of Echo Park in Los Angeles for two years, preparing the script and producing her film (Breslauer 1992). And even though she had seen the solidarity the girls created, she did not understand how that solidarity was
sustained. Her young critics at SFIFF did not protest the specific por-
trayal as much as the cultural logic that Anders seemed to have missed.
For Anders, the critical problem was patriarchy, and the evidence was
women fighting women over men. The young women vehemently dis-
agreed. There was more to it than that. Their comments addressed what
it means to be a gang member: the variety of girls who join, issues of protection and loyalty, the gang as a voluntary association. Generally, they
seemed to be speaking more to the audience than to Anders—filling out
the film.

GG, a former member of East Side Norteñas, remarked on the variety of girls in gangs. "Some of us go to school and we get good grades, and some of us drop out, but we don't make people join. That's up to them." TC, who had rarely spoken in public meetings, also stressed the variety of gang members and the solidarity among girls in gangs who back up their partners. MG, a founder of Da Crew, had her hand up for a long while as other audience members critiqued the fact that a White woman portrayed Latinas and portrayed them as gang members. Finally, MG just stood up and falteringly stated, "Why did you do it like that? Why didn't you show the real fights. . . ?" Interpreting the comment as a question, Anders explained that she did not want to portray violence. She had kept most of the violence off-camera because she intended to focus on the personal relations among the girls. MG remained standing. Her statement was not a question. "Why did you show them fighting like that? Throwing down over a boy? Uh-uh, we don't do that. You didn't show the reasons we fight." Spurred by MG's critique, the young women began waving their hands, insisting on being recognized. Anders admitted that the girls she worked with in Los Angeles would agree that the fighting is not over boys. Nevertheless, she had heard the story she used from her daughter: a situation of two girls holding guns to each other over a man. Insisting that the incident really happened, Anders made it the major plot of the film because she was concerned about the divisions among women that arise because of men. At this the Latinas of Fruitvale clamored a unanimous "Ahhh, no!"

When other members of the audience were critical of Anders—as an outsider, a Euro-American, representing Latina youth—the Latina teenagers didn't seem to side with that criticism. They seemed equally uninterested in other critical questions presented by the audience members. Audience participants challenged Anders' intention, asking her questions such as "Why weren't families portrayed in the film?" or "Why represent Latina youth solely as gang members when there are other Latino youth subcultures?" These types of questions tended to emphasize Anders' outsider position in the Latino community. At one point, a Latina who had been trying to get in a question finally stood up and addressed the girls who had been hoarding the discussion time: "Make your own films! That's what *we* have to do!" To which the girls responded, "We did!" When Anders directed her attention to the woman who had questioned her authority to represent the Chicana/o community, the girls continued to talk among themselves, their bodies huddled over the theater chairs in intense discussion. Since they were taking up so much of the discussion period, Anders invited the girls to speak with her later. The Latina youth had a lot to say but had only one question: How could she help them with the video they were producing?

NOT A GANG STUDY

Dorinne Kondo (1990) has written about ethnographic "setting tropes," narrative conventions that invoke the experience and journey of an ethnographer in an unfamiliar setting. The convention brings order to an otherwise chaotic, open-ended experience called fieldwork. For two and a half years, I conducted field research among Latina gang members in the community of Fruitvale in Oakland, California. But instead of "setting" my fieldwork in the mean streets like so many other gang studies, I begin this study with a story of girls in gangs at a public meeting where the representation of Latina/o youth was under debate and discussion. At this public forum, my informants spoke directly to a wider audience—thus dislodging any privileged position I might have thought I held as an ethnographer. As I listened to the girls participate in this forum, I began to realize that this would not be a study of girls in gangs, but a study of girls in gangs speaking on behalf of themselves. After all my hard work to build trust and confidence, was my role now secondary, even superfluous? My role was shifting. I felt anxiety, but also a different possibility. When the girls spoke for themselves, I was released from the gnawing problem of doing a gang study.

Throughout my fieldwork, I had confronted images that constrain and limit the complex lives of our youth: in academic literature, in the few serious cinematic portrayals, in news and media coverage. Even as Chicanos enter various research fields, attempting to avoid traditional approaches that portray gangs in terms of deficiency and pathology, the persistent image of Latino youth is that of gang bangers—gangsters, hoodlums, and violent delinquents. During the course of my research, I was constantly anxious about my particular contribution to Chicana/o scholarship—another gang study? A sympathetic account might attempt to deconstruct the image of otherness, but even this sort of gang study would risk reproducing stereotypes. In creating the very object of study—gangs—otherness is constituted. Because it would locate youth on a local level—in the "street," the " 'hood"—a gang study would continue to demarcate the disciplinary field as well as segregate youth from the rest of society. I propose, on the contrary, to examine how the girls resisted their localization and objectification. I follow them out of conventional "turf" to examine their discursive practices as the tactics of the oppressed in counter or subaltern public spheres (Fraser 1989, 1992). This move entails close attention to the girls' video, *It's a Homie Thang!*, as well as an analysis of how they intervened at various sites of public discourse about gangs.

The public sphere can be understood as those locations where individuals join in a discussion of issues raised by the administration of the state. In Habermas' (1994) ideal public sphere, individual citizens form a public by articulating general interests and ultimately arriving at an objective goal. In this view, the ideal public sphere should not be "distorted" by particular interests. But the actual clash and engagement of discourses is messier and more uneven. Thus, the problem is how to bring identity politics and difference into conceptualizations of public conversation. In the study that I am constructing, I attempt to look at problems of representation at various locations, intersections, of discourse. I am not proposing a complete picture of a subcultural group— girls in gangs. Instead, I bring together discrete incidents, plotting a narrative of my subjects' (and my own) struggles around representation. I trace particularly the girls' growing awareness of self-representation and my own struggle with authority. The data which I select to analyze are not drawn primarily from the culture of the street, but rather shift attention to sites where the girls challenge prevailing representations of Latino/a youth, gang youth, and girls in particular. My research is thus not a gang study. It shifts the paradigm of research from the turf to the sphere of politics, from gang subjects to civil subjects.

OVERVIEW

Chronicling the various sites of discussion and the ways in which the girls develop their stakes in a politics of representation, "Rollin' through Oaktown" introduces the community of Fruitvale in Oakland, California. I briefly take up the debates about the development of an urban underclass in order to consider spatial practices found in Fruitvale that reveal the multiplicity of discourses which accommodate and challenge the conditions brought on by economic restructuring. The next chapter, "An Ethnographer's Tale," both enacts and queries the "arrival scene," a way of "locating" the ethnographic encounter. I examine the power relations of fieldwork—how the researcher determines the topic of research, the conduct of the study, and the writing of the investigation. Showing how the girls successfully contested my research goals and methods, I examine how, finally, we developed a co-discursive partnership reflecting our different stakes in the issue of representation.

In the chapter "Mediating Images: *It's a Homie Thang!,*" I describe the production of the girls' video project—how it began, how they changed the topic, and how they produced a distinctive auto-ethnographic documentary about girls in gangs. Finding the film's major message to be a dialectic of difference and similarity—we are not like you/we are like you—I point to a more complex ending, a third space expressing a utopian goal for marginalized communities. The video stands as an addendum, possibly a correction, to my ethnographic representation. I have tried to present it, therefore, as more than just evidence or data. In effect, the video qualifies my power to represent.

Considering "Affinity and Affiliation" relations, I extend the video analysis, discussing the culture of solidarity I found among the young women of Oakland. Examining the everyday practice of "hangin'" or "kickin' it," I propose that the defining characteristic of the girls' culture is a form of romantic friendship. In a gang context, intimacy takes on a public role. Employing feminist theory of the public and private spheres, I show the social practices through which the girls transform a collective culture from the private into the public. I term this transformation "the publicization of the private."

Examining specific "Cross-Sites for Cross-Talks," the girls speak out about their lives in public meetings and at community agencies. On these occasions, the subjects of my study enter into dialogue and debate about public images, public policy, and public affairs regarding Latino/a youth and gang youth, particularly girls in gangs. I analyze various strategies the girls use as they participate in public discourse and develop a practice and politics of representation that aims to end their objectification and to intervene in generalized images and understandings.

In "Dialoguing Difference," I am not proposing to have found an ideal public sphere but include the site in order to consider the communication process that begins with acknowledging difference in our dialogues for democracy. I have also provided as an appendix some "Frequently Asked Questions" about gangs and about the young women who participated in my research project. In it I refer to other studies about gangs and girls in gangs for the reader to pursue.

Through this progression I analyze intersections of dialogue—from the push and pull of ethnography, to the independent video, to the several cross-sites of public discourse. Employing Nancy Fraser's (1992) notion of multiple, overlapping—and what she has interchangeably called counter and subaltern—public spheres, I examine the limits and potential of democracy, from the ethnographic encounter to the sites of conferences where images and policy toward gangs are discussed. Implicit throughout is Chéla Sandoval's (2000) analysis of the processes and products by which women of color respond to their objectification: the "methodology of the oppressed." What drives this study, then, is a concern for how the Chicana adolescents I got to know in Fruitvale negotiated their identities and representations through a surprising range of political spaces.

I began with an ethnographic vignette, hoping to unsettle the typical image of girls in gangs. Experiences such as this throughout my research have impressed upon me how various liberal, radical, and leftist spaces restrict youth participation—refusing youth the status of citizenship. Exhilarated by the possibilities of public activism, the girls from Fruitvale brought a raucous, contentious, and unbounded style to orderly, regulated, and methodical meetings. They expanded discursive space, broadening the issues and interests of subaltern publics struggling for democracy and social justice.

ROLLIN' THROUGH OAKTOWN

Any system of representation, in fact, is a spatialization of sorts which automatically freezes the flow of experience and in so doing distorts what it strives to represent.   DAVID HARVEY, 1980

Debates about the emergence of an urban underclass examine poverty under new relations of production, evaluating the transnational nature of corporate capital and the technological shift that has impacted upon the working class in the United States (Wilson 1987; Katz 1993; J. Moore and Pinderhughes 1993). One of the most salient arguments in this debate interrogates the differential wage structure that produces a racialized income and opportunity gap between White communities and communities of color—that is, race matters. Such endeavors to account for the communities that have been devastated by the shift are eminently needed. However, evaluating the modes of survival and endurance primarily through an economic premise reduces the cultural practices by the people in the blighted areas—their contestations, resistances, accommodations, and creativity. Under this economic theorem, the accounts of inner-city life reintroduce the earlier culture of poverty paradigm that was challenged by social movements against racism and colonialism.

The underclass model perceives the structures of society—in this case the corporations and the state that are crucial for working people to thrive—as the cause and perpetrators of the poverty. In an economic environment of social service cutbacks beginning with the Reagan-Bush administrations, the underclass analysis depicts the jobless as victims. Portraying the unemployed and the children of the unemployed not only as people who have few choices, the analysis conveys a lack of agency among the poor. The prevalent depiction of the jobless and their children in these communities as plying trades of criminality reduces the more realistic view of their various modes of everyday survival. Culture under this rubric is one of hopelessness and wantonness.

Herein lies the underclass model's problematic contention in which culture is prescribed and determined solely by the economic forces. Social groups give expressive form to their social and material life experiences by developing distinctive patterns, "handling" the way social relations are structured and shaped through diverse ways (Hall and Jefferson 1975; Thompson 1960). How life is met, challenged, and experienced provides the terrain to understanding how social groups negotiate their social and material existence. The range of "handling" or negotiating meaning, values, and ideas—the way the social relations are structured and shaped by the dominant institutions—is the activity of cultural production. Indeed, anthropology has distinguished the notion of "Culture" by defining its locations and settings in relation to the history of colonial domination. Pluralizing the field of resistance(s), the concept of *cultures* not only conveys the relationship of domination and subordination but also offers a multiplicity of points of contact and interaction. Thus the subaltern elaborate a number of alternative styles and norms of inventing and circulating counter discourses, interpretations, identities, and practices.

I propose instead to take a different route in looking at these communities. By "rollin'" through Oakland, the process of spatialization displays a plethora of signs revealing the discord, dispute, and contention to the totalizing domination of capital in the community of Fruitvale, a predominantly Mexicano/a and Mexican American community. Through description one can see the setbacks of corporate flight and the loss of manufacturing industries, as well as the effects of the technological industries in Northern California and the development of the service economy. While offering a perception of a neighborhood with strong community-based organizations, a review of the community-based spatial practices displays an ethnic working-class economy that thrives at a time when the well-being of people is greatly reduced by a federal regulatory and political environment that encourages the abandonment of communities of color. Moreover, through a spatial analysis, one recognizes agency—political, social, and cultural. Returning agency to the communities that are struggling within a disruptive period of capitalist development that eliminates spatial barriers in the drive for flexible production on a global scale provides insight to the myriad cultural practices in the contained space of barrio life.

MAPPING FRUITVALE

In describing Oakland, one maps it between two points of memory—between San Francisco and Berkeley. Both cities are remembered through a variety of histories as hubs of social unrest during the sixties. San Francisco is marked by its counterculture, its iconic hippie culture. Berkeley is remembered as the setting of political resistance—the place where the sixties free speech movement originated. Both cities are remembered as points of protest and defiance against a post–World War II America and its "victory culture." San Francisco and Berkeley were emblematic of the times when American myth and reality were pried apart.

In other imaginaries, in the memories of different groupings, in the memories of those who were not part of the American Dream, Oakland is a prominent place—it is the city where the Black Panther Party originated. It is the place, to some the birthplace, of the Black Power movement, and thus played a role in generating identity politics in American life. In such a tumultuous place, the Black Panther Party began a struggle to end racism "by any means necessary." The slogan galvanized a generation of youth of color that still has its effects today—even in this time now called "post–civil rights."

Thus to attempt to tell this story of one ethnographer in the city of Oakland, the context has to be set. The concepts—of ethnic pride, of international solidarity with developing nations and groups fighting colonialism, of cultural nationalism as well as leftist politics that sought to build new political affinities—are still part of Oakland. The movements of the sixties and seventies left a mark, even though at times that mark seems so small. The concepts of people of color working together and fighting "the system" are found along the city blocks that make up the community of Fruitvale in the city of Oakland. Thus, my job, in one small way, is an attempt to reconstruct one community in order to understand the character and nature of the research among the young women I met.

Exiting Interstate 80 at Fruitvale and driving east you first cross the railroad tracks. Just beyond the freeway and tracks is Jingletown. The somewhat Victorian-looking homes that line the freeway were first settled by migrant workers looking for a steady job who had tired of following the crops and sought stability from seasonal work. Finding room and board, men and women waited to find steady work so they could live and raise their families in Oakland. Mona Younis describes Fruitvale's beginnings:

Named by a German immigrant who planted an orchard of cherry trees in the mid-1800s, Fruitvale was once a major fruit-growing and canning center. Historically a center of Latino community and culture, the area was annexed to Oakland in 1909. . . . The orchards that

made this area a favorite resort for affluent weekend visitors are long
gone. (Younis 1998, 225)

Driving east just under a minute, you get to Fourteenth and Fruitvale.
Immediately the landscape shifts, resonating what Davis calls "the spic-
ing of the city" (2000). On one of the corners, a national hamburger
franchise offers fast food with the option of even faster service at the
drive-through window. Catty-corner is a national chain shoe store offering shoes at bargain prices. However, the other businesses contend
with big-bucks commerce. Immediately next to the shoe store, a clothing store stretches out onto the sidewalk, where T-shirts, pants, and
windbreaker jackets hang from the awning and racks, obstructing the
walkway. Pedestrians maneuver through the cache of clothing to get to
the corner crosswalk.

Across the street a small market advertises carnes and vegetables
for the community. Lettuce, tomatoes, and potatoes—the bins explode
with the pale green husks of tomatillos, the sundry bright yellows and
deep reds of chile peppers, the sandy color of jícamas, the golden pink
of mangos, and the deep orange of papayas. The mix of sweet and spicy,
earthy and delicate scents accentuates difference in a condensed space.
The restructured economy produces the mixed consequences of declining employment in the manufacturing industry and at the same time an
increase in the service sector. While Oakland itself has not gained direct
employment from the Silicon Valley industries, the new technological
economy has produced a sector of highly paid employees whose conspicuous consumption produces low-paying jobs in a service economy.
In the pursuit of these jobs, the long-standing Chicano/a community of
Fruitvale has been impacted by the massive immigration of Mexi-
canos/as and Centro Americanos/as producing the "third world cities"
within the United States.

Fruitvale is a main thoroughfare of commerce where small businesses
draw from the dominant economy. Catering to the lifestyle and means
of livelihood of low-paid wage earners, the intersection becomes con-
gested with cars battling for the few choice parking spaces in front of
the businesses. People stop to pay bills, cash checks, and send money to
hometowns at buildings announcing "Envía dinero a México" (Send
money to Mexico) and "Tarjetas de Telefono" (phone cards) and offering cash advances on employment or welfare checks. Some run out of
their cars to buy a quick lunch at the vans that sell tacos and tortas de
carne asada, carne adobada, and chile relleno, while others park to shop

at the discount clothing stores with brand-name knock-offs. On Fruit-vale Avenue are rented and owner-occupied homes, storefront churches, bars, bridal shops, laundromats, Mexican and Salvadoran restaurants, and street vendors selling ice cream and raspadas, or hot roasted corn and salted nuts flavored with red powdered chile.

Long a very small community of predominantly Mexican Americans, Fruitvale's population swelled during the 1980s with Mexican immigration. The recent arrivals have brought a type of tempo tropical to the cityscape, and the Mexican-origin community is now sprawling to encompass a wider demographic reach.[1]

In this bustle of consumption, spotting the commercial terrain are a series of moderate to large buildings that identify the climate of Fruit-vale: the Spanish Speaking Alliance Center, La Clínica de la Raza, the César Chávez Library, the Narcotic Education League. Along other thoroughfares in Fruitvale, one finds multicultural coalitions and organizations such as People United for a Better Oakland (PUEBLO), Coalition Forums of Oakland (CFO), and Fruitvale Community Collaborative (FCC). The organizations that stand along the main avenues arose from a particular moment in the history of the identity politics movement. Some of the organizations began with start-up funds provided by War on Poverty programs, others groups emerged in direct affiliation with the civil rights movement, while many more sprang from the youth and student movement of the late sixties, the Chicano Power movement. While many of the organizations and coalitions disappeared, those that remained kept a steady marching pace with the shift in politics that marked the seventies and eighties—the shift from liberal welfare state to Reaganomics.

The decrease in social services is characterized by the increasing fight for limited funds; however, the main vision of these organizations continues toward empowering the community by providing information and educational services and advocating development that puts people before profits. These organizations still develop leadership from the neighborhoods, training people to lead, advocate, and represent their voices in the political forums of Oakland. What makes this concentrated area remarkable is that so many of the organizers have kept their goals and ideals, organizing and mobilizing, while at the same time adjusting their groups' political tactics to meet the times.[2]

Nonetheless, while these organizations have struggled to survive and register important gains to keep the service institutions running, the forces of Reaganomics, the turnabout in affirmative action, the recession caused by the shift from manufacturing to high-tech industries, and the rise of the banking and investment sectors of capital have made the day-to-day living conditions of the people of Oakland and in Fruitvale a rough-and-tumble situation.

In the neighborhoods of Fruitvale one finds a mix of owner-occupied and rental homes with a few apartment buildings interspersed here and there. Homeowners maintain their houses. Some houses announce efforts of remodeling and reconstruction with new paint, new roofs, or large receptacles holding old wood, plaster, light fixtures, and other scrap items. Real estate value is not the sole reason for renovations. Families remodel to make room for extended families to live and socialize. One also finds new cars sparkling on driveways, not so remarkable when one considers the dominant corporate-consumerist urging to "spend money now." Since there isn't enough money to save, more spending goes toward the most important and necessary items, such as cars to get to work, in times of a structural shift to fluid capital. In these neighborhoods one sees groups of youth hanging around on corners, sitting on the steps of homes, or loitering in apartment parking lots. Most people tend to recognize the youth as children of the community rather than perceiving them as criminals. Common community concerns often are expressed as a need for youth programs and not necessarily for more police. In fact, community concerns focus on issues of police accountability and misconduct.[3] But it wasn't always that way.

MAPPING HISTORIES

Early-twentieth-century cities were the product of immigration and assimilation, where the children of immigrants cut off ties to the language, culture, and habits of their forebears' countries and in that "whitening" process captured power. While city growth and status corresponded with nineteenth-century capitalist development, administration and governance sometimes competed and sometimes corresponded with projects of manufacturing, finance, and real estate interests. Similarly, today's global city reflects the current economic restructuring of late capitalism and the flows of capital and trade in a new world order as well as the transmigration of kinship networks, social movements, and cultures. However, the global or transnational city is also the historical result of nation-state policies in particular contexts of social and economic relations. While the earlier city centers were attempts to construct a universal identity as American citizenry, the new global cities through the adaptation, accommodation, and transformation of the built environment reveal the conflicts and contestations of making place in the interstices of a world power.

Making place is an act of agency, where people produce a way of doing things that reflects new identities within and outside of the power structures. Making place not only marks a core and periphery but registers the interconnection with the development of capitalism from nation-state to global power.

Fruitvale has only recently become a site for deliberating about California's large Latino population. However, Oakland's Mexican population began arriving in significant numbers in 1910, when the Mexican Revolution and other factors forced 10 percent of the Mexican population to immigrate to the United States.[4] Oakland's Mexican immigrants ended up along the railways of West Oakland. Working in the railroad industry, the canneries, and small shops, by 1930 the Mexican population in Oakland had grown to approximately 3,200.

During World War II, Oakland became the site of a number of military- and defense-related industries, and Oakland's port was expanded for shipbuilding and repair (Younis 1998, 222). As a center for war industries, jobs at the Kaiser Corporation and the Moore Dry Dock Company and other shipyards brought workers from across the nation. Migrating from the South, the African American population tripled within five years, with Blacks accounting for nearly one in ten of Oakland's residents in 1945 and growing steadily thereafter (Younis 1998, 222). Mexican Americans came from Colorado, Texas, Arizona, and New Mexico seeking jobs in war-related industries. "These new workers, both men and women, were settled in temporary government housing and expected to report to work at one of the military installations the next day" (Lujan 1995, 10). Augmenting the Southwestern migration, in 1942 the federal government signed an agreement with Mexico to initiate the Bracero Program. Enacted as a source of low-wage labor for the agricultural industry, five thousand "guest workers" were brought to Oakland. Mexican Americans and Mexicanos worked as cannery workers for the Del Monte and Dole factories.[5] Additionally, during the war, Chinese Americans were mobilized to work in the Bay Area's shipbuilding and other defense plants. "In early 1943, Kaiser employed more than two thousand Chinese workers, the majority of whom were local residents" (Johnson 1993, 55). While Oakland's shipbuilding and war material production brought prosperity to the area and attracted retail establishments to further develop the central city, racial segregation in housing did not emulate the wartime effort that produced interracial work sites.

While the labor shortage stimulated recruitment of Black, Chicano/a, and Chinese workers during the war, the city began a decline during the postwar period. The postwar prosperity of economic expansion, abundant cheap energy, and employment growth meant increasing federal expenditures for defense and suburbanization—freeways and mass manufacturing of affordable automobiles. The Keynesian economy of state-managed growth stimulated the demand for products and the development of mass consumerism and accelerated the development of regional shopping centers and suburban industrial sites. Thus, the downtown core of the city significantly diminished. Younis notes that in Oakland the "conversion from a manufacturing-based to service-based economy, competition between central cities and burgeoning suburbs, had discernible impacts on the city's economy" in the postwar period (Younis 1998, 223). Encouraged by tax advantages and access roads for supply and distribution, industries and businesses developed with the burgeoning suburbs. Funded with generous federal housing subsidies (Veterans Administration and Federal Housing Administration loan guarantees), the suburbs and hills of Oakland became predominantly White and middle class. Those who remained in the center city suffered from the loss of public projects and services. Additionally, as housing construction occurred in the suburbs, affordable and adequate housing construction in the city's center was curtailed. Oakland's Black and Chicano residents cramped into old, deteriorating, single-family dwellings.

As the residential and industrial relocation exacerbated segregation, by the 1960s one-quarter of the city's population lived in poverty. In the 1960s suburbanization meant a loss for city-dwellers in private-sector jobs. At that time, Oakland historian Hayes (1972) noted: Oakland had lost five big employers since 1960 and innumerable small ones. Cal Pak (food processing), whose employment fluctuated between 1,000 and 5,000 seasonally, had moved to the central valley. Most of the job loss due to move-outs was accounted for by large firms. Merchant Calculators took 1,000 jobs with it when it left. Nordstrom Valve left Oakland for Texas and Nebraska, taking 1,200 jobs and a $5.7 million annual payroll. These plants were among the largest in the county. In one-half decade, between 1958 and 1963, Oakland's employment dropped by 3,200 (Hayes 1972, 49).

While suburbanization more than halved the city's White population between 1960 and 1990 (Younis 1998, 222), the African American population increased to 47 percent (Oden 1999, 44). A 1966 study of household poverty in Oakland conducted by the University of California's Survey Research Center found that while Mexican Americans (White with Spanish surname) made up 10 percent of the households, their unemployment rate was at 12 percent (Pressman 1975, 27). Oakland became "a city of parts: a Black ghetto in the Flatlands and the well-to-do in the hills" (Starling 1986, 40).

Confronted by job scarcity, Oakland's West Side Black and Chicano/a communities found the government, financial, and commercial interests (City Council, Bank of America, and *Oakland Tribune*) primarily concerned with reviving the downtown central business district.[6] While labor segmentation occurred as unemployment rose among people of color, it was accommodated and reinforced by a geographical fragmentation of the city. The "temporary" war housing deteriorated, producing a blighted inner city. Additionally, housing discrimination reinforced patterns of racial segregation between the hills and flatlands of Oakland. To top it all off, the West Oakland community confronted the concerted effort of the federal and regional governments' support for the suburbanization process—the postwar development of the freeway systems. Cutting through communities and forcibly displacing residents, the construction of the Nimitz freeway in the late 1950s relocated the Mexican American community from West Oakland into the Fruitvale area at East Fourteenth (Lujan 1995, 11). The Nimitz freeway was a harbinger of the developing freeway system of the 1960s and 1970s that undermined local businesses in favor of the development of suburban malls and provided suburbanites with quick access to jobs in the white-collar business district.

As corporate interests worked with the local government to revive the central business district, two policies by the federal government and the City Council would later affect the development of Oakland as a transnational city. First, the federal government passed the Immigrant Reform Act of 1965, which removed national origin restrictions against Asians. Migration produced as a result of U.S. cold war policies encouraged skilled workers from Asian countries to settle in the United States. While previous residential restrictions on the Chinese community forced the development of Oakland's Chinatown, the liberalization of immigration law gradually permitted Asians to purchase homes in a small section called China Hill in the San Antonio district that borders the community of Fruitvale (Younis 1998, 223). Second, the City Council incorporated Oakland's Chinatown into the central city planning in

1966 (Oden 1999, 142). These postwar policies would later enhance Oakland city government's capacity to lure Asian capital investment in the central city in the 1970s when the U.S. economy faced a gasoline shortage and a loss in manufacturing and in the early 1980s when California entered a recession. Younis reports that by 1990:

> employment in manufacturing and wholesaling, "once the backbone of the economy," had dropped to 15.7 percent of the labor market. . . . The plant closure project found that more than 500 companies in the Bay Area, most of which were East Bay companies and Oakland's main labor market, have closed or relocated since 1981. Only 60 percent of those who found themselves unemployed by the business closures secured alternative employment; 66 percent secured jobs at significantly lower salaries. (Younis 1998, 223)

While plants shut down or relocated to other parts of the world, Oakland attracted the attention of emergent Asian investors, as the Port of Oakland could increase their export capacity and facilitate trade (Oden 1999, 14).[7]

The recession (1973–1975) showed that the postwar economic growth could not continue. As inflation combined with a depressed economy, the executive branch responded to the budget demands and deficit increases by cutting federally supported programs designated for the rehabilitation of cities. In Oakland, the city's growth machine plainly represented White Republican corporate interests of pro-growth downtown development. While unemployment increased, Mayor Lionel Wilson, aligning with the Kaiser Corporation, Clorox Corporation, and World Airways, complied with the Reaganomics "trickle down" approach to the communities of the flatlands (Oden 1999, 61).[8] The deindustrialization of restructured capital produced a kind of reindustrialization in a different form, into non-unionized, low-wage jobs. While the middle-class segment of the skilled and unionized blue-collar workers shrank, a few obtained jobs in the white-collar technological industries; at the same time a less skilled and lower-wage reservoir of production and service workers grew.[9]

The segmentation of labor is reproduced in the social life in communities like Fruitvale. It is expected that Latinos/as will soon become the majority in Fruitvale; they now comprise more than one-third of the population, followed by African Americans (about one-fourth).[10] In 1992, 90 percent of Fruitvale's employed residents worked outside Fruitvale (Younis 1998, 235). The reindustrialization was accompanied by passage of the Immigration Reform and Control Act of 1986. The reservoir of lower-paid and less skilled workers now incorporated previously undocumented workers. The law allowed those who had lived in the United States for four years amnesty and a green card. Many who previously worked in rural areas moved to the cities in search of better wages. Now working in "plant nurseries, construction firms, foundries, ship-yards, cement companies, furniture factories, rubber factories, paper factories, restaurants, hotels and motels, car washes, and butcher shops . . . toy assembly, garment sewing, and electronics production . . . and in housecleaning and child care," as few as 10 or 15 percent of all documented and undocumented Mexican immigrants work in agriculture in California, Texas, and Arizona (Hondagneu-Sotelo 1997, 119).

With the restructured economy, global capitalism has facilitated new sociocultural practices of transnationalism for immigrants, affecting barrios and colonias in the United States. Global capitalism facilitates crossing boundaries with courier companies, money-wiring firms, travel agencies, and van and bus businesses.

The Immigration Reform and Control Act of 1986 provided legal residency to formerly undocumented workers, thus easing border crossings into Mexico to rekindle familial and village networks. In addition, the Mexican economy benefited from the wages of the new Mexican communities by 5 billion to 7 billion dollars (Smith 2001, 78). Driven by the destabilized peso, the international debt crisis, and declining living standards, immigrants to California included poor and middle-class Mexicans. Thus, in cities like Oakland experiencing an increase of immigrants, cultural traditions and language are reasserted and ethnic enclaves expand and produce an ethnic economy. While anti-immigrant proponents of California Proposition 187 complained of a "cash drain" from immigrants sending money to their home countries, the new transmigrants have contributed to the growth of local businesses through consumption and services in their immediate communities.[11] "Currently there are some 150 Latino stores serving the primarily Spanish-speaking Fruitvale district (Lujan 1995, 12). Transnational cities like Oakland reflect the scope of spatial restructuring. Mexico lost an enormous territory in 1848, and immigrants six decades later, during the Mexican Revolution, reasserted language and customs, but the new transnational Mexicans entering in the period of structural transformation have changed the landscape of the older barrios and colonias. In this setting, place does not assert a universal identity nor a singular identity but reflects the conflict and contestations for making place.

REVISITING THE UNDERCLASS DEBATE

Now, these areas are generally depicted as communities under siege by drug warfare and violent gangs, tempering the American imaginary. Delineating various forms of organization and distinguishing between turf gangs and drug gangs, the Oakland Police listed eighteen gangs within the community of Fruitvale. Still, the police and City Council have debated whether a gang problem exists in Oakland. Interestingly, the fact that the two political bodies debated the issue discloses the social construction of a public problem.

In their extensive study *Panic: The Social Construction of the Street Gang Problem* (2002), McCorkle and Miethe review the discourse on gangs in Nevada and provide a comparison of statistics and analysis of gangs in other states. They uncover considerable variance between the actual statistics to violent crime that is gang-related, far from the image that police, public officials, and the media describe. Additionally, the description of "the problem" exacerbates any rational discussion, since the definition of a gang varies not only from state to state but from county to county.

Finding a sizable gap between the rhetoric and the reality of street gangs, McCorkle and Miethe reiterate what so many other gang researchers have frequently pointed out, i.e., the majority of youth in the inner cities are not gang members. The gang is but one of many subcultural groupings found among youth. Reporting that gang crime represents only a small proportion of all serious crimes in schools and other settings, they divulge further inconsistencies in defining gang-related crime. Additionally, they charge that random sweeps and profiling— such as the Los Angeles program has entailed—of youth who live in particular areas, have tattoos, dress in a particular style, or have a stylized walk criminalize more than half the youth of color as gang members, thus raising the potential for more police surveillance and more personnel and funding for the police. Finding that the majority of gangs are not of the corporate (Carl S. Taylor 1993) or entrepreneurial (Jankowski 1991) type, these authors note that most turf gangs are minimally involved in the sale of illegal drugs. Since most street gangs are not highly structured and coordinated, the involvement with street sales is episodic and disorganized, far from the media image of sophisticated drug trafficking operations. Examining the processes of agenda setting and policy making, McCorkle and Miethe state that since

> law enforcement bureaucracies compete for a finite pool of public
> dollars, the intense competition . . . inevitably involves persuading

policy-makers (and the public) of the urgency of the crime problem and the need for greater investments in law enforcement to contain the threat.

Persuading others of that threat (i.e., claims making) will routinely involve symbolic representations that distort and dramatize either crime in general or, as is more likely the case, some particular aspect of the crime problem. Thus, there is every reason to question many of the claims made by law enforcement regarding street gangs in other parts of the country. (McCorkle and Miethe 2002, 197)

Although they recognize that gangs exist and commit serious crimes against persons, property, and the public order, the authors insist, however, that the 1980s prognostications of a crisis and subsequent claims of a malevolent conspiracy against the public did not reflect the objective risks posed by gangs.

Writing at the millennium, one can see the structural shift that pummeled (and is still affecting) communities of color. Living in a different city, now owning a home in a predominantly Mexican American community, I know the aftershocks of the structural shift. Men and women work part-time hoping to find full-time jobs, while others are too discouraged to seek work. There are gangs in my neighborhood, and police patrol regularly. High unemployment, loss of jobs in the manufacturing industries, a prolonged recession, scarcity of resources, and cutbacks in social services illustrate the dire straits of communities battling for the livelihood of families.[12] Limited opportunities in the job market, high dropout rates, and teen pregnancy are signs of the times.

As I traveled through Oakland during my fieldwork research, I often thought of the debates about a new urban underclass. The underclass paradigm argues that the lack of economic opportunity facilitates destructive behavior, adversely affecting kinship structures and educational attainment and fostering welfare dependency and joblessness. While Wilson's concept of an underclass defines a particular stage of capitalist transformation and applies to a segment of society that has been hard hit, popular discourse took to the concept, applying it liberally to all areas of the inner-city poor. Regrettably, it was also too facilely used to label youth in gangs.

The concept of an underclass evidently illustrates the effects of structural transformation. But is it useful in explaining youth gangs? Dismayed by such a construction that severs ties between youth and their parents, I often thought that the deluge of media images of violent youth roving in gangs was a shell game, a con game of smoke and mirrors. Having read Georgi Dimitrov's 1945 polemic against fascism, I recall how he described the competitive power struggle among the various sectors of capital. As I examine the panic over youth gangs, the criminalization of youth of color, the way he described finance capital as the lumpen sector of the capitalist class resonated with me. Unlike the manufacturing capitalists who produce commodities, finance capital can be construed as pimps and pushers—they produce nothing. The turf wars on the streets were allegorical dramatizations of the larger rearrangements between finance and manufacturing capital that encouraged the abandonment of factories as finance capital and transnational corporations pushed their political agendas against local communities. This is not fascism, but it certainly depicts the cutthroat license of finance capital during economic restructuring.

AN ETHNOGRAPHER'S TALE

If ethnography produces cultural interpretations through intense research experience, how is such unruly experience transformed into an authoritative written account? How, precisely, is a garrulous, overdetermined, cross-cultural encounter, shot through with power relations and personal cross purposes circumscribed as an adequate version of a more-or-less discrete "otherworld," composed by an individual author?   JAMES CLIFFORD

In the summer of 1993 I moved to Oakland to conduct an audience reception study of media representations of Chicano youth, focusing particularly on gang genre films that have constructed images of deviancy among youth of color. The research featured interviews with Chicana teenagers, tracking their reception of films like *Boyz N the Hood, American Me,* and *Bound by Honor.* Timing was crucial. Hearing that Allison Anders' *Mi Vida Loca,* a film about teenage Chicana gang members in Los Angeles, would be released that summer, I planned to take a group of girls to view the film and, straightaway, interview them. Hoping to employ both reader response and audience reception theories (Radway 1984; Bobo 1988, 1995), I focused on teenage girls' interpretive practices, analyzing the ways they questioned and critiqued portrayals in the films of the Chicano community and gang membership. Since these films carry strong moral messages about gangs, my project would investigate how these messages were being received by Chicana teenagers. The difference between what I set out to do and what actually happened during fieldwork is the crux of my tale. In what follows, I show how the girls I met contested my research goal and research method— how a project that began as an audience reception study changed into a study of girls in gangs. My tale evokes the fumblings and fortunes of fieldwork, bearing in mind current critiques revolving around relations of power in ethnographic research.

Motivated by a commitment to social change, feminists and critical anthropologists have produced profound examinations of the power relations in ethnographic practice: the researcher's control of agenda, process, and writing. Their interventions offer critical ways of understanding the representational practices associated with fieldwork—including this tale of the field.[1] The term "tale" evokes an author crafting a story: choosing, emphasizing, hiding, and revealing. I begin with an ethnographer's tale in order to emphasize a distinct feature of social research: the subjective narrative as a constructed text. As an ethnography—writing about a people, a group, or an aspect of culture—the tale is not just fabrication, but a selection and heightening of events in order to describe a place and time. Introductions to ethnographic studies often begin with an arrival scene that serves to orient the reader in an unfamiliar place. Such accounts work in a very particular way within ethnographic social research, often taking the form of a personal narrative of initial blundering and feelings of otherness in the researched community. Arrival scenes tend to appear in prefaces, introductions, appendices, or they are written as a separate essay, discussing the woes and wonders of fieldwork. They transmit to the reader the author's extraordinary experiences, reporting how the ethnographer arrived and was tested and accepted by the community. In many ways the blunderings and halting access reported can be compared to an initiation. The social scientist is seen to be undergoing transformation, a rite of passage that marks a shift from knowing about a culture through texts to knowing a culture from experience. Thus, the tale functions to prove that the ethnographer has prevailed, engaging with the "foreign place," thereby authorizing his or her representation of a culture and people.

I have two purposes in telling my tale. The first is to introduce my informants and to present the dialogics of our research relationship. But in using this problematic narrative form—the story of my rite of passage—I do not intend to lead the reader into an otherworld, revealing the gang's mysterious culture. I employ the convention as a way of emphasizing the agency of research subjects. Indeed, my tale describes not one arrival scene but a series of comings and goings between field site and academy, the continuing challenges of maintaining connection and resolving discord between myself and my interlocutors. I trust that my naive tale does not exploit and betray (Stacey 1988) the girls who participated in my research but instead helps to explain my changing focus. The analysis of field dilemmas can contribute to critical debates about power relations between researchers and informants.

The second purpose is to raise the thematic of representation and self-representation that will be explored. The tale authorizes not so much my representation of girls in gangs as my research interest in the politics of representation. My interlocutors in Oakland were members of an all-girl alliance called Norteñas With Attitude (NWA). The girls effectively challenged my initial research concentration on media images. But as my tale will reveal, issues of representation did not disappear in the shift from media to a study of gangs. They took an unexpected turn. Through

conflict and tension, the girls and I developed a co-discursive partnership that rearticulated our understandings of representation. Narrating
the girls' active participation in knowledge creation, I have been brought
to recognize how they empowered themselves to change the research
and influence my writing, both in "the field" and now as I struggle to
detail the events of our ethnographic encounter.

NEGOTIATING THE FIELD

To describe the Fruitvale community of Oakland is difficult because it is
like the neighborhoods I grew up in and have lived in all my life. It's easier to conceive the area by specifying what it is not. It's not a middle-
class suburban neighborhood—White, African American, or Latino. It's
the inner city. But it is a California inner city—extending out, not up.
There are a few apartment complexes sprinkled among the mainly single-
family homes that dominate the neighborhood blocks. Some homes have
grass or concrete lawns, some yards are dirt-filled; some houses are
painted, some need paint; some are occupied by owners and others by
renters. The NEL Centro de Juventud, where I conducted my research,
is like many community centers I have worked in. Providing supervised
social and recreational activities for youth, the center's main objective is
drug prevention and intervention services to youth and their families.
Funded primarily through federal, state, and county agencies, the center
sometimes receives project grants from private organizations for community outreach and educational programs. The Centro de Juventud is
one of the many specialized programs of the incorporated Narcotics Education League that was founded to combat drug and alcohol abuse in
the Latino community.

Located on Fruitvale Avenue, one of the hubs of the Latino/Chicano
community in Oakland, the Centro is a one-story brick building—
sweaty-hot in the summer, sweatshirt- and jacket-cold in the winter.
While the Centro schedules various cultural, educational, and recreational activities, it is mainly a drop-in center, a place for teens to "kick
it"—to hang out, meet, and talk with friends. Because there is no requirement to participate in organized activities, the easygoing setting
seems to fit a style that attracts youth who otherwise would not be drawn
to more programmatic activity centers. For many, the Centro is a "safe
place," an alternative to the drug scene and possible violence of the
parks, streets, and, in some cases, porches in the neighborhood.

The Centro's various activities can be mapped through its allocation

of space. Upon entering the lobby, a small hallway leads past the director's office to a nook of the building—the library. While there are two
computers in the room and two large lounge sofas, a large television
with a sophisticated VCR occupies the room. From time to time, and
with permission, the library is used by the Centro's youth to watch videos, mainly Hollywood feature films. Moreover, this out-of-the-way
room stores office supplies and records of Centro projects and propos-
als. The library keeps several folding tables and chairs as well as chalk-
boards and easels with chart paper. In a corner are rolls of butcher paper and stacks of poster boards indicating that the library is not a place
for books but is the brain center of the Centro. This is where staff and
youth discuss, plan, and mobilize to carry out projects. From this library, other activities—not directly Centro projects—have been forged.
High school youth came together to develop a list of educational complaints, organizing a major walkout at schools which are predominantly
attended by Latino/Chicano youth. At other times, youth have conducted surveys of police harassment, organized for federal funds for
summer jobs, and developed plans to lobby the City Council against the
mandatory curfew laws for teenagers. Other times, the library is used to
organize mural projects as well as anti-graffiti projects.

From the lobby entrance, other passages define the Centro's everyday
activities. There are two large auditorium-size rooms, one of which contains a large basketball court with a stage for meetings and assemblies,
and the other has pool tables, ping-pong tables, and an arcade of video
games and pinball machines. In the hallway separating the two audito-
riums are offices for the peer counselors who work at the Centro and the
administrative secretary. In this area of the hallway are the public phone
and water cooler, two central technologies that produce noise, excitement, and congregation. Frequented by the boys who play basketball,
the water cooler produces a lot of horseplay among the teenage boys,
and girls group by the phone.

When first arriving at the Fruitvale Centro, I met with the director,
Rosalinda Palacios. I had worked with her in the campaign for La Raza
Unida Party, in Chicano pinto (prison) reform organizations, and in the
early seventies Chicana consciousness-raising groups. The director and
I agreed that my project would begin in August 1993; July would be a
time of volunteer work so the youth could become familiar with me. I
felt that the girls would not be reluctant to talk with me. I brought the
confidence of a community organizer, work I had done before returning
to the university. Employment in community service offered me grass-

roots involvement and practical skills of communication. Organizing around local issues required knocking on doors and listening to how people discussed issues that affected them. It also entailed the ability to sit for long periods, to take in the environment, to talk about everyday topics, and to know when to move the conversation toward an organizing agenda. Generally, I found that no matter which community I was in, people were comfortable talking with me, often inviting me to sit a spell. I felt skilled at the art of, as the youth say, "hangin'."

On that first day, Palacios gave me a synopsis of the youth center's goals and projects while we rode around Oakland in an old Ford pickup to purchase equipment (boxing gloves, tennis paddles, weights, kitchen utensils) for the Centro's activities. Later, as we hauled out the goods, she introduced me as a university intern to the staff and peer counselors. Seven members were young men from the neighborhood. Two were young women, Beatriz and María. The director announced that we should promptly get together to organize the discussion group for the girls who attended the Centro, and then she left us. María and Beatriz first asked general questions—about my schedule, what school I attended, my major—then asked about the rap group. They expressed first surprise and then eagerness about a discussion group just for girls. While I didn't have time then to explain exactly what my project was about, I gave them the general idea—that the girls would get together to talk about films and what they thought of them. They expressed enthusiasm about watching movies, especially the films I had singled out. I told them that, additionally, the discussion group would go to see the film *Mi Vida Loca* by Allison Anders and that I would then interview the girls about their reactions and responses to the film. Beatriz was excited about the all-girl excursion for a film about girls in gangs. María seemed a bit reserved throughout the exchange and finally asked why was I exclusively interviewing girls. I answered, a bit too abruptly, that most films and studies of Chicano youth centered on the boys, and I wanted to study what girls thought about these movies. My answer seemed to satisfy her. It was later as she questioned my field goals and methods that she became interested and invested in my project.

While I was confident that the Centro's youth would participate in my research, I was nevertheless an outsider, and I came to count on the two young women as mediators for the success of my project. María and Beatriz knew most of the girls who came by the Centro, and they provided valuable time and insight to my work. When the group finally met, both María and Beatriz would go through the Centro calling everyone into the library. Moreover, during the sessions, both would interpret my questions—breaking them down to everyday language. They were mediators bringing a more favorable relationship between me and the girls who joined the group. While I did not know this at the time, both María and Beatriz talked up my project to many of the girls, recruiting them to participate. María, particularly, was a source of local knowledge of the girls and their attitudes and behaviors. As a peer counselor she arbitrated hostilities between youth who frequented the Centro. Many times during the group discussions, she mediated disagreements as well as counseled the girls when topics became intimate. During those times, I was thankful for her presence and intervention. Her expertise as a peer counselor and the girls' deep trust in her provided me with invaluable insights to the problems the youth faced. Her participation, moreover, abated my anxiety about the project.

My hours at the Centro were from four to eight o'clock Wednesday and Thursday afternoons, and from five to twelve on Fridays. During the summer the Centro stayed open until midnight because it sponsored the Friday Night Live activities initiated by Mothers Against Drunk Driving. Funded by special county allocations, the program permitted youth centers throughout Oakland to remain open late. Generally, I found the Wednesday and Thursday shifts long and boring. I drifted from room to room at the center attempting to converse with the peer counselors or with some of the youth. Many times, I would station myself at the lobby entrance and take responsibility for the sign-up sheet. Everyone coming into the Centro had to sign in. There were two sheets for members: under fourteen, and fourteen and over. If someone was over nineteen years of age and not a member of the Centro, I would send them to the secretary's office. Sitting at a small desk, I would read the newspapers or leaflets that were laid out on two display cases in the lobby. This gave me something to do, a chance to read about the community I was working in and the services provided, and most important, to gain a familiarity with the names and faces of the youth who frequented the Centro. Usually, preteen boys would be at the center, and sometimes they would come around to where I was sitting. Rarely would the conversation be directed at me. Mostly the boys would bicker and fight. Once in a while, a few preteen girls would sit on the steps of the lobby and talk with me, but their attention was directed at the boys. Again, there was bickering and fighting.

While I dreaded the long evenings on Wednesdays and Thursdays, I looked forward to the Friday Night Live (FNL) programs. The first stretch of Friday would go pretty much as the previous nights. However, at about seven we would temporarily close the Centro and prepare for the evening program. The senior peer counselor would discuss assignments and what rooms we would work. It was a time when we relaxed with one another and talked about the week and weekend plans. There was usually a meal for the evening, prepared by two peer counselors. In addition, there was one sporting event in which all would participate in one form or another. I looked forward to the program, not only because of the assignment, but also because most of the teenage girls of the Centro attended the Friday events.

At my first FNL in July, the youth were lined up outside the Centro and were frisked by two peer counselors before entering. From the doorway, the boisterous noise of the youth echoed in the lobby. I was assigned to check off the names of the youth on the Centro's list as each person came in. A group of girls ranging in age from sixteen to eighteen arrived at the door talking loudly, jokingly pushing each other. As they lined up to enter the Centro, a peer counselor looked them over and asked several girls to remove red or purple bandannas from their ponytails, foreheads, or pants pockets. Others were asked to remove their purple jackets. After the first couple of girls signed in, they gathered in the lobby where I was working. Then as the rest of the girls said their names to me, the group began to shout each girl's nickname, bursting into laughter. Most of the girls wore dark red or burgundy lipstick; some outlined their lips with black eyeliner pencil. Their eye makeup was heavily applied; the most prevalent was black eyeliner and black mascara. Some wore long ponytails, knotted at the very top of their heads, giving them more height, with long bangs arranged to fall over one eye. While a handful wore shorter hairstyles, bell-bottomed pants, ribbed tops covered by a net vest, and platform shoes, most wore red or black oversized baggy pants (called "Dickies"), large, loose T-shirts, and Hush Puppies, high-top tennis shoes, or Doc Marten copies.

When most of the girls were inside, a large group went to the women's bathroom, and others went to the game room. The Centro director had pointed some of them out previously, telling me that they were members of four girl gangs in the Fruitvale area—Da Crew, Las Norteñas, East Side Norteñas, and Fresh Bitches In(effect)—who had formed an alliance called Norteñas With Attitude. On the first FNL night I maintained my station until after dinner. No main sports activity was planned for that evening, so once again I drifted from room to room. After I had attended several FNL-sponsored activities at the Centro, the senior peer

counselor assembled the youth in the game room to announce a volleyball game (boys against girls—this was cheered wildly), to go over rules
of conduct in the Centro, and to give miscellaneous information. Then
he introduced me to the assembly as a volunteer and allowed me to talk
about my research project. As I explained my project, the youth gathered in the auditorium were respectfully quiet. The silence continued as
I listed the films we would see at the Centro. However, when I described
Allison Anders' film about girls in gangs and that we would go to a theater to see the film, one of the girls bellowed out, "Yeaaah!" Another responded, "'Bout time!" And there was general cheering. When the assembly broke up, not one of the girls approached me to find out more
about my study or about participation. I roamed around the Centro
again until the volleyball game, and it was then that each girl whenever
she hit the ball yelled out her gang affiliation and the others would
chant, "N-W-A, N-W-A, N-W-A," accompanied by wild cheers.

Feeling at home with the neighborhood, the center, and the youth as
I met them, I began my work with a zippity-doo-dah zeal. I had a project, a community, and an adequate theoretical approach for an audience
reception study. While preparing for my field study, I had studied various theories and critiques of reader response and audience reception
with Jacqueline Bobo. Conducting interviews with Black women about
the film *The Color Purple,* Bobo defines audience reception studies as
an examination of "the way in which a specific audience creates meaning from a mainstream text and uses the reconstructed meaning to empower themselves and their group" (Bobo 1988, 93). While the research
method could be survey, interview, or discussion group, the methodology empowers audiences by acknowledging their interpretation. Audience reception theory broadens the interpretive lens, providing polyvocality to texts that are usually interpreted by critics and professional
intellectuals. Audience reception theory intervened upon previous media
studies that perceived the viewer as passive. Breaking away from the idea
of false consciousness—that audiences are passive receptors of dominant ideology, reader response and audience reception studies turn to
mass audiences to get their interpretations, how audiences negotiate
meaning from popular and public images. What interested me particularly about audience reception was Bobo's concept of an "interpretive
community." Her concept defined community through a social dynam-
ism of forces. Interviewing Black women who had viewed the film,
she examined their responses to the social thought developed by Black
women writers and critics. Thus, she breaks from a binary of lay(wo)man

and intellectual to examine the politics and ideology of interpreting films. For her study of a particular audience of Black women, Bobo finds that her informants bring together various viewpoints and insights to a film. While they bring their everyday experience to a film's representation of everyday experience, an additional factor for examination is the discourse of Black women cultural producers—scholars, writers, critics. The complexity of representation and representational practice, Bobo asserts, "articulate a social force to creating new self-images and social change" (Bobo 1988, 101). I felt that the Centro could offer such an interpretive community. The girls would be from the local area, already organized through networks of friendship and participation at the Centro. While they would bring together their everyday experience to a film's representation of youth or urban life, the Centro and the various political associations of Fruitvale were also a vital part of their everyday experience. The organizations and institutions, founded in struggles for civil rights and the identity politics of empowerment, were a social force that would be part of the girls' perception and consciousness. At least, I would test this idea.

Since I would be focusing on gang genre films, I felt prepared. I had taken a course on street organizations with José Lopez at California State University in Long Beach. In this course I read a particularly important study by James Diego Vigil (1988), whose description of the various types of gang members gave me a language for understanding my own preteen experience in the neighborhood I grew up in. I could describe myself as a "situational" gang member, intensely involved for a temporary period. While I had appreciated the style and demeanor of the cholos and cholas of my neighborhood, I didn't walk the walk or talk the talk. I claimed a gang identity with the kids on my street to prevent threat, harassment, and assault from bullies from other neighborhoods. I was also familiar with street culture, since my oldest brother was a pachuco and my other brother was a cholo.[2] Looking back on this experience, I felt that I had enough familiarity with youth/gang films and media reports on gangs to understand that the street cohorts of my youth and those of today were different. How different still takes up a lot of my thoughts. I remember there were guns and drive-by shootings. When a neighborhood kid was stabbed and nearly died, I remember the stories of guys who went out and killed in retaliation. I knew stories of the guys who did time for it. I remember going to school loaded from cheap wine, and I saw girls passing out from barbiturates and dopey from sniffing glue. What I remember of my preteen years was that none of this seemed unusual. By 1965 the preteen experience was a memory I tried to forget. I thought all that was a cholo thing, and I had nothing more to do with it. I was someplace else. In 1968, when I entered community college, a lot of the values of pachuquismo resurged as I became involved with the student movement. I think of those values—loyalty and trust, carnalismo, familia—as they were transformed in that moment of political consciousness.[3] And I realize how they have colored my own sense of activism and commitment to social change. What I was unaware of during the early part of my study was how much they would be brought to bear during "academic" fieldwork.

Preparing for the discussion group, I also worked closely with María. During the first weeks of "volunteer" time, she was respectful toward me but distant too. We began to talk more frequently and more energetically as we exchanged ideas around the two survey sheets that I wanted the girls to fill out. My first study asked about the community of Fruitvale. I framed the questions in a way that I hoped would encourage them to give their worldview as teenagers in an urban barrio. When María and I reviewed the first list, I asked María whether these topics would be relevant to the youth who would attend the rap group. She hesitated, then responded that she did not know if the girls would talk to me about their groups, but if they did, I would have a lot of material for my project. I was surprised and insisted that the examination was about the community, not about gangs themselves. María responded, "Yeah. But if they talk about the gangs with you, then you really've got something." María suspected that my questionnaire was likely to provoke discussion about gang life. I insisted that the questions were background research, just a mapping of what the Fruitvale area was like for the youth of the community. My investigation ranged from particular status categories—age, religion, schooling, employment—to relations at home—chores and responsibilities, relations to siblings. In addition, I asked how long the respondent lived in her neighborhood—this would indicate how closely she identified with the community. I asked whether the respondent felt safe in her neighborhood and how she characterized herself to her group of friends (dominant, follower, easygoing). The sampling would also provide information as to their knowledge of organized street culture. I asked what the main crew/gang in the neighborhood is called; what its territory includes; what other gangs or crews are in nearby areas; what their boundaries are. The inquiry was framed to detect respondents' knowledge of street organizations in order to understand how they would interpret and judge a film. I was not seeking answers that only an in-group would know. The inventory seemed to me a set of general questions about everyday life in a barrio—particularly neighborhoods that have a large number of street cohorts that influence youth culture. María understood my questions as raising issues that could only be answered by gang members. While the survey seemed impartial to me, María detected that many of my questions were those that only an insider would know and therefore could ask. In my concern for breadth and a certain neutrality, I was unaware that I revealed my past through these seemingly descriptive questions. When I asked her if many of the girls would attend, she said yes, "because it's about gangs."

The second survey focused on media habits. María suggested introducing "action" films as a genre and asked me to clarify what would happen after we viewed a film. The media survey ranged from viewing habits to genre, from how often the girls went to the theater or viewed films at home, to a list of films they may have seen and liked. It also included television habits. A second set of questions provided information as to the respondent's judgment and concerns: Is it important that a teen film resemble real life? What do you feel should and should not be in a teen film? What qualities or characteristics do you like to see in a female character? A third set of questions aimed to provide me with their thoughts on gang films (*American Me, Boyz N the Hood, Bound by Honor*): How closely do you think the characters resemble the people you meet in real life? Do events in the movie resemble life? How closely do you relate to the male characters? female characters? Once again, these questions provoked a situational identity with street organizations, and again María felt that my questions would be interpreted as "about" gangs. During the weeks of revising the questionnaire, María would ask me questions about myself, background questions that I figured were to size me up—had I ever been in fights, what barrio I ran with (i.e., had I ever been in a gang). I realized they were the questions that would test me as to whether I was up to the challenge of interviewing girls from the barrio and to locate my social class position. I reciprocated by asking questions about her, and we came to some basic understanding of each other. She became more invested in my study.

The idea for a discussion group was received well by the girls who frequented the youth center in Fruitvale. Nineteen girls attended the first three discussion sessions held in the center's library. My plan was to conduct unstructured interviews with the girls in group discussion and to follow up with personal interviews. At this initial meeting, two things occurred that determined the future of my project. The first indicated what the girls would eventually want me to research, and the second determined the way the meetings would run. As I asked them to say their names so that I could get to know them, one of the girls asked if they could say what gang they were in. I said, "Well, I usually identify myself as Keta and as a Chicana and that I dropped out of college and am now back. . . . So, yes, however you identify yourself." The girl who had asked the question then said her first name, followed by the nickname she went by among her friends and what gang she was in. The girls all began to cheer and repeat the name of her gang affiliation. At other times, the girls would shout "N-W-A!" And so it continued. All of the girls had identified themselves as either members of Da Crew, East Side Norteñas, or Las Norteñas. There were no members of the group Fresh Bitches In(effect), the fourth girl cohort that made up the alliance Norteñas With Attitude.

What struck me was that all of the girls had identified themselves with a gang. Having expected a broad cross-section of Latina urban youth, I intended to examine how the dominant messages of the films—anti-gang and anti-violence—were being interpreted when compared to the hyped-up violence that occurred in these films. What did Chicana teenagers think about these films? How did they feel about these films when gang violence occurred in their neighborhoods? Were the films glorifying gangs? Violence? Since all the girls identified themselves as gang members, I wondered how this would affect my study. I warily thought, well, this might be productive. Possibly, a different approach to my study could be developed. Maybe by locating their gang worldview, I could make a tighter comparison between the films' messages and the girls' commitment to their social milieu. And at the same time I felt that I had to bring in other girls to the rap group to participate, to try to even out the responses I'd get.

The second thing that happened came when I attempted to clarify questions of my survey. Another girl asked what we would we be talking about. I responded, "A lot of things . . . about your lives. So we'll take up what you want to talk about." "Sex?" one young girl asked, and I said yes. They immediately began a discussion of birth control and pregnancy, guessing at their parents' reactions if they came home pregnant. They were testing me, waiting to see how I responded to their transgressive discourse. The girls talked about pregnancy and parents as if it were a conversation among themselves. I did not try to stop the conversation or redirect it. Instead, I intruded at times with questions for clarification or information, an interruption which the girls accepted. They would address their answers to me as well as to one another. While I was relieved that the session had not followed a question-and-answer format, I was also aware that they had taken control of the discussion.

At the second meeting, the survey on media habits guided our discussion. This was not as successful as the first get-together. At this time, and in subsequent meetings, a tension developed as a result of my two-pronged (media and actual life) approach. From the last week of August to mid-October, only three girls attended regularly, while the others were inconsistent. When more girls attended, some expressed frustration with my questions about movies. But discussions about gang life were usually animated. They wished to discuss their lives, while I kept attempting to bring back the discussion to media habits. This, I believed at the time, resulted in infrequent attendance, and the experience became frustrating for me as well. The discussions on their lives, I had assumed, were to get at demographics—a process of situating themselves through class and social identity. Personal but not intimate. The background information was needed to assess how the dominant representations were being decoded and recoded through identities formed around race-ethnicity, class, gender, and sexuality. However, I felt them pulling me toward a study of gangs, something I had not intended, since my academic background was media, communications, and a bit of literary criticism. My project was becoming something else, and I resisted. Rationalizing my resistance, I assumed that my method of group discussions was not a viable method for an urban ethnography. I believed at the time that an ethnography of gangs had to be conducted in the streets. Moreover, since attendance had dropped, I clearly was not in a position to conduct a more extensive ethnographic study. The girls were rejecting my research goals.

Yet each week a group appeared at the Centro asking when the discussion group would start. The girls wanted to talk about their lives. Since my project was going nowhere fast, I reviewed my proposal statement, sharply focused on responses to media images. I saw no real conflict between a study of lived experience and a study of cinematic representations. Was the tie between the two goals too abstract or too academic to hold the girls' interest? In any event, I had no alternative. I downplayed the media aspects of my proposal and focused on those questions which examined the girls' knowledge of life and culture in the Chicano/Latino community. This brought into focus the following issues: Are the anti-gang, "just say no" campaigns viable, relevant to girl

gang members' experiences and youth cultural codes? How do they negotiate between the patriarchal Chicano cultural system, and the male-
centered arrangements in youth gangs? What does their gang membership mean to them? What needs are met in girls gangs? What could
replace them? How is their gang structured? What are its origins? What
are the affiliations with the boy gangs of their community? What do
those affiliations mean? How hard and fast are the loyalties to the male
gangs? How hard and fast are the loyalties to their own gangs?

These questions seemed to me at the time more directed at the girls'
interests. And they provided me with a contingency plan, adapting elements of my original project to an emerging study of girls in gangs. I
found, additionally, that my formula of investigation was changing.
Moving from prepared questions in a semistructured interview, I im-
provised a question for discussion on the spur of the moment. As the
content of the group discussions became more of a drawing force in the
girls' lives, my undisciplined approach may have looked like the method
found in "experiential analysis."[4] Issues of representation, however, remained a latent element in the changing work.

The fall of 1993 had been a period of adjustment for me. While I recognized that the study would have to change, I nonetheless persisted
with media topics. This drew criticism from the girls. At one point when
I attempted a discussion of the film *American Me,* MG said, "We're supposed to be talking about gangs. . . . Wha'z up with this?" And she
turned to another girl and started a different topic. TC, another girl,
was trying to answer my questions but soon fell silent. María, the peer
counselor, turned to me and said, "I told you. We gotta talk about the
gangs."[5] Thinking that the gang discussion was not enough for my
study, I attempted a discussion of La Llorona in order to discuss Chicano myths as narrative forms that regulate the social and sexual behavior of girls.[6] Once again, MG protested and drew FN and others into
a separate discussion. María asked why I was talking about this, and I
explained that I wanted to investigate the girls' thinking about how
women are thought of in our community. Beatriz, the other peer counselor who participated from time to time in the discussion group, then
said, "Well, why don't you ask? All these guys call us bitches and hoochies and don't have respect for us." Her remarks caught the attention of
the girls, who then began a general put-down of guys. This meeting in
the final week of October was the last time I attempted to push the initial study.

As the research topic of gangs developed, the discussion group meetings changed. Generally, the sessions were not the interview and response format. Meetings were casual enough so that the girls could come in and out of the discussion, sometimes leaving for chips, getting a phone call, talking to a boy outside the Centro, and returning to the rap group. While I started the conversations with a topic, most of the time the girls would change the course of the discussion to what was pressing to them. They used the Wednesday sessions to catch up with each other, clarify rumors and gang events and talk about incidents at school. They were in conversation, determining the contents: gang rivalries, the loyalties the girls have to their gangs, and fights among the members of Norteñas With Attitude or with rival gangs.

During the winter of 1993–1994, I started the sessions with questions that I needed for clarification, asking the girls to expand on events they had told me about earlier, either from the discussion sessions or from the conversations in the car when I drove a group of girls home. I attempted to broaden the questions in order to understand whether an incident was particular to a situation or if it was constitutive of girl gangs. The girls were rarely frustrated by my going over previously discussed material. They were patient about my confusion over the names of rival gangs, the names of the girls they fought with, which girl was in which gang, who were the boys they liked. In addition, as they spoke about a fight or about their gang, they willingly answered my detailing questions: Who said that, who was there, who else knew, did this happen at school, did you do anything before that, who was with you? Rather than resent these interruptions in their stories, the girls usually became excited, often reminding each other of the sequence or the context of an event, contributing to the story. At other times when my questions were unclear—especially when I was attempting to get at questions of identity and at the same time trying not to put words in their mouths—they would turn to each other and reformulate my questions. Like the discussion of La Llorona, sometimes my questions were too abstract. In one instance, I wondered about first-generation immigrants. Earlier gang studies noted that first-generation youth do not join gangs. Attempting to inquire about a rival gang's immigrant status, I interrupted MG in a story about a fight. I asked, "Are they Mexicanas?" One of the girls responded that the rivals were Sureñas. "But do they speak mostly Spanish or caló?"[7] At which MG asked: "What's your point? That girl was gonna beat me up." I insist: "But you just said everything in Spanish—did she say it in Spanish?" MG: "Yeah . . . so?" I go on: "But you hardly ever speak Spanish or caló. . . . Did you respond in

Spanish?" MG: "She's Mexican, Keta. We're all me-hee-ca-nos here." Throughout the time of field research I had noticed that the girls' speech was predominantly English, influenced by Ebonics, and punctuated by slang of urban Black youth. I noticed as well that the girls identified Sureñas as coming from Mexico or Central America. I was interested in language and generation, seeking an understanding of their significance to ethnic and racial identity and gang identity.[8] However, my questions were sometimes ill timed and inappropriate to the girls' discourse, particularly when they were attempting to tell me another story. They also reflected my academic interest, and many times I paid in embarrassment for my intrusions. I would have to seek answers through other means at other times.

By the end of the first year, we had discussed the structure, origins, and activities of the gangs. The girls expressed satisfaction with my study. They informed me that they had been part of another discussion group at another community center with a graduate student, Angela Gallegos, from the University of California at Berkeley.[9] The girls were attuned to the content and process of research, and they had reshaped my project to talk about gang life.

Two significant events occurred during my first year in the field, both of which emanate from the NEL Centro de Juventud's principles advocating youth rights. One development was the participation of the Centro's youth at a conference on gangs sponsored by Latino police officers. At this conference the majority of the youth participants were members of the discussion group that I initiated. At the conference the girls challenged many of the assumptions about and images of gang members. The girls' participation in this civil gathering and later participation in other academic and community public forums shifted our understandings and stakes in the politics of representation.[10] The other critical twist occurred at the end of my first year in the field. The Centro's director informed me that the Parks and Recreation Department would have funds available for a video project and asked if the girls would be interested in doing a short public service announcement (PSA) to be aired on a local cable network. When the video instructor came to speak with the girls, I emphasized that this would be their project, and therefore attendance and dedicating two hours after school to another lesson would be up to them. I had not seen the video project as part of my own research, since it began with the topic of teen pregnancy, and by that time I was conducting a study on girls in gangs. My field notes of those early meetings on the video project are sketchy. Since I had become closer to the girls, my notes centered on the informal discussions we had—talking to them about problems at home, what was going on with their relationships with boyfriends, or new leaders and problems with membership, and, of course, more fights. But eventually the girls changed the topic and format of the PSA to a documentary about their gang, and it became integral to our work together. In the next chapter I will provide the background for the shift and interpret the video, *It's a Homie Thang!* Now, suddenly, media representation was back in the picture—but in an entirely new way.

REPRESENTATION IN A SUBALTERN PUBLIC SPHERE

This ethnographer's tale offers insights into the tensions and conflicts I found in fieldwork. Inasmuch as this research experience is now—perhaps too neatly—narrated in the woes and bliss of fieldwork, I will examine how this garrulous experience comes to be an authoritative account. By writing about how my entry was negotiated, on what terms it was granted, and how the contact and relationships were maintained, I attempt to de-emphasize the celebratory categories of unity as an insider, a woman from a low-income, working-class Chicano/a community, with a bit of firsthand experience with gang culture. I have come to recognize that shared similarities of race/ethnicity, gender, and class are not the sole connections that legitimate my authority to represent the girls. But it is mediated from the ethnographic encounter. I mark my identity as an insider to propose an examination of other differences— power relations before, during, and after field research. Through thick description, my tale evokes these relations in order to show how the girls were co-participants in my project's aim—from its restricted perception of representation as media images to a broader examination of the politics of representation. This entails questions concerning the purpose of my tale and consequently of my project to articulate the relationship between representation and its effects in the public sphere.

Feminist theory that once assumed that the commonality of womanhood and positionality in the sexual-social hierarchy would produce non-exploitative research relations now confronts the hierarchical relations underlying feminist scholars' research (Baca-Zinn 1979; Stacey 1988; Reinharz 1993). Recent feminist debates question the processes of fieldwork and writing. In attempting to formulate a less exploitative and

more egalitarian research relationship, feminists such as Diane Wolf insist that researchers acknowledge and examine a triple axis of power relations between researchers and informants:

> (1) power differences stemming from different positionalities of the
> researcher and the researched (race, class, nationality, life chances,
> urban-rural backgrounds); (2) power exerted during the research pro-
> cess, such as defining the research relationship, unequal exchange
> and exploitation; and (3) power exerted during the postfieldwork pe-
> riod—writing and representation. (Wolf 1996, 2)

Wolf notes that all three dimensions are interrelated and mutually determining. Appraising the relations between researchers and informants,
Kum-Kum Bhavnani (1988) adds that often the researcher's power is un-
spoken, hidden in the researcher's decision about the topic of research,
how to conduct the study, and how to write the investigation. From the
moment of conceptualization through the final writing stage, researchers hold power. But it is not absolute, or unmediated.

Thus while recognizing the power of the researcher, I also want to underscore the active agency of research subjects in the ethnographic process. The observations of Niobe Way in her essay "Using Feminist Research Methods to Understand the Friendships of Adolescent Boys"
(1997) have special significance to my deliberation. Mindful that a feminist approach to research entails an examination of positionality, Way
emphasizes that research is an inherently relational process that involves
shared stories, actual bodies, and real voices. Describing her semistructured approach to interviews, Way highlights the agency of the people
being studied:

> The narrative in an interview or the responses in a survey are never
> simply a pure or "innocent" representation of voices of the "Other"
> . . . but are jointly constructed. In my research, this relational as-
> sumption led me to allow for both stability and spontaneity. For
> example, although there was a specific set of interview questions be-
> ing posed to each participant, there was also room during the inter-
> view for the participant and the interviewer to follow new and
> unexpected pathways. This semistructured approach to interview-
> ing explicitly acknowledges the interviewer's agenda (e.g., to under-
> stand a particular phenomenon or topic from the participant's per-
> spective) and the participant's agency or power (e.g., to introduce

important new knowledge that the interviewer had not anticipated).
(Way 1997, 3–4)

When the participants introduce new knowledge, the responsive
researcher's agenda and project shifts. In Way's formulation, whether
based on survey or participant observation, the final text is a product of
relational dynamics. She appreciates the authority of the informants—
who know, understand, and recognize their role as co-participants in the
research project. Once the informants enter the relational field, agreeing
to participate, they develop stakes in the project. Way implies that there
is a type of compact, a contract between interviewer and participants
that arises from the relational dynamic. Knowledge creation is what
the participant informant agrees to as part of the relationship. This I
consider the most prominent power of the participants to shape the
research.

The topic of research, then, ultimately affects the authority of the researcher in the field and the authority to represent. An examination of
how an ethnographer acts within conflicting relations, defining and
redefining the research topic, necessitates an examination of methods
and methodology. Such an examination is necessary at the outset of my
thesis to lay out the stakes of my project—its challenge to the representation of girls in gangs and its location of the girls in public discourses
of representation. In the sections that follow, I explore Wolf's triple
axis—positionality, field relations, and representational power of the researcher—and at the same time, offer an examination of the dialogics,
the relational dynamic between researcher and informants.

POSITIONALITY AND AGENDA

My potentially intrusive role as researcher converged with cultural expectations regarding gender and age. In fact I accepted several positions
which were, by and large, simultaneously enacted. I was a volunteer and
researcher as well as a confidante and an elder woman friend.

Space mediated our complex balance of power and trust. For example, constituted as a separate, private space, the location of the Centro's library encouraged trust. The library was set aside to provide intimacy, allowing for immediate access to the girls' lives through the
discussion group. The notion of divulging intimate information to an in-
sider/outsider invariably produces a hierarchical division. The space

worked to maintain my position as researcher, where I could safely perform my subject position as observer. The library as a space for interviews "naturalized" my presence at the Centro and created for the girls their own subject positions to "tell" me about themselves: it provided a stage for their performance as subjects of research—girls in gangs.

Additionally, age and education marked our differences. My presence as an older researcher, clearly of another generation and in some cases older than the girls' parents, could have become a point of tension—preventing the girls from talking to me about certain subjects. The generational difference, however, became a factor of trust—setting up a dynamic relationship between the young women and myself. I believe that the girls would have talked to an older Chicano because age in Chicana/o culture still garners legitimacy and respect. In this instance, I held on to the boundaries of age difference. The result was to accentuate my lived experience in contrast to their lived experience. While focusing on connections and similarities, points we had in common, difference was registered additionally in terms of social and class identity. The fact that I was in college, upwardly mobile in an institution of higher education, was probably an even more notable difference between us. As a college student, I could be categorized as a "nerd" or "square" who is attentive to studying and therefore passes through public space from home to school, unlike girls in gangs who carve out space in the streets. Here, my status, and age—a woman with life experiences who had dropped out of school and was trying again—made a bridge for trust. Thus cultural tradition regarding generation and life experience determined by age coalesced so that the young women were confident with me.

This aspect of being an older insider allowed "talking and listening," thus reducing conflict and tension between us. This was further aided by the fact that I conducted my study through the NEL Centro de Juventud, a youth center that not only serves youth with recreational activity but maintains counseling and educational goals to empower youth. Further, the monological interview set-up—I ask the questions and they answer—was convergent with their prior experiences in discussion groups. Thus, I was positioned as a facilitator and/or counselor for group discussion. This categorical position therefore precluded critiques regarding my authority to question the girls, subsequently removing the pressing requirement for disclosure of my own background, status, socially mobile difference.

The young women, in fact, did not ask about my background or experience until the second year of fieldwork. Becoming a confidante and woman friend, I believe, resulted from other categories of Chicana/o cultural relations: one, the role of aunts who share trust with younger children and adolescents; the other, the compadrazgo and comadrazgo system of extended familial relations.[11] While I discuss this social network in another chapter, I will remark here that comadres are not necessarily relegated by age nor defined through age relationships among women of Mexican heritage. Comadres can belong to the same age cohort or be intergenerational—an older and younger woman bonding through the system of compadrazgo. So, I believe that while the young women and myself were cognizant of the range of differences between us, the terms of elder, confidante, and woman friend were within the range of cultural experience that we shared.

One other aspect of positionality between researcher and subjects can be located during the shift from audience reception research to a study of girls in gangs. During this period of redefinition, I could have walked out on the project. The girls, I believe, knew this. During the fall months I was attending class at the university. My commitment to school took up evenings and days of studying as well as driving 150 miles to campus and back to Oakland. On the usually scheduled days of the discussion group, Wednesdays, I had an early-morning class and several times arrived late at the Centro. Eventually reacting to my late arrivals, one of the young women, MG, was angry with me. She insisted that if I was "serious" then I must be at the Centro on time and not cancel meetings without notification. I had a lot of handy excuses about being late—school, classes, meetings with professors, school committees, etc. These excuses provided them with the understanding that "school" could be the reason I might stop doing the interviews. Additionally, in the girls' view, "school" (advanced education) is serious, and therefore I could drop the research project if time were a conflict.

They saw me as a researcher but also as a student with demanding tasks of homework and exacting teachers. These are categories of which they were aware, and they utilized them to help understand what a student-researcher does. At the very next meeting of the discussion group, María, the peer counselor, and MG suggested that I take courses on days other than Wednesday and that I make time for a "serious" study of Chicana adolescents. By determining my subject position, by de-emphasizing the student with responsibilities to teachers in favor of the researcher responsible to her informants, the young women acquired greater influence in redefining my study.[12] I had to move my class schedule to one day a week (Tuesdays, all day) to make sure I worked at the center on Wednesdays. Additionally, I had to make sure weekends were flexible, in case there was an activity or gathering I needed to participate in: weddings, quinceñeras, or the possibility of observing other gang activities up close.

METHODS AND RELATIONSHIPS

This brings me to the second axis of power: methods and the quality of relationships between researchers and informants. Methods such as participant observation or survey interviewing and open-ended interview allow people to tell their stories. While giving voice may not change structures of patriarchal capitalism and racism, methods employed in the field have empowerment potential. "Informants" become active agents in formulating and determining the research topic. This involves critical examination of the methods—from semistructured interview to participant observer in the discussion group—and content of the research topic. As my project shifted from audience reception to a study of girls in gangs, my research method also changed from interview to a type of experiential analysis (Reinharz 1983). In each of the methods, their viewpoints and worldviews were aspects of the study that helped to shape it. I wanted them to be in conversation, to set up a type of equality.

My tale of the field reveals how the topic of research was a crucial point of contention. Inspired by innovative works on spectatorship and audience reception, my idea was that I would be in the field for a brief period (three months) and then move back to the academic base and find a different group to interview.[13] The research relationship based on a semistructured interview method would nonetheless be reduced to the following formulation: I ask the questions, they answer—with room for unstructured discussion. The ethnographic approach in my proposed study would take up the social aspects of the audience, their environment, and the politics of their everyday lives, but always in order to understand their relation to and interpretation of the films we would discuss. My research questions concentrated on the following: What constitutes these youth as "authorities" on the gang films? What attributes qualify their interpretation and use of the films' images in the ways that they wanted? Central to my mind, on commencing the study, was the question: In what sense are the informants, brought together under my aegis, a "community?"[14] Accordingly, my questions about how the subjects perceived their neighborhood and the social issues confronting their community would establish organic connections among the informants.

Audience reception study opened space for other interpretations—
to register the effectivity of fans, to see dominant images coded and decoded (Hall 1980). Drawing on the Gramscian concept of hegemony, in
which the strategies and tactics of readers contest and challenge and
reinterpret dominant ideas, audience reception theory was seen as a
means to understand better the work of ideology (Bobo 1988). Since the
struggle over representation is critical to breaking from past paradigms,
the methods employed necessarily relinquish some of the researcher's
control over the process. From the beginning, my own research relationship was set so that I could look into the girls' lives and ask questions
about their feelings. The field practice of reciprocation and exchange
then revolved around what I would provide them through this academic
endeavor: possibly the opportunity to see their opinions in print; to give
them voice, to legitimate their views.

A primary focus of my study was a reaction to gang films: Where are
the girls? This critical, not-quite-so-hidden aspect of my study was a
response to the lack of images of girls prior to Anders' film. This was
heightened by the dearth of literature at the time about girls in gangs and
the clear need to refigure media and sociological studies that construct
gangs as exclusively a male domain. Through reception theory, I was
hoping to get at the girls' perception of life in a barrio where gangs had
become quasi-institutional (J. Moore 1978; Vigil 1988). Thus, my study
would not be a sociological investigation but would provide a sociological context for reception theory. Since representation was the focus of
my research, the fact that I wanted to ask my subjects about dominant
images of gangs in movies and television news coverage provided the
means to feature girls in street groups: to mark their absent presence.
However, what I was asking had limited currency for my interlocutors.
Of what value is it to talk about the absence of women in films, since it
just amounted to a criticism with no results? Since the gang films prior
to Anders' did not have girls in them, since most news stories and features focused on young men, the girls felt the drive and impulse to talk
about themselves. My research topic had to change because dominant
media representations were largely irrelevant to my subjects. The girls
needed to present their world and worldviews to fill, not analyze, the
gap. The fundamental aspect of my study—representation—was the
catalyst to change the study. From media representations to their stories
and self-representation of girls in gangs, our different understandings
converged.

The principles of audience reception allowed for a process which
broadened the method and relationship from discussion group facilita-

tor to participant observer. If I were to represent the girls, then I had to be given more intimate details about their lives. Methods, methodology, and personal politics converged. Representation meant that the specific topic of media images had to be reworked and resituated to produce a study of girls in gangs.

While my social position as university researcher sanctioned me to ask questions, did I have the definitive power in the research process? Upon reflection on methods and the quality of the relationship in field-work, I must answer yes. But it is a qualified response, because the girls could (and many times would) turn away from me to begin a different discussion that they felt was more relevant to their day, to events that were happening around them. When the informants "have the power of knowing their experiences and deciding what to tell me and what not to tell me" (Way 1997, 3–4), I recognize the agency of all participants in the research process. Recognizing their control to create knowledge, the informant tells or does not tell, adds and elaborates.

While I formulated questions as best I could, however haphazardly, my questions revealed the authority to articulate scholarly and academic concerns because of my familiarity with both media theory and social science analysis about gangs. However, as the girls decided when to participate and not to participate, it was up to me to catch up, to listen, and to develop questions based on their concerns rather than purely academic ones of my own. While in the first portion of fieldwork (i.e., media representations) the tension was most stressful, challenges emerged nonetheless during the revised study of girls in gangs. This occurred at times when I was particularly focused on comparing the girls' responses to other sociological studies of gangs, work that influenced the kinds of questions I formulated (Vigil 1988; Jankowski 1991; Campbell 1991; J. Moore 1991).[15]

For example, when I was attempting to see the prevalence of gang membership in families, the majority of the girls insisted that family relations do not determine their participation. In a few cases, the young women knew of family members who had formerly been in gangs. In other cases, the girl was the only family member to have joined. My speculations and questions about family links seemed unsuitable. I found that my questions about family influence not only resulted in very little response but additionally obscured the strong bonds of solidarity that they produced and developed within their social group. The reasons girls form or join street organizations can be quite different from those that motivate boys. Since the space of the streets is predominantly a gen-

dered regime and therefore creates the conditions for street cohorts—
where boys hang out and construct a culture of aggressive masculinity—
public space operates upon young women differently.[16] Since the young
women are challenging their confinement to the domestic sphere, their
flight to the streets challenges patriarchal relations within the private
sphere. However, in the public gendered space, they are now susceptible
to being categorized as sexual objects. The formation of an all-girl street
organization contests this sexual objectification. The pattern in which a
girl finds a group of similar girls in public space is serendipitous. If the
individuals coalesce, then it arises from their determination to defend
their right to enter and be a part of public space. Therefore, when I asked
questions influenced by other sociological studies, I did not get at how
they made a girls' culture through an eclectic yet purposeful borrowing
and selection from various cultural forms found in Chicana/o, African
American, and Euro American cultures. We had to agree to different
questions.

WRITING AND REPRESENTATION

Negotiations during field research prompt an examination of the third
axis of the relational dynamic—the power of interpreting responses and
events from participant observation. Narayan (1993) argues that even
though insiders may discover personal and cultural roots during research, one must nevertheless recognize that the researcher moves between the academy and the field. The act of traveling between two sites
reflects "vectors of power," therefore highlighting the social and political context that produces the ethnographer's mobility (Narayan 1993,
24). Heeding her observation, I recognize my social position. Regardless
of the similarities between the girls and myself, my social position is
clearly at variance from the majority of the Mexicano/Chicano working
class. As I will enter the ranks of the middle class by income and occupation, I recognize my socialization as a middle-class Chicana that
evolves from life experience and intellectual development. Claims to in-
siderness would not erase my academic and personal history.

My ethnographer's tale attempts to explain my presence among girls
in gangs in the neighborhood of Fruitvale. Moreover, my selection of
particular events strives to establish that this is not a conventional gang
study but a study of representation itself. The tale is not about the dangerous streets of the inner city nor dark and rainy nights that render the
Chicana/o community a mysterious, strange, and fertile ground for the

otherworld of gangs. Even though the girls wanted me to write a study of girls in gangs, my project has remained focused on the politics of representation. Acknowledging my responsibility to take up their interest, defining the (changing) research topic, I take the authority to write about the representation of girls in gangs based on their own efforts to represent gangs. This aspect of the research project is both the hardship and boon of my fieldwork, the dilemma of process and product as they become defined in the field. Writing and representing, enacting ethnographic authority, I hold to a vision of social change. Fieldwork was caught up in this process. Thus I have come to recognize how, through a stressful push and pull over who was in control, our co-discursive partnership reflects negotiations across differences, an ongoing alliance.

The response of the girls to my position as researcher and our agreement on the research goal became a way in which they could speak about their everyday lives. Works by Vincent Crapanzano (1980) and Jean Duvignaud (1970) focus on change and self-awareness through the ethnographic encounter. Crapanzano particularly contests the fiction of "invisibility" and "disinterested observer" often allegorized in fieldwork practices, an attempt to ensure that what "really" happens is not disturbed or altered by the ethnographer's presence. But what happens or what is written when the ethnographer disturbs or alters the field? Can invisibility ever be achieved? Crapanzano contests the neutral self-effacing bias in ethnography, noting the dynamics of the encounter and the subjectivity of the ethnographer: his or her politics and interests that are mobilized for inquiry. Duvignaud offers a framework to examine how ethnographic "interrogations" provoke self-consciousness and arouse latent attitudes that call forth different forms of collective consciousness and identities.

Through the interview process, with my naive questions about everyday practices, my interlocutors had to put into words things that they took for granted. They had to find words to explain to a college graduate what their everyday expressions and practices meant. As Duvignaud notes, "but finding words is troubling. How to explain what is taken for granted. Thus, putting into words, finding verbal expression of the everyday, finds a form" (Duvignaud 1970, 268). That form is the arrangement of ideas in a broader context, taking the everyday out of its everydayness and relating to broader structures of power. So they came to a point at which they understood that they knew things that I, the interlocutor, was neglecting. They discovered that they knew things that I, a college graduate, did not understand. Finding verbal expressions, putting ideas into form, the girls developed a greater awareness of their identity in the course of presenting their everyday lives. Duvignaud's ethnography specifically identifies ethnographic contact as a material force in which informants acquire a vested interest in the researcher's larger project. Developing this awareness and articulating their worldviews, our "enclave type of subaltern public sphere" (Squires 1999) became a base from which they could articulate concepts of representation to a broader public in face-to-face contexts.[17]

Niobe Way's (1997) "relational dynamic" emphasizes that fieldwork methods of listening and talking are crucial to the politics of representation. Beyond what she has stated, I stress that by making "representation" explicit as an epistemological foundation of our research, we increase the informant's potential to influence the ethnographic product. The girls' drive or impulse to talk about themselves and present their world, combined with the fundamental aspect of my study—representation—became catalytic junctures of cooperative work. What evolved between us as a result of our fraught relationship was a broader and more elaborate conceptualization of representation. While a focus on representations in media became restrictive to the girls' desire to speak about their experience, I found social science representations of gangs and the dearth of studies centered on girls also circumscribing. When the prevalent concern is representation, feminist-insider ethnography becomes a way to avoid recreating inequality. When the desire of both researcher and informant is focused on altering dominant views or increasing knowledge about the subjects, then goals converge, at which point the informants have proficiency to influence the ethnographic product. However, representation remained problematic even in the shift to the gang study. The girls' stories and worldviews highlighted an additional aspect of representation that I had not foreseen: an investigation of self-representation and the re-presentation of girls in gangs.

The ethnographic contact is riddled with unexpected denouements, one of which is that the subject acquires a vested interest in larger structures. The girls and I entered a dialogue about gangs at a point where media representations have saturated the depiction of inner cities. The topic of gangs is an ongoing conversation with a history, and we entered a conversation never having the first or last word. The dialogics of our ethnographic encounter, then, not only marks myself and the girls in conversation but registers the broader social forces affecting our understandings and negotiations of representation. In this context, the term "alliance" seems an appropriate term to describe the co-discursive partnership that developed between us. Alliance is an interactive model that allows people to come to terms with the implications of power and privilege. An alliance model, rather than limiting unity upon points of commonality, accounts for differences and offers the possibility of re-visioning traditional conceptions of power.

While the tale I have told in this chapter illustrates the challenges to my authority as a researcher—complicating and reconfiguring the re-search method and topic—I recognize my contravening power: to rep-resent. However, there is still another form of agency from the girls that conditions my authority. The young women produced a video about their gang membership and about their lives. Therefore, by using the metaphor of alliance I can suggest how my thesis and their video are interrelated products of the ethnographic encounter. Alliance portrays the dialogical relation between our two texts—speaking to each other, against each other—while at the same time highlighting our different approaches. Alliance appears as the best metaphor for our different understandings of representation and our different uses of each of our texts. Both are partial stories, located observations. The girls wrote their own script about what they believe is important to understanding the gang and girls in gangs, while my text is about problems of representa-tion. My writing is supplemented by their video. The girls' work re-asserts their authority, establishing their voice as both oppositional and collaborative. Inasmuch as my text reflects the more academic concerns of the research—my interpretive elaboration on the problems of repre-sentation—their video registers a different view of what they believe are the fundamental questions to be explored in a study of gangs and girls in gangs.

MEDIATING IMAGES

It's a Homie Thang!

> The interpretive process, however, always operates on two distinct levels:
> the people we study interpret their own experiences in expressive forms,
> and we, in turn, through our fieldwork, interpret these expressions for a
> home audience of other anthropologists. Our anthropological productions
> are our stories about their stories, we are interpreting the people as they
> are interpreting themselves.   EDWARD M. BRUNER

Considering the use of film as a tool of field research, Margaret Mead in
"Visual Anthropology in a Discipline of Words" (1974) enumerates the
various objections that would be raised by anthropologists about film
usage. While the objections regarding training and aesthetic qualities and
cost have become less of a consideration, the major problem that Mead
outlines is still under debate—the relationship between the ethnologist,
the filmmaker or team, and the subjects being filmed. Recognizing the
subjective factors of interpretation, that a filmmaker imposes his/her
view of culture and people, Mead sets out a list of "safeguards" for the
use and dissemination of film that represents cultural behavior, sacred
ritual, and heritage. One safeguard that she offers is the inclusion and
participation of the people who are being filmed—inclusion in the planning, programming, filming, and editing. Attempting to hinder the "hazard of bias" (of the filmmaker), Mead discerns ethnographic film as a relationship between the subjects' own cultural framework and that of the
filmmakers, allowing for a comparative corrective for different cultur-
ally based viewpoints which visual texts could provide (Mead 1974, 8).

In a different context, yet with a similar perception, Jean Rouch
(1974) attempts to reconcile critics inside and outside social science
about the uses of "sociological film." Developing a history of film from
both fiction and nonfiction to elaborate on the observational powers
that film provides, Rouch raised a critical question about ethnographic
and documentary film: "For whom have you produced this film, and
why?" Rouch unabashedly responds: "For myself." However, as he elaborates on this reasoning, he notes that film as a research tool extends the
ethnographic written record. Not only is the social scientist "there," but
the audience, as much as any written text can offer, is also there. He then
complicates his answer by acknowledging that in the process of filming
and editing, his prime audiences are the subjects of his films. The camera, in Rouch's formulation, is a tool which provides for a different type

of communication between the filmmaker and his or her subjects—offering what some call "shared anthropology" (Rouch 1974, 96).

I have extracted minor and secondary arguments from Mead's and Rouch's comprehensive essays because they suggest a way to consider the relationship between visual and written texts that emerges from the ethnographic relation, particularly the relationship between myself and the young women I worked with in Oakland. In the chapter "An Ethnographer's Tale" I examined the power relations between myself and the young women through a critique of ethnographic practices based on feminist concerns for more equal relations in the field. I became increasingly aware of the relations of power that are produced in the ethnographic context. Endeavoring to describe the dialogical relation between myself and the girls, I examined the arrangement and distribution of power between us, inevitably confronting this question: Who has the power to define whom?

The video, *It's a Homie Thang!*, emerged in this ethnographic push and pull over representations. It was produced by the participants of the Narcotics Education League's Centro de Juventud discussion group with whom I conducted my field research. The video explains the gang through the experiences and life stories of its female members. It begins with the participants' interpretations, giving significance to the "facts" of gang life. Developed for future investigators, it also serves as a primer for gang studies. The video provides information and insight into the gang worldview, and in this sense, the video can be situated as a realist form of ethnographic documentary. The video is made for information about gangs, from "our" point of view, with "our" voices directed to an outside audience/"public" which is capable of going beyond stereotypes. *It's a Homie Thang!* can be understood as an experimental moment of auto-ethnographic film since it situates the girls' voices as authorities on their own worldview. And I believe, because the video became the vehicle for the girls to represent themselves to a broader audience, their video is a contribution to ethnographic documentary film.

The video is one of the most challenging products of our ethnographic encounter. Because a visual text is constrained by time, the question becomes how to present my observations and analysis that came about from months of fieldwork to an audience that has not had the benefit of the same amount of time in the field.[1] My concern therefore focuses on audience, the consumers of the video. Because visual texts provide signifiers that can reconstruct and reconstitute a text's message, the analysis I provide can be construed as my attempt to control the text's meaning. However, my pleasure in viewing the video *It's a Homie Thang!* has always been in relationship to and dialogue with an audience—with no guarantee that the meaning of the visual text is fixed, unvarying from viewer to viewer, or will remain the same over time. My chapter assumes that three interpretations are possible: interpretation by the anthropologist, interpretation by the participants of the culture being studied, and interpretation by the readers/audience.

Foremost, I show how my conception of the video as an ethnographic product situates it in the realm of the public sphere. As a tool for self-representation, crafted by the girls themselves—speaking for themselves, their social identities, and their social network—the video amplifies their voices to a broader public, beyond the research relationship between myself and the girls. According to one young woman, the video gets at these basic questions in order to move to a higher or more intense level of dialogue to engage the subject of gangs. The video addresses the most frequently asked questions about gangs and particularly girls in gangs: How was their gang organized? What were the origins of their gang? What is the source of gang rivalry? These questions that make up the script content of *Homie* are the typical questions about gangs that the young women were asked, not only by myself as a researcher but by journalists and by people who attended conferences when the young women spoke about their gang membership. While I elaborate on the interaction of the girls with various publics in the chapter "Cross-Sites for Cross-Talks," their video can be placed in the developmental process of the girls' increasing awareness of the problems of representation. I would like to situate my presence in the context of the community center in which I worked. Many of the activities that the young women participated in involved speaking about their gang identity, about the significance of the gang to various professionals. This factor allows for a different kind of relationship between the ethnographer and her informants. That is, many events happened not solely because of my ethnographic presence. The NEL Centro is a particular kind of center for youth. The young women spoke at a police conference. There they addressed police officers and social workers. They spoke at a free clinic. They spoke at various conferences in various venues where they emerged as authorities—as young people in gangs. This is not expressly a direct outcome of my presence. The Centro is youth-centered and lobbies for youth. The Centro's program gives youth a voice, provides youth with a forum to voice their opinions. The Centro's leadership holds that youth should frame their own programs. It is an activist center. These events would have happened without me.

What I think did happen as a direct result of my presence emerges from my questions. When I first began, I asked the naive questions. Many of the young women had not articulated what their gang membership was. Through my interrogation, the young women became more fluent, articulating the meaning of the gang and its significance in their lives.

It's a Home Thang! is in direct dialogue with media representations. It was not intended as a home movie for family and friends; rather it was meant to circulate as a research tool for the study of gangs, specifically girls in gangs. Its intended audience is adults and particularly people who work with teens in social services, as well as future researchers concerned with girls in gangs. Therefore, the video does not propose to provide an anti-gang or anti-violence message to teens. The video is a representation that will approach various audiences with varying ideas, desires, and expectations. As an ethnographic product scripted and directed by the girls, the video produces a polyvocality between my text and their video text. When treated as an ethnographic product, the video both challenges and qualifies my ethnographic power (authority?) to represent the girls.

Because the video in fact creates a co-discursive relation between my thesis and their product, generating two different conceptualizations on issues of representation, I provide in this chapter the background for the production of the video as well as an analysis of what I found to be the major message of the girls' text. I begin this chapter by marking the stakes, interests, and ideals that guided me in the field through a description of the process to produce the video. Through ethnographic background, I show how the girls constructed an audience, marking their processes: how the video project began, how they managed to take control of the video project, and as a result how they developed the idea of who they wanted to reach with their video. Through the production of their video, they became increasingly aware of the need to address a broader audience about the subject of girls in gangs. By understanding their own stakes in representation, the girls and I became critical partners in developing a working relationship and goal to produce their video. By becoming the authorities on gangs, they became the authorizing agents of representation.

While the video decenters the social scientist's voice of authority, it is nonetheless the ethnographer who must select, explain, and interpret. Thus, I describe and interpret the video's major and minor messages. Finding that the video produces a major message through a dialectic of difference and similarity—we are not like you/we are like you—the video constructs an ideal audience. At the end of this chapter, I also offer a second interpretation of the video's minor message. I contrast the public persona that the young women present at the beginning of the video with the private persona developed in the video's last section. I analyze their statements—the vernacular poetics—everyday speech that they use that may seem nonpolitical and inconsequential. However, as we listen to our subjects, the vernacular presents a poetics of resistance and insight.[2]

CONTEXT: MAKING VIDEO(S)

As mentioned earlier, the video project was introduced near the end of my first year in the field when the Centro's program manager, Rosalinda Palacios, informed me of funds from the Parks and Recreation Department for a video project and asked if the young women might want to make a PSA for a local cable channel. The project provided an instructor who would teach them how to use the camera, develop a script, and learn editing. Additionally, the video instructor presented the various themes commissioned by the citywide proposal that the young women could take up. Since the video instruction was set during the regular hours that I met with them, I attempted to arrange alternate meeting times for my research, and the discussion group meetings disappeared.

Highly motivated by the opportunity to present teen views, the young women began with one of the proposed topics, teen pregnancy. The girls developed various questions to pose to teens: What would you do if you got pregnant? What would your parents say or do if you got pregnant? Would you have an abortion (and why or why not)? Why do you think girls get pregnant so young? What happens to your friends when they get pregnant? Do things change? What or how? This project, however, did not work out for them, and they began to complain to me that the project was boring. There were several factors as to why the topic became "boring." One reason was that the girls realized that the video instructor proposed that the girls go into the neighborhood and interview people. One of the girls, SP, felt the project would fail: "No one's gonna stop and talk to a gang-banger." TC, who became proficient at handling the camera and creating angle shots, expressed her discontent with the man-on-the-street approach: "We're going to go out and videotape and what? All we get is a bunch of people talking." The idea of the on-the-street interviews created anxiety for them. Additionally, what had been the exciting aspect of the video project was that the girls were interviewing each other. During this phase, the girls followed a question-an-swer order, stiff with the interview format and uncomfortable with the questions. Once in a while to cut the tension they would ask: Are you a virgin? or a hoochie? When were you popped? Moreover, conflict de-veloped among them on the topic of abortion. Some girls were in favor of abortion, while others were opposed. The girls seethed in disagree-ment. Their perceived unity, assuming that everyone had the same opin-ions and ideals in the gang, revealed itself on the issue of abortion. (I be-lieve that the issue produced unease among them. The differences among them on abortion altered the images they had of each other. The issue of abortion therefore disturbed the imagined community they felt they had attained in the gang.) This division had never been so publicly expressed. While the girls did talk among themselves about abortion, the polite and discreet way to deal with it was to avoid these discussions in any public manner. However, with the video as a public forum, the girls' disagree-ments could not be hidden or evaded. The topic was so hot and divisive that the girls began to argue with one another during the taping. They wanted to change the project.

In a discussion with the video project instructor, they expressed their wish to change the topic to gang life while at the same time recognizing a dilemma. Since they were members of gangs, they felt they could not advocate a message contrary to their lived experience: "We can't say, Don't join gangs." Because the video project proposal mentioned that the video would be used as a PSA for an Oakland cable network, we—I include myself—were stuck. While the Parks and Recreation Depart-ment video proposal advocated youth perspectives that would articulate their concerns and understandings of issues that affect their lives, the content and message were prescribed. Video topics would have to en-compass "drug and alcohol education and violence abatement" (OCTF 1994). Moreover, since the content goal of the PSA is educational, to provide the public with information, the goal proposed "to create aware-ness and engage concerned citizens in methods of cooperative resolu-tion" (ibid.). The form of the PSA, additionally, constrained the content. The PSA for commercial and public television is restricted to three to six minutes, thus inhibiting elaborate explanation or subjective explo-rations of the themes. While the PSA should highlight and illuminate is-sues that impact upon the community, the television genre contains the implicit structure of recommending methods of resolution or emphasiz-ing existing programs as the means to broach resolution. Both form and content manage to provide a quick and accessible message for the viewer.

Therefore, to air the perception of youth in gangs without a message of cessation or suppression would be controversial to the project's goals as well as antithetical to the genre of the PSA.

After a long discussion in which we (the video project teacher, the young women, and I) could not decide what to do, the peer counselor, María, suggested that it was okay to do a video on gangs: "They always show how the gangs are bad; how kids shouldn't join gangs. But you can tell them your story, why you're in a gang." She emphasized that the video would fulfill the educational component of the proposal. Since a public service announcement provides information and the proposal strongly advocated youth views, the girls would be presenting their views from their perspective. Thus the format shifted from the genre of the PSA to a documentary through interview—providing information about a group, culture, or subculture. We then moved quickly to undertake a different kind of documentary about the girls and their gang membership. Until then, again, I had not seen the video project as integral to my own research, but with the shift in focus, our projects dovetailed.

Not only did the discussion become more animated, but the new topic led to a more elaborate set of questions and detailed locations for filming. Moreover, it initiated a narrative structure.[3] As they developed a list of questions and possible answers, they began to script the subtopics of the video. The topics they chose provided a variety of opinions and experiences that they felt any one of them could discuss and elaborate upon (without the disagreement they experienced earlier). The video about their gang membership reaffirmed their unity, and everyone could participate—speak about the gang—without a lot of dissent. Furthermore, since I was eliciting responses about the gang, the girls had a greater repertory of questions and topics to address.[4]

While the video production was in process, the program director of the Centro, Palacios, was called by the director of the Bay Area news division at ABC, who wanted to do a story on the project. ABC's news director had heard that the video was about "why girls should join gangs," i.e., a recruitment video! Somewhere between the PSA and a documentary about girls in gangs, the media got the idea to do a story about the production of a gang recruitment video. I informed the news director that it was not a video to urge girls to join, but she still insisted upon sending a news crew to the Centro. I told her that it was the girls' project and they had final approval, not me. When I presented the issue to the girls, they were angry. MG stood up, striking her fist on the palm of her hand, "They always do that. It don't matter what we say; they say what they want." She went on to protest the media's disdain toward the Mexican community and the poor, complaining about the media's stereotype of gang members: "But this time, we got our video. Let them come and videotape us, and they can say what they want, but we'll have ours. We can say, that's what they want you to see, but this is what really happened; what we're really doing. 'Cause we'll have it all—what they want people to see, and what we really said." This was the longest speech I ever heard from her.

During the drive home later that evening, some of the girls talked about the newspeople who would cover the videotaping of the following week.

TC said, "We should have another video camera, so we could show how they are with us."

I responded, "That'll be a multimedia event, cameras on cameras on cameras."

MG asked, "Yeah, but where we gonna get another camera? Does the teacher have another video?"

We all grumbled. Where to get another video recorder?

Then another young woman, QG, came up with another possibility: "Keta, you should have your tape recorder on, so we can get more about how they are."

Then I began to laugh. "TC, maybe you can just turn the camera around and we'll have two cameras looking at each other."

MG, smacking her fist into her palm, exclaimed, "That's right! We'll turn the cameras on them. Ask them why they thought we were doing a video to tell girls to join gangs. Just 'cause we're Mexicans. They wouldn't do that with White kids."

So we decided that we would tell the video project teacher about our plans. We had a meeting with him the very next day in which MG, TC, FN, and I were going to discuss editing a video of our trip to Los Angeles—taking out all the cursing, tattoos, smoking, etc.—in order to show it to their families. As FN said, "You keep the originals of what really happened and give us the copies we can show our moms." (Yet another story on controlling media and self-representation that I will elaborate upon in this chapter.)

With the video instructor, we talked about what we wanted to do. I suggested that if we turn the cameras on the news media folks, we had to be prepared with questions and not just let them answer the questions with a yes or no, that we had to pin them against a wall with well-developed questions. The video project teacher said he'd bring another video camera to record the interaction between the news and the girls. We figured what else we would ask the news media. I was assigned to call the station to give them the go-ahead. At home that evening I complained to my roommates about the media's presumptions and subsequently recruited one of them to bring their home video camera to take in everything that happened.

On the day we were to meet the news crew it began to rain. Huddling together, the girls discussed moving to another location, possibly the Centro. But since we were at the park, we could not call the news station to tell them of our change in plans. We waited and waited and finally we realized that the news crew was not going to show up. Deciding to go to QG's house, since that's where they kick it, the girls were determined to forge ahead on their project. Once at QG's place the girls quickly took their script to assign everyone their jobs and talked about the content of the scenes they were going to tape. Once everyone had her job assigned, they went to work. The news crew didn't show up, but the girls were now on a whole different footing. There were three cameras on the set. There was the professional camera, the one that the video instructor had taught the girls to operate. He also brought another camera that the girls could operate when the news crew came around. And then there was the home video camera that my friend brought with her. The young women used all the cameras. The girls never smoked on their *Homie* video. But on the home video cassette that I have, the girls are at the side watching the taping, smoking, and drinking. When the girls are on *Homie,* their tattoos are covered, but in the video I have, they display their tattoos. In the extra home video, the girls took my friend's home video recorder and taped around the scripted scenes—showing off their tattoos, poking fun at the women who were on the set, running in and out of QG's house, and generally having a good time. When talking to MG about what to do with this extra video, she simply stated, "There's the fake video, and you got the real one, how we really are."

In the two ancillary videos where cursing, tattoos, smoking, and drinking are unconcealed and are subordinated to the public video that will be viewed by either their families or audiences, the girls express a sophisticated understanding of the construction of representation. At the same time, their statements that the uncensored videos are the "originals" and not "fake" complicate the girls' claim that *Homie* is a representation of the real. This doubled perception and conception of the real provides for a complex unraveling of the video(s). On the one hand, the goal of documentary is to provide information about others. Within the realm of representation, the characteristic mode of visual media renders people as objects, to be seen, to be looked upon. Thus the people are depicted for illustration, for spectatorship. Because representation is filled with power relations, the contestation attempts to re-present a pre-existing object, that is to re-depict, to re-symbolize. In this sense, *Homie* as a documentary reflects the girls' interest in changing the way people think about them. They take the tools of production into their own hands. Thus it is a self-conscious effort, and their performance for the camera is consciously constructed. It is a performance of toughness and the revelation of their social network, the poetry, of their personal lives and ideas. The documentary, then, is to represent their "real" stories. The documentary genre works for them because of their conscious effort to change the way in which they are depicted. Thus, the film represents what the filmmakers think more than it represents "reality" or actuality. However, the form is constructed. So, they understand their text as a "partial truth" (Clifford 1986). It expresses their lived reality, yet they withhold other areas of their lives in order to contest dominant representations of gangs and particularly girls in gangs.

On the other hand, the ancillary videos complicate use of the realist form as a tool for countering dominant images. The realist form of documentary and ethnographic film has been perceived as a form of self-representation to empower a group, to image and imagine the voices and subjectivity of the "subaltern" (Mercer 1994). Because the realist format points to an actuality outside the spectator, particularly to the outside social world, it is assumed that the form articulates the truth of the subject. (Film in this instance operates as an indexical sign rather than as an iconic sign.) This implies a conviction that the camera can express the lived reality, and certainly the girls' hope that the camera can capture the authentic. Utilization of the realist form of documentary assumes that the form is objective and holds no ideological meaning. Since documentary operates on the use of realist forms to articulate the truth of the subject, there is the belief that the camera can express the lived reality. Therefore the question remains as to whether one can contest or subvert the dominant meanings and ideologies through this form.

The context for the video *It's a Homie Thang!* produced for a television audience ("citizens") is the attempt by the young women to intervene in the public sphere. Given the intention of the video project, to provide a voice to a marginalized segment of the community, that is, youth, the young women developed their political strategy to deal with the ABC news misconception of their intent. Miscoded by the news network and under the dominant televised stereotype of gangs, the young women endeavored to intervene upon dominant discourse in the public sphere. Their efforts to explain gang membership and the subsequent conception of what they were doing by the news media illustrates the always-present danger of being misrepresented. Striving to control the conception of their project, the young women through the multiplication of cameras attempted to exert damage control.

These political strategies to enable their authority and to intervene on the images and stereotypes are further witnessed in other areas of the production of the video. The most self-conscious moment in the video is the first section, "Language." The section was not originally scripted for the video. During the taping of *Homie*, the young women realized that they had been using "bad" language in various scenes. There are moments when the young women attempt to censor their language, but finally they give up their effort and return to the language that they conventionally use. This subsequently brought about the first section, in which the young women attempt to explain what kind of film the viewer will be watching: girls in gangs, uncensored.[5]

In yet another instance of the young women's attempt to record the details of their lives, they recruited María, the Centro's peer counselor. María, appearing in the first and last sections of the video, was recruited into the video because of her familiarity with the gang culture and her close counseling with the young women. They see María as a veterana, one who is a former member of a gang. While María was never a gang member, but rather occupied a more peripheral status within the gang milieu when she was a preteen, she had developed considerable respect among gang members, male and female, among the youth of Fruitvale. Her street knowledge, her ability to move in various circles, her keen interest in racial justice and knowledge of ethnic pride struggles, made her a very articulate young woman whom many youth admired. Therefore, she was recruited to the video because of her ability to articulate sentiments and views shared by the young women. QG, who particularly wanted to speak about the style of recreation found in the gang, became camera-shy and asked María to participate in the video with her. Feeling more comfortable with María's presence on the scene, QG was able to defer to María's expressive ability.

An additional strategy to legitimate their voices was to bring into the video the reluctant ethnographer, myself. Throughout the video instruction and production, I had naively insisted that the video was their project and I had no influence. I had unrealistically assumed that my role was as a "distant and disinterested observer" of their project. By providing rides to the location shootings, I ensured that the young women showed up to each of the classes on video. Moreover, the discussions with the young women about how they felt about each stage of the production registered my ethnographic presence and visibility. While the young women scripted and edited the video, assuring the authority of their voice, the video's narrative structure, nonetheless, reflects my progress in the field. I started with the naive questions of the social science researcher, and, as a result of my interrogation, they developed the script to answer the most frequently asked questions about gangs— How did your group start? How did you meet? How do you join a gang?

One example occurs in the video when a young woman states: "It's not because we're born bad but what we go through." Speaking directly to the camera, she then asks, "Huh?" (meaning "Isn't it so?"). In the context of the video, this is a question directed at the audience. Yet in the filming, she posed the question to me, the ethnographer and academic. As a researcher, with institutional authority and knowledge, I was asked by VR to either elaborate or agree. At the moment of filming, however, I was surprised that she was asking me to enter the film. I responded, "This is your film. You say what you think." The response of the other young women was to tease VR for looking to me as the authority on their video. In another section, my voice intrudes into their text. I ask, "Why can't you walk away [from fights]?" However, there are many more moments of my presence. The young women position themselves as ethnographers, asking my questions. They interrupt each other in order to clarify slang and acronyms, much as I did while taping my interviews with them. While the girls may have been poking fun at me or taking on my ethnographic identity as a role model, the imitation, nonetheless, emphasizes that they are the constructing authority in producing their video about gangs.

The video presents an unusual look at gangs. The informants or performers are young women. They are from three all-girl gangs. The young women who participated in the video project also have an unusual problem, one that parallels yet differs from the one I faced as the ethnographer. In this video they attempt to speak on behalf of all gang members while also attempting to mark a difference. I must admit that when I was in the field I was asking and developing questions from previous studies: How was their gang organized? What were the origins of their gang? What is the source of gang rivalry? What do they feel when they are fighting? What are their relations to the boy gangs in the neighborhood? I did not develop particular questions or hypotheses to examine variance. Many times I did not get responses from the young women that diverge in a sharp way from the studies already written about gangs. Thus, in many ways their video universalizes gang members. Imitating my naive questions, putting my questions to each other, they translated to themselves the importance of their knowledge. The questions ceased to be my questions but became a response to the ethnographic encounter. They understood that I was neglecting things that were more important (Duvignaud 1970). The girls then began to distinguish and differentiate their positions and points of view.

Therefore, as a researcher and social science ethnographer, I am now confronted with the problem of representing the significance of their video. What follows in this chapter is an analysis of their video as a text, like any other text. In order to give authority to their voice and subjectivity, I analyze the video the same way as I would analyze a movie, a novel, a professional documentary, or an ethnography. I analyze the video by comparing and contrasting each of the video's intertitled sections to the opening scene to get at the significance of the text/video. The video's major message emerges through this dialectical reading: We are not like every other teenager, and we are like every other teenager.

CONTENT: VIDEO STRUCTURE

While *It's a Homie Thang!* provides a distinct contrast to news media features and documentaries about gangs, its format is based on television news features. Its twelve-minute length and original exposition were developed for a local Oakland cable network presentation that aired in the summer of 1994. In an attempt to re-present an already depicted grouping, the video presents some interesting moments in which the young women pose or perform a stereotype, the streetwise and street-tough image that abounds in society. However, unconventional features erupt with the introduction of the private lives, yearnings, and wishful thinking of the young women, complicating the usual media representation of gangs. The two aspects of self-presentation introduce a dialectic of difference and similarity which becomes the major theme of the video: We are like everyone else, and we are not like everyone else.

I will interpret the film's major message by comparing and contrasting the video's opening section to the sections which follow—images and scenes that are oppositional, redundant, or complementary.[6] The video is scripted in six sequences marked by the following intertitles: "Language," "Membership," "Herstory," "Enemies," "Fights," "Poetry."[7] Each of the sections provides basic answers to common research questions about gangs. Why did you join a gang? What is good and what is bad about being a member? How did you join? What do you do? Through these questions, the young women provide their particular accounts of joining or of why the gang is important to them. The personal stories reveal nuances of gang life and different levels of commitment to the gang. These glimpses of life history provide a sense of the variety of street gang members (Vigil 1988). While surveying these individual experiences in the gang, the video underlines the group values—especially the value of members backing each other up.

Language

Homie opens for about a half-minute with a group of young women who are cursing and calling one another names when the "Language" intertitle scrolls up on the scene. One of the young women, QG, speaks to the camera explaining the use of name-calling against foes as forms of harassment and the contrast of name-calling among friends, homies. "It's like when we talk to our pa'tnas, we don't mean it, but, you know, to other people, sometimes we mean it, sometimes we don't." Another, MG, turning to the camera, and as a consequence addressing the video audience, says, "Yeah, it depends who you're talking to. Like [to QG] I be, like, 'Shut up, bitch.' I mean, that's my pa'tna. I can tell her that. But, when it's like today, when we was almost like nearly got ranned over, I talked a hella shit to some lady. I mean, but I wasn't doing it, like, just saying it 'bitch,' 'ho.' I was doing it serious, so the bitch could walk out." Continuing their explanation, the opening section ends with the title of their video, *It's a Homie Thang!*

The video's first section, "Language," is based on two types of acknowledgements that inform the viewer that they will be seeing something about gangs. First, the opening operates on the stereotype, on the viewers' preconceptions about gangs. The scene reasserts the stereotype, the familiar image of gang members. The opening works to distance the audience by showing how the viewer is unlike the gang members. Second, by turning to the camera as a form of direct address, the young women construct an audience. The audience, a figurative "you," already has an idea of what gangs are, and it is different from us, the gang members.

The major theme is developed in "Language." A group of teenage girls is gathered at a park. They are conversing in a pastoral setting, which contradicts the notion of gangs as urban and street-based. A sense of distance is produced by the long shot that displays the full bodies of the young women. Their clothing is an androgynous dress of baggy pants and oversized T-shirts. The long shot allows the viewer to gaze upon them. The intended effect works to provoke the notion of otherness: how other the girls are in relationship to the audience. Similar to their direct address to the audience, the girls' relaxed playfulness highlights their willingness to perform for an audience in order to disclose their world. The long shot permits the viewer to look at their performance of unruly behavior. It registers their comprehension of what being looked at constitutes, the positioning of themselves as other, different from the viewer. It registers their complicity with being looked at. However, it is now under their authority.[8]

While subsequent sections attempt to breach the distancing produced in the opening, the stereotype that lies behind the opening is of a coarse subculture. Yet, the introduction undertakes a project to bring the viewer into their world values. The intertitle "Language" works like a parental advisory found on television broadcasts or CD jackets to warn consumers of the adult content. Language, accordingly, is a notification and consequentially becomes conventionalized as the rapid-fire exchange neutralizes the ruffian effect of name-calling. The intertitle and the girls' explanation are a conscious changing device allowing the viewer not to be excessively judgmental, as there will be a further unraveling of their worldview.

Video Title

The second section, running about two minutes, works without an intertitle, as it is introduced by the video title, *It's a Homie Thang!* The scene is still in the park. Now, however, the young women are standing along a rock wall, lining up as though for observation in an allusion to criminalization. The camera renders long shots that show the entire group and medium shots that frame the faces and upper bodies.

The young women standing along the wall perform their street toughness. As the camera pans across the group, one young woman, VR, says, "People stereotype gang-bangers, and we're just like everybody else." Another, DD, coolly nodding her head and using her chin to express her direct address to the viewer, speaks to the feelings of youth who are so labeled: "Just because we dress like this, or whatever, that don't mean that we don't know anything or we're stupid. Or we don't have any feelings." MG then clarifies the differences and similarities. She first uses her hands to signal her gang affiliation. "We chill the same way, it's no different in how we kick it, we kick it the same way. But it's just that we down for the big DC [Da Crew] and FF [Fifty-fourth Street turf gang] on mine." Then further utilizing her body as a metaphor, she pushes her hands down as if thwarting off any penetration of her body. "We got love fo' some muthafuckas. But other muthafuckas don't get shit up in this muthafucka." Her body language speaks. She expresses that she is not to be messed with, will not be beaten by any rival. VR speaking to the feelings of youth who are marginalized directly addresses whether these stereotypes are true only of gang members or of youth in general. Directing herself to the camera, she then states the questions: "It's not like we're born bad; it's what we go through. Huh?"

Because the girls address the viewer, the frontal positioning of their bodies produces a mixed economy of the gaze. Usually invoked as the power of the dominant to look at the dominated, the gaze produces the object of the frame as exoticized or deviant. In this section, the young women invite examination by lining up. The camera pans across, focusing on faces and bodies as each of the young women speaks in turn. However, the invitation to look upon them is authorized by their direct address to the audience. In this instance the young women address the viewer by naming the stereotypes that operate in his or her mind to mark the young women's otherness and deviancy. Each speaker insists that they do the same things and feel the same as other youth. Direct address facilitates their control of the gaze through their self-positioning as authorities of a gang worldview.

The sections that follow, "Membership," "Herstory," "Enemies," and "Fights," work in a redundant or complementary relation to the opening section of the video, marking difference from the viewer. In these sections the street tough represents the general gang member. In addition, the location of the scenes suggests the various representations of the urban landscape where the lives of these urban youth unfold.

Membership

The footage on "Membership" is shot as two scenes in the park. In the first scene, three girls are lying on a blanket, facing the camera, a panoramic view of the city of Oakland behind them. While the city is covered by the misty fog of a rainy day, it is nonetheless touched by sunlight. The young women are laughing, looking down at the grass. Then they look at each other and sometimes to the camera. The scene seems to move into their private sphere of girls' talk. The young women are immersed in casual conversation.

In this first scene the young women discuss how and why they joined the gang. MG, positioning herself as the interrogator, asks who can get in. VR responds that anybody can join: "It don't matter what color you are, you just gotta be down." DV chimes in, "Just as long as you're down, it don't matter how old you are. . . ." VR interjects, "Can't be no punk. . . ." DV laughs and clarifies, "Yeah, you hear some little girls talking shit, you know. Some little girls, you need little girls to handle them." They then discuss what forms of initiation they went through. DV notes that she wasn't jumped in (initiated through a fight), while VR states she had to go through three rounds of fights to become a member. Their laughter continues as the film cuts to the next scene.

In the second scene of "Membership," three young women discuss what they get out of being in a gang and what problems are created by their membership. Reporting that she gets "protection" from the gang, GG notes, "Just having somebody be there for you. Sometimes your family ain't with you. . . . It's like sometimes your family be tripping off you. And you need friends and being friends, sometimes you consider them your second family." MG turns to the other young woman, DD, to respond. Since DD is reluctant to speak, MG rephrases the question. "What do you see cool about getting in? Or what's the bad part about being in a gang?" DD responds that the constant potential of being mugged is the biggest downside: "The bad part is that you got to watch your back every time you go out. You can't just go out to anyplace. You got to be watching your back every time you're walking or something. And the good part is you get to meet a lot of people. You get to kick it with them. Do what you like to do. The same like what she says."

Because GG and DD do not want to be the sole respondents, they question MG, kidding throughout. GG asks her what she gets out of being in a gang, and DD laughs and adds, "You get to kick people's asses?" MG laughs with them, then shakes her head, disavowing that this is her form of recreation. "No. What I see is that I can call somebody and they'll come. I'll have people can be with me when, like if, they jump me. I can get people back on them. That's the good part. But I don't see no bad shit. That's because I'm in it. The bad shit is that you gotta get jumped in and jumped out, but I'm never doing that."

The cityscape behind them suggests their attempt at controlling their lives in the urban atmosphere. Their self-positioning, looking from the top of the hill to the city, alludes to their point of view or worldview about gangs. The perspective from on top of the hill, where the gaze can connote the domination and authority over material space, suggests the young women's notion of controlling territory, turf. This perspective from above additionally allows for meditative self-reflection to be above the fray. While this section concurs with the opening section on "Language" (i.e., we are not like you), the personal stories and self-reflexivity allow the viewer into their thoughts and perspectives, which begin to chip away at the polarizing differences.

Herstory

The "Herstory" section has three scenes. It begins with three girls sitting on a back porch, and the camera angle is low. GG tells how East Side Norteñas began as a group of friends who socialized and then became a gang. While GG continues to narrate, the next shot presents the camera crew. One young woman holds the portable microphone, while another is behind the video camera shooting the scene of the three young women on the back porch. The scene of production is further emphasized as the camera pulls back to show onlookers who are not immediately participating in the filming. María, the peer counselor, directs the onlookers to move away from the camera's angle. The intended effect of this scene in "Herstory" is to underscore that the young women are not only telling the story but producing the story for the larger audience.

The next scene returns to the three girls on the porch and the intertitle of the section appears: "Herstory." The camera angle is still low. As GG, with the hood of her jacket around her head, concludes her story, FN makes faces as if off camera and then covers her mouth. GG continues while MG nods at her, then GG stares out to a distant point away from the camera. As each takes a turn, clarifying the various meanings of their gang affiliation, the other young women look at their nails or speak to someone off camera. The presentation of their origin stories is relaxed. If they are not speaking, they just wait, seeming bored.

Whereas the video can operate on the level of generalities about the gang, a specific contribution develops in the "Herstory" segment. It introduces the radical departure from universalistic descriptions of gangs as boys' groupings. "Herstory" is set on the back porch of the home of one of the young women. While they are near the space of home, their discourse contradicts the confinement to the roles designated by the domestic sphere. The section offers a transition from the universal to the particular—to the situated history of the three all-girl gangs.

The young women assume a more relaxed posture, not the bravado of toughness. They are at ease. They become more relaxed through telling their origin stories. Once again directly addressing the video viewer, they let the audience know about themselves and their particular location within the gang milieu. As they once again include the audience, as in the section on "Membership," they return to their joking. The relaxed scene, allowing the viewer to come into their world, is registered by the few moments when they are distracted by events going on around the production of the video or when two of the young women stare at the camera as if they were unconcerned with being looked at.

"Herstory" provides the viewer with the information about the three gangs the young women belong to and how they developed a broader alliance through the formation of Norteñas With Attitude. One young woman notes that NWA "was just a joke at first. You know, snatched it from Niggas With Attitude [urban gangsta' rappers]." Reflecting on this alliance, the girls construct an account of a "golden age" when all three groups were a formidable rival to the Sureña gangs of the area. By offering the particular stories of the three girl gangs, "Herstory" addresses the organizational structure of their alliance and allegiance. Their particular form of solidarity and camaraderie—the culture of the girls in the gangs—however, is demonstrated in the last section of the video.

In the following sections, "Enemies" and "Fights," close shots enable an intimate connection with the worldview of the gang member. As in "Herstory," the girls are no longer up on the hillside of the park, but rather the sections are filmed within the confined space of a porch. While "Membership" provides the contemplation of unrestricted space, allowing the young women to laugh and joke, the constricted space of the porch in "Enemies" and "Fights" denotes the metaphor of cramped urban space. Although the porch is situated in the domestic space, it can also signify the location of the gang in its urban setting.

Enemies and Fights

In "Enemies" two young women speak directly to the camera. Seated and facing the camera, they discuss the range of ways they consider someone an enemy. Their points are punctuated by fists slapping onto open palms. They attentively listen to each other, gesturing agreement. FN asserts, "The only time I hate a girl is because she probably claims the opposite shit that I do. Or, she's done something to me or one of my relatives." Notably, the young women are no longer smiling or joking, nor performing the bravado observed in the earlier park scenes. The message of the young women is of gaining respect and reflects the seriousness of attaining and establishing respect from others. MG adds, "They're treated hella different. . . ." FN interjects, "If the bitch don't claim Norte, then she's just gonna get disrespect." Finally, MG concludes, "[There] ain't no love for a muthafuckin' enemy . . . the bitch can go to the hospital, we don't give a fuck." At this universalist level, the gendered identity of the speakers seems to disappear. The representation of all youth in gangs carries the responsibility and burden of explaining all gang members.

Similarly, in an attempt to explain the violence in which they participate, the section on fights reveals the girls' dissimilarity from other youth. "Fights" opens with a computer-generated puzzle format to build the scene—a format which augments the wipe or dissolve used in film editing. GG sits directly facing the camera, while DD sits sideways along the stair steps with her upper body turned to the camera. The voice of the researcher, my voice, floats in. "What leads to fights?" GG shrugs, "Just . . . bitches dogging. . . . " DD interjects, "Bumping into you, talking shit." GG then summarizes, "Just feeling like fighting, you know. Sometimes you just be walking down the street, somebody might mug you." As GG speaks, her arms cross her body. They open then close across her body. DD speaks to the camera, "See, if you back your shit up, if you're down for yourself, you'll back your shit up right there." She then turns her head to some distant spot and then turns back to the camera. She lifts her chin to make her point when she speaks about the need to gain respect from rivals through fighting. "It don't matter how many of them or whatever." As she concludes, she smiles, slightly sheepish, then stares off to a distant point away from the camera: "You gotta pull yourself. . . . You can't be no little punk."

The close-up shots, which convey the serious nature of their involvement with symbolic and physical violence, work at suggesting the very personal thoughts of the subjects conveyed through their body language. Close-ups reveal the soft lines of DD's face, the full cheeks and soft lips that conflict with the tough words. The soft curls and the soft cloth material of the sweat jacket, combined with the way in which she positions herself (sitting sideways), allow only a part of her body to be viewed. DD's sitting position is curved, expressing her susceptibility to the violence as well as her need to protect herself from the dangers of the street that she describes. Unlike the eye-level shots in those sections which pronounce similarity, the medium shot expresses the drama of their words through the bodies filling the space of the scene. The camera's low angle, which in cinematic film speeds up motion and causes confusion, signifies the precariousness of violence in which the girls participate and registers the fragility of their existence.

These two sections ("Enemies" and "Fights") work in part by repeating the redundant message of the video's opening section, We are different. However, difference is no longer a performance for the camera. Through their perspectives about enemies and fights, they mark their social contraposition. The low camera angle, additionally, destabilizes the dominant gaze; it is not equal. The viewer is in the lower position, thus the young women are in the higher position of experiential knowledge and authority. The viewer is in their world, up close and personal.

The discussion on enemies and fights initially alienates the viewer, emphasizing part of the major theme of the video—We are different. Because the young women are attempting to impart their social reality, they neither change their language nor attempt to disguise their close association with the aggressive behavior that is produced by their connection with the gang. Yet, the scene is an attempt to bridge the division with the viewer. Through the close-up shots, through the reduction of space suggested by the boundedness of the porch, the viewer is now brought into a close relation with the young women. The viewer is able to see their subjective reality through the claustrophobic space of the porch. Additionally, the innerscape of DD's precarious position in this world is revealed. Throughout, her eyes glance away from the camera and then back to the camera. What becomes evident is the pain of the life the young women have encountered as a result of their gang membership. Difference, then, is recognized and made comprehensible. Thus, the camera's revelation of body language bridges the video's initial distancing effect of otherness.

"Membership," "Herstory," "Enemies," and "Fights" work to repeat the video's opening message. Restated in different ways, the fundamental information about gangs is repeated for the viewer. The intertitles summarize the content of these sections, representing what will be presented. Yet, while the total content constructs the image of the "universal" gang member, the viewer receives the particular information of each of the speakers. Statements such as "I joined," "I think," "I left," or "I won't leave" reveal the different investments each person has in the gang.

Likewise, the close-ups, by reporting particular looks and body language, divulge the risks and stakes each of the youths encounters through
her participation in the aggressive culture of gangs.

Within these frames, the specifics of the peer group are elaborated.
Likewise, the sections re-invoke the distinctive characteristic of Chicano
gangs. That is, they are fighting gangs (J. Moore 1991; Vigil 1988). Covering each other's backs (the promise to defend one's friend in a fight) is
the distinct form of group solidarity that brings the particular peer
group of the gang together. The importance of backup is elaborated in
the "Herstory" section. As GG ends this section about fights, "[Your
home girls] think so high of you, you should stay up in that position,
where you are high, where you're not tripping off the bitch. If [she's] got
funk with you, you handle it right there and then."

Poetry

The last section of the video, "Poetry," contains three scenes. "Poetry"
attempts to reintegrate the viewer through a major theme, We are just
like everyone else. The scenes are again at the park but at different locations from the initial scenes. From "Herstory," the location of girls in
gangs, the video now reaches toward more intimate space. No longer
looking out at the city nor performing street-tough bravado, the young
women impart their expression of girls' culture. The effect of the last section presents an oppositional relation to the video's opening, from difference to similarity, leaving the viewers with a feeling that they have
gotten to know the young women in the video. The similarities, We
are just like everyone else, are revealed through a representation of girls'
culture.

During the scripting of the video the young women included the section on poetry as a way to express the distinction between boy and girl
gang members. One young woman stated: "The guys always go around
writing their names and the gang on liquor stores and fences. Even on
the centros [Chicana/o-operated centers in the Fruitvale community].
We don't. We write about how we feel in poems." The deleted section,
"Kickin' It," was to similarly show how the young women expressed the
contrast of their experience of private and public spheres.

In the first two scenes of the section "Poetry," two young women,
MG and VR, introduce their poetry and journals. These form a textual
space where each of the young women expresses and writes how she is
feeling. The two young women note, in particular, the use of poetry to

prevent intragroup rivalry and fighting among the gang members. Poetry marks the space of the personal. The poetry is about love lost and love gained. The production of the poetry as a form of writing characteristic of the private sphere can be opposed to graffiti on public walls. Similarly, the last scene denotes the recreation and pleasure of girls' culture. At the video's conclusion, the otherness that began the video is lessened. The viewer has since become perceptually familiar with their gang culture (difference) and can understand their adolescent female culture (similarity). The introduction of unusual topics such as "Poetry" and "Kickin' It" addresses the particular form of female solidarity that operates in the gangs.

The final scene of *Homie* works as a denouement. (This scene was originally scripted as the section called "Kickin' It.") It begins with two teenagers talking and situates "girls' talk" outside the domestic sphere. The two young women are sitting by a reflective pool in the park. The video's message "We are like everyone else" is sociologically closer to girls' culture in general. In the "Poetry" section the computer-generated puzzle assembles each of the scenes. QG begins to develop a spatial opposition as imaginative as it is geographic. She establishes that "down there" (in the streets) is the likelihood of violence, while "up here" (in the park) she can relax in friendship. María patiently listens, then elaborates on the recreation of being "up here." The camera pans to the gentle lapping of the nearby pool. As each of the young women speaks, there is continual smiling and nodding of agreement. Then as they discuss the privacy of the area and the ability to share private thoughts with each other, they get up and skip up the park stairs. Their narration continues as voice-over, when the young women continue to ascend the stairs and move higher behind and beyond a large redwood tree that is beside the stairs. Through voice-over narration, María continues, "We can talk about things that we can't talk about with our moms or our family." The camera follows the line of the tree to its pinnacle and stops on the blue skies.

The denouement of *Homie* occurs when the girls ascend the steps of the park. After explaining the security of peer friendship that cements the group, the two young women skip and run up the park stairs—an idyllic resolution to the viewer's inquiry about gangs and girl gangs in particular. The video's major message—its dialectic of difference and similarity—turns people who have been objectified by mainstream media and academic discourse into subjects who speak and have a purpose for being in the film. As they go up the stairs and step outside the frame, the girls halt the spectacle. They are no longer to be looked at. They invited the gaze and, by controlling the gaze throughout the video, take authority once again to end their performance as objects for study. Through the oscillation of presenting themselves as like you/not like you, the girls refuse being othered.

Yet, the happy ending is disorienting. Utilizing the genre of realism, the denouement seems only somewhat related to the represented event, thus breaking narrative coherence. The denouement remains puzzling because from a realist form of documentary, the ending marks a shift in genre to romance. Does the documentary form, its realist structure, effectively challenge and change the viewer's mind? A characteristic of all visual media is that the mode of representation renders people as objects, to be seen, to be looked upon. Thus the people/objects are spectacles. Can description of "what it's really like for us" break the gaze that situates them as other? As exotic or social curiosity? Does the realist genre, the use of news media feature, its narrative form, effectively work to say the opposite of dominant images? Does their video get at the issues of social construction of race, gender, class, sexuality—challenging the social constructions that operate in society—categorizing, rendering, evoking emotions, feelings, prejudices, the notions of the otherness?

With the young women's ascent of the stairs, the topography of the video shifts. In the last scene of "Poetry," a third space is now registered—a space that lies outside both the streets, "down there," and the park, "up here." Aware of the images of gang members that circulate in society, the girls attempt to provide a different view. However, the realist style limits them. They reach a point at which they cannot explain any more or any more clearly.

The effect of this mobility, however, is to create a nonconclusive ending. Thus a different genre erupts in the video at its very end, subverting the form used throughout the video. They turn to romance as a way to break from the limitations of the realist genre.

VERNACULAR POETICS

Since the intention of the video is to answer the basic questions usually asked of them about gangs, the young women scripted scenes that would acquaint audiences with girls in gangs. The documentary impetus to show a wider range of Chicano culture does not work for the purpose of the young women's video. Moreover, the video overlooks analysis of youth in relation to the broader society which a documentary on gangs would include. The video not only answers the basic questions posed by outsiders, it also discloses the social network of peer relations among the young women. Since female subjectivity is centered, the girls move from being spoken about to asserting themselves as speaking subjects. The exposition of the gang becomes the primary shaping force illustrating their social identity. However, in its genre structure an implicit message of the video discloses the worldview of the youth in relationship to the larger structures of society.

The video's "romantic" ending is a rupture from most documentaries about gangs as well as a break from the video's overall documentary form. Fredric Jameson's conception of romance offers a way to examine the contrasting genres of realism and romance found in the girls' video. Jameson suggests that romance is an aesthetic act resulting from the dialectic of everyday life and utopia. Romance is ideological, "inventing imaginary or formal solutions to unresolvable social contradictions" (Jameson 1981, 79). Jameson notes that realism, as a genre, restricts forms of representation to place, incident, description of everyday life, while romance offers a struggle between two opposing forces or lower and higher realms and a resolution that offers a possibility of transforming ordinary reality through the journey or crusade.

The film references the streets "down there" as a place of danger and of violence. In the section on "Membership" the city is the background of the scene in which the girls explain their street identity. In "Herstory" the porch denotes urban space as they discuss the violence in which they participate. Similarly, in "Enemies" and "Fights" the street-tough bravado is expressed. Moreover, in the final setting, "Poetry" discloses the girls' more personal thoughts and their stakes in peer friendship. "Up here," the park, is defined as a space of freedom. Yet, "freedom" is marked in two particular ways. First, it is a place where one does not have to fear a rival, does not need the defensive posture and performance of meanness, but instead is a place to relax with friends. Thus freedom is about revealing a self that is vulnerable, tender, compassionate, and understanding. Second, freedom is figured as a place one can talk. Freedom in this sense is a freedom from authority and control, including adult regulation of behavior.

"Up here" is the tactical, visual, experiential realm where one can relate to the social material world in a different way, yet it remains a place of refuge in the real world.[9] In the video's final scene, however, the two young women ascend the park stairs. Running up the stairs alludes to a higher ground that "up here," at the park, still cannot bring about. The stairs form a symbol for a still unattainable utopian level. With the last scene of ascension, the minor message of the video, then, becomes important. The final scene works as climactic irresolution. The romance of flight or ascension is puzzling and therefore does not offer closure. Where are they going? What are they reaching for higher up?

While the video endeavors to chart social identity in the gang, a topography of space maps the movement of the young women from the park to the urban space of the back porch and back to the park. Each of the spaces elaborates the cultural style, social activities, and coping strategies of socialization that establish the gang subculture as a lifeway (Vigil 1988). Considering that the video was conceived as a PSA—restricted by the timed format and structure—the video's realist form takes on a political component through its use of a narrative structure designed to reinterpret a pre-existing object. Through this form the young women attempt to articulate the "truth" of their experience. The video, as a mode of counter discourse, allocates a competing story to the dominant media representation of gangs and girls in gangs. The cinematic mechanisms—the scrolled intertitles, the direct address, and the use of the puzzle as the editing wipe—lead to the conviction of wholeness: this is the gang world.[10] Additionally, the performative aspect of street-tough experience and the use of the stereotype as a fixed construction in the mind of the viewer allow the young women to work through the dominant image. While not setting up a directly oppositional characterization to the stereotype, the young women attempt to say, "We are not only this, but more."

In *Homie,* an overarching problem of autoethnography emerges. The video constructs a series of imaginative performances to characterize the girls' own view of their experience and consciously projects a desired truth to a broader audience. By retelling their herstory, the young women attempt to have their voices acknowledged by outsiders. While the young women present the issues of language, fighting, and enemies, and as they allow the viewer into their personal space through poetry and forms of recreation, their re-presentation depicts subjects who seem autonomous from dominant political and social influences. The girls in the film seem to exist outside the influence of social structures, economic relations, or patriarchy.

While the video does not explicitly address larger structural dynamics that contribute to the existence of gangs in economically underprivileged communities, the video implicitly addresses the girls' positionality in society. Benmayor, Torruellas, and Juarbe (1997), analyzing language and immigration examine the discursive practices which reflect the situated use of language within speech events and larger structures. Utilizing the analytic of vernacular poetics provides a way to comprehend and particularize how the young women articulate their situatedness within the dominant discourses and social structures.

In the opening section MG remarks upon her use of language: "But, when it's like today, when we was almost like nearly got ranned over, I talked a hella shit to some lady. I mean, but I wasn't doing it, like, just saying it 'bitch,' 'ho.' I was doing it serious, so the bitch could walk out." MG does not clarify why she was nearly run over. Her remarks imply that the near-accident was sudden and random. When she challenges the woman to fight, MG asserts her presence. The statement alludes to the problem that possibly the woman did not see MG and her friends. She begins to address the problem of invisibility, even though it is not clear whether this obscurity is produced by the fact that she is young or that she is racially marked and therefore invisible. Her need to lash out demonstrates any number of possibilities in terms of her subjective experience. In the section following the title of the video, the girls line up against the wall and problematize difference. While VR calls up the generic "people" who stereotype gang-bangers, DD similarly calls up a universal "you" that misunderstands youth in gangs. While they address the stereotypes of gang members produced by a generic, universal "you," the "we" of the video begins to draw a wider net of representation. VR questions: "It's not like we're born bad; it's what we go through. Huh?" Implicitly she asks: Is it because we are gang-bangers? Is it because we are youth? Is it because we are Mexican? Through the questions, an indirect macrostructural dimension of the video arises. The appeal, i.e., We are just like you, begins to chip away at deviance in its criminal sense, and the young women seem to be asserting an "unnamed" social identity as a minority group. The difference and sameness of which they are speaking are those of Chicana/o youth in general and begin to address the larger structural issues of a low-income community, speaking to the feelings of youth who are marginalized. It implicitly questions whether the "you," the viewer, thinks of "us" as different and act accordingly toward us, as minorities. Deviance is registered racially and ethnically as well as through gender. The implicit or minor message of the video questions whether the construction of difference can be reduced to the institutionalized alterity of gangs.

In addition, the performance of the street-tough pose alludes to another performance, that of racial identity. Race appears in this instance as a performance in language and body movement. Appropriating the language of Black urban youth, the girls race their language, enunciating a coded identity.[11] The girls' performance is a syncretic mixture of the urban language of African American youth and the posture of barrio locos. The loco stance is of a swayed back and tilted head in order to look down at another person. The young women in many ways seem to reinstate the stereotype of the "gangsta" rapper whose music functions as the CNN of the ghettos and barrios. Like gangsta rappers, the young women participate as the source of information, the representatives of the life and worldview of urban youth. As one of the young women notes, the name Norteñas With Attitude was appropriated from urban gangsta' rappers, "but it's all good." Like the rap group's records, they broadcast the conditions of urban youth of color, the "street knowledge," through the medium of their video. However, unlike the rappers, the young women give their worldview as young women. Their parental warning in "Language," like warning labels on records, marks the street life they will depict as outlaw, urban, and therefore colored.[12]

Because of the temporal structure of the PSA, the video cannot present a comprehensive representation about gangs or an examination of the broader structures that affect them. However, the articulation of their subject position is expressed through the vernacular poetics—of the streets, down there, and the park, up here—through an examination of language, locations, and scenes of the video. Similarly, the movement up the stairs as metaphor expresses the space of imagination, of possibilities of something yet to be attained. The romance of ascension then performs an ideological function in the sense that it marks the young women's aspirations and imaginings of a space that is beyond the given complexities of their social world—of marginalized communities. This dramatic scene becomes the attempt to rise above the very real world of Oakland and of ethnic/racial marginality. When the girls changed the topic from teen pregnancy to gangs, a shift also occurred in the structure of the text—from journalistic man-on-the-street interview to narrative. The changed topic, moreover, produced the "authoring process."[13] The girls have negotiated across space and enter the broader terrain of public discourse. The girls attempt to re-articulate their gang identity, that is, they attempt to assert the social identity as gang members and at the same time attempt to draw a connection with the viewer. The ability to move to a different image is not only limited by a lack of formal training and education in film and film criticism, but ideologically bound. The girls have limited resources to create an image which is not already deep in ideology. The girls appropriate various video techniques from news media to MTV in order to re-present themselves. At the same time, the girls use a powerful image of type and stereotype. The capacity of any powerful sign is its ability to pull in several directions at once. The representation becomes dynamic through the oscillation between the two poles of the major message—like and not like you. Thus, the girls re-accentuate, use the familiar image and accent the differences, in order to unsettle the dominant image of gang members. The ambiguous, impossible fantasy ending reopens the text to other interpretations.

In *Homie* the girls discuss the danger of the streets, the importance of watching one's back, and their particular view of violence, stressing a sense of difference from the audience. Their introduction of unexpected, even romantic, topics such as "poetry" and "kickin' it" addresses the particular form of female solidarity that operates in the gang, a sense of belonging located at the boundaries of private and public. In the following chapter I will pursue a related message of the video: the characteristics and quality of the girls' investment in the gang. Offering further levels of interpretation, I interweave the video text with ethnographic observation in order to examine the nature of gang solidarity.

AFFINITY AND AFFILIATION

> One supposes social anthropologists themselves live lives in which
> friendship is every bit as problematic as kinship, and probably a good deal
> more problematic to handle; in our professional writings about the cultures
> of the world, however, we dwell at length upon kinship and have much less
> to say about friendship.   ROBERT PAINE

In Vered Amit-Talai's examination of teenage girls' friendships (1995),
she argues that the characterization of adolescence as a stage of transition and impermanence has anesthetized critical studies of adolescent
peer relations. Inasmuch as time is a constituent characteristic in the
construction of adolescence, peer relations become a footnote to social
and cultural organization, discussed only as a problem of socialization.
If the intensity and importance of teen peer relations are understood,
they are analyzed through the essentially transitional feature of adolescence. Amit-Talai observes that such characterizations disassociate adolescent friendships from other social roles. Comprehended as contingent
and impermanent in the life cycle, friendships are reduced to private,
free-floating relationships. Amit-Talai also notes that disciplinary studies tend to locate such relations in the personal realm and the private
sphere, always marginal to economic and social production as well as to
state and institutional structures. In the previous chapter I interpreted
the major message of the video *It's a Homie Thang!* through what I have
called a dialectic of difference and similarity. In the video's final section,
the girls' entreaty that they are similar to other teenage girls is produced
through the presentation of their solidarity group. The video focuses on
two aspects of the peer group: interpersonal communication, and fun or
recreation. The introduction of unusual topics such as "poetry" and
"kickin' it" addresses the particular form of solidarity that operates in
the girls' gangs. I posited that the strength of the girls' project is the representation of their peer group. This chapter interweaves the video text
of *It's a Homie Thang!* with ethnographic observation in order to examine the culture and mode of solidarity that operates in the girls'
gangs, expanding on the emergent message of the video—a claim for the
specific quality of their investment in the gang.

While some gang studies examine honor and respect in relation to the
development of gangs, this chapter reviews the bonds of friendship and

solidarity found in the girls' gang—subjective responses to a social world that relegates youth in general to the margins. By locating and questioning the distinct boundaries of private and public, I reopen the domain of girls' culture. I have found that the young women utilize forms of unity and solidarity borrowed from the domestic sphere, reworking them to consolidate a feminine culture in public space. This domesticization of the public and the publicization of the private is a key transactional mode of girl-gang culture. Negotiating a presence in the public space of the streets, the young women exchange and transfer the values from one sphere to another.

The conventional conception of private and public spheres imagines separate, complete, and bounded realms in which the public sphere customarily stands in contrast to the private. Understanding the variable uses and meanings of the concept for examining culture and society, Jeff Weintraub (1997) notes the following ways in which the concept is advanced: the liberal economic model in which the public sector is that which falls under state administration and the private sector is the market economy; the "republican virtue model" (which Habermas also has described) in which the public sphere encompasses community and citizenship as distinct from state sovereignty and the economy; the "sociability" model in which the public is symbolic display that has little to do with self-representation and collective decision making; and the historical model, shared by many feminists, which challenges the binary opposition of private/public as separate spheres where privacy defines domestic or familial, as contrasted to a public defined largely as the economy of wage earners.

Re-examinations of the public/private split have been productive in criticisms of paradigms that have analyzed institutions of the family, the state, and the economy when the private sphere is constructed as a nonpolitical realm. Feminist scholarship makes clear that the defining characteristic of separate spheres is the relegation of women to the private or domestic domain, a separation that has functioned to subordinate women. In the conventional sense of the dual sphere, the home and the hearth are retreats from the world of politics and must be safeguarded from the intervention of the state. Under the myth of separate spheres, the private realm's relations of patriarchy tend to be assumed, and thus its political nature remains unexamined. Since politics and power are defined as public displays, the study of alternative politics and forms of empowerment produced in the private realm by women and children, sibling and kinship relationships, and community networks are

demeaned and insufficiently analyzed. The ideological effect of the pub-
lic/private-sphere split is the concept of the home as a feminine space
where patriarchy offers safety from work, commerce, and the state.
Overall, feminist criticism has specified that the dual-spheres paradigm
is about power. Recognizing the active interrelationship of the two
spheres, feminist scholarship attempts to restructure the theory of difference without reviving binarisms of public and private that reify male
authority and female dependence while closing off the interconnections
of work, family, and the state. My own research confirms this analysis,
showing that the myth of separate worlds obscures a dynamic production of girls' culture in distinctive public spaces.

MEANING TOUGHNESS

R. W. Connell in *Gender and Power: Society, the Person, and Sexual
Politics* (1987) identifies "the street" as an institution for analysis of gender relations as important as the more familiar structures of family and
state. Generally, the street is conceptualized as a particular kind of
space—urban space—through which the citizen navigates to reach
other institutions and places of production. In sociological studies, the
institutions usually considered are: the home, family, and workplace; the
apparatuses of the modern welfare state, which regulates and adjudi-
cates in both family and work; and to varied degrees the church and
community services such as education and health. Because these arenas
are considered definitive societal institutions, the street tends to be emp-
tied of institutional force as an intermediate level of social organization.
Remarking upon the irony that one of the most famous sociological
texts is called *Street Corner Society* (Whyte 1955), Connell notes that
the street, like other institutions, has its definite social milieu and its particular social relations. Exhibiting the same structures of gender relations as the family and the state, the street as milieu "has a division of
labour, a structure of power and a structure of cathexis" (Connell 1987,
134). Recognizing the street as a setting for intimidation of women, from
low-level harassment to assault and rape, Connell notes a major structure of power: "the street then is a zone of occupation by men" (Connell
1987, 133). However, because the street is a more loosely structured environment than other institutions such as the family and state, Connell
remarks that the street allows room for diversity and experiment. Characterizing style as a form of theater found in the streets, he notes that
the street as institution allows for negotiation and renegotiation about

forms of gender. Connell's reassessment of the street—as a site of negotiations and transactions between private and public—provides a critical context for examining girls' gang culture as exemplified in the video
It's a Homie Thang!

Homie introduces a number of contrasting images and performances
that mark the tension between public and private spheres. Participation
in the world of gangs, a quasi-institution of the streets, presents a number of anxieties, stresses, and apprehensions for the young women.
Transgressing expected social behavior, they take up defiant behavior
generally considered masculine in order to assert mastery over urban
space. By creating a group of street peers for social support and recreation, the gang validates one's identity as inviolably superior to other
groups in public space. In this context, *Homie* is a study of street identity, the way its makers have transgressed expected female social roles
and attempted to survive in the public sphere.

In the video's sections "Language," "Membership," and "Fights," the
girls enact the street tough, through posturing and repetition of swear
words. The bravado in these sections asserts difference from the audience. But while their presentation is for viewers expecting a documentary about gangs, the bravado is doubly parodic. The girls perform an
exaggerated toughness and streetwise behavior akin to Judith Butler's
concept of gender performance (1990). Since gender is not a fixed category nor a biological essence but a creation of society, Butler argues,
what is considered feminine or masculine is performative, a way to construct different roles in a hierarchical system. Thus the girls' bravado asserts an attainment of mastery in a masculinized sphere. The girls simultaneously adopt the masculine coding of the public sphere while
subverting the gendering of this sphere. It should be noted that sphere
in this sense is different from space, the geographical material world.
Sphere describes the discursive structure which functions as an access to
public life.

Performance allows an examination of other gender destabilizations.
The assemblage of a street-smart identity includes the production of a
self that can be read by others. In the video when the girls line up against
the wall, the camera pans across them, allowing time for the audience to
take in their dress style. The androgynous clothing—oversized baggy
pants and large, loose T-shirts—provokes the notion of otherness. While
a few girls wear more conventionally feminine styles—body-hugging
bell-bottom pants and short-ribbed tops—androgynous attire is the
dominant style. Accentuating a visual otherness, most of the girls out-

line their lips with black eyeliner pencil and fill it in with dark red or burgundy lipstick. The style differences may not be notable to an out-sider, but they are important to the girls as signs to be read in public: This is a gang-banger. The girls note the ways their group is identified as a gang. MG and SP state that the other girl groups were solely "cliques"—informal gatherings of friends. SP, who associated with members of the second generation before joining, states that when her schoolmates took on the name Da Crew, it made the group different from the other cliques at school:

> There were some fights back then, but it wasn't a lot. Then the other cliques [Las Norteñas and East Side Norteñas] started to get names. And we started kickin' it together. The other cliques were different. They did different things. They dressed different. Not like us, with baggy pants and T-shirts. They'd dress more girl-like, not real loose pants. They were more like a club. We called one group gang-hoppers because they would hang with one of the boy gangs and then another, you know, party with one group and say they were down with them, then move to another when they got new boyfriends. Our gang, it's different, because back then we would have boyfriends from wher-ever, but we were just down for Da Crew. We didn't make no claims for any one of the boy gangs.

Street codes manifested in dress style, posture, and language are markers of the social identity that one establishes to create a presence in the public sphere. The style asserts an identity different from other street organizations and social groupings of girls. Thus the transgressive dress and style are both a derivative of and resistant to the gender order. An exaggeration of "girl" through the pronouncement of lips and hair com-bines with an assertive use of clothing to hide the body. The result is a mixed economy of gender.

The fantasy of independence and predominance—coded as mascu-line—motivates the girls' performance of bravado. Their street knowl-edge dictates that they take on the persona of the street tough to ward off danger. However, insecurity and apprehension are produced through the breach of acceptable feminine behavior, and the tough pose is com-monly understood to be a mask hiding vulnerability and fragility. My own ethnographic research with young women in gangs confirms this view. However, other facets to the toughness bear explaining—the meaning of meanness. Disrupting domestic roles and expectations, the young women move into a sphere conventionally designated as male and thus as risky for women. Internalizing the fantasized masculinity as independence, the diversions (in both its connotations, of turning away and of play) found on the streets include spatial mobility, away from the confinement and restriction of the home.

While performance implies mask and the ability to play any number of parts as in a theatrical drama, performance as enactment of the self begins to break down (or modify) the implication of artifice. One becomes the person one performs. Affecting toughness is thus not merely a public image; it is also an enabling ethos—a disposition, character, or fundamental value. Toughness displays that one is not accessible; it may project impenetrability. Jack Katz (1988) finds that the styles of the bad-ass and the street elite project an ability not to give way, not to give up or to give in. He notes, moreover, that the image gives the impression to others that the bad-ass can suddenly thrust the forces of chaos into the world of anyone and everyone nearby; the street elite and bad-ass "generate dread," portending violence (Katz 1988, 128). Meanness backs up the persona. Meanness is the juncture of the symbolic and the physical where the infliction of physical harm is imminent.

While the girls' adoption of a street-tough image may be an exhibition of masculinity, a parody that destabilizes the domination of men in public space, it enables the young women to handle themselves in a public space. For the danger and fear that accompany stepping into the public space of the streets, away from the family, are real. In the video section "Fights," DD looks directly at the camera and says: "See, if you back your shit up, if you're down for yourself, you'll back your shit up right there. It don't matter how many of them or whatever. You gotta pull yourself. . . . You can't be no little punk." The menacing public image the young women summon says they are not to be messed with. Consequently, the internalization of the fantasized masculinity of a street elite enables survival. Meanness, the menace of violence, is the actualization of self through affiliation in a gang.

By taking up public space, the girls run several risks. There is danger from other girls who take up the codes of the street gang (e.g., those who police the territory). There is also danger from boys who will act upon their conceptions of the proper behavior of young women in public. The symbolization of streets as masculine, the effect of spatialization, moreover provides the basis for the operation of power, surveillance, and discipline. One of the consequences of transgressing the gender order is violence. Therefore, the achievement of toughness must be backed up with meanness. Having transgressed social roles and expected modes of behavior, the girls produce a self with agency. In the sections "Enemies" and "Fights," the girls' attitude is relaxed and their discourse is matter-of-fact expository. The flat tone of voice resonates with an aggressive ethos. Meaning toughness is the realization of self, as one who means what one says. Thus street-tough meanness is part of the ideology of the social environs which the young women are entering. And being street-tough is not just a mimicry of masculinity through pretense. It is a performance which supplies the means, knowledge, and opportunity to make possible a self that can be affirmed in the streets, a self that is consequential in the public sphere.

SUSPENDING SEX/GENDER

The occupation of public space additionally produces reactions in the community and society at large that commonly would designate the girls as cheap, sexually indiscriminate, and careless. The aspect of carelessness has taken up the majority of social research, as most studies on urban young women, particularly young women of color, take the form of pathologizing accounts of teen pregnancy. Viewed as agents, however, the young women are defining their participation in the masculinized territory of the streets and rejecting the patriarchal norm that stigmatizes their behavior as promiscuous. On this level of contestation and contention, Rosa Linda Fregoso offers keen insight into the ideological construction of young women in the streets as promiscuous and provides a possible account of an interactive model of dual spheres. In her essay "Pachucas, Cholas, and Homegirls: Taking over the Public Sphere" (1995b), Fregoso analyzes the private domain of the home in both the dominant society and in Chicana/o culture. Identifying the economic realities that determine relations in the home, Fregoso emphasizes that few working women benefit from the dichotomous opposition of public and private, since many are either the sole providers or must work to supplement the family income. Registering the ideological effect, Fregoso notes the internalization of ideals that define masculinity in terms of authority and classify economic success as public. The street as urban space is an arena women must navigate in order to reach the broader institutions and places of production. Many women working outside the home view the home as separate from the world of work, commerce, and the state. Since urban public space is designated as the realm of men, the home—as a feminine space—offers safety.

Expanding feminist analysis of the role of women to include young

women, Fregoso notes that the social role of the young woman in the
domestic sphere is to service the family. Young women, therefore, function as an extension of the reproductive role of the wife and mother in
the family. (In this instance the reproductive role is associated with domestic work in the sex division of labor or housework, the myriad tasks
required to produce on a daily and intergenerational basis those resources—physical and psychological—that permit the ongoing performance of the work that is directly subordinated to capitalist and/or state
institutions.) Fregoso registers the control of female sexuality as the
foundation of the private sphere for Chicano families and for society as
a whole. Fregoso's analysis of the control of sexuality enables us to analyze the transgressions that are categorized as deviancy or pathology in
young women's gang activity. Fregoso remarks on the home as a space
of confinement (or re-confinement for women wage workers):

> Masking as a concern for their safety, the confinement of girls to the
> home is first and foremost about protecting sexual property, about
> policing sexuality. And this is precisely the masculine familial project
> that pachucas interrupted and disrupted. Their bodies refused to be
> contained by domesticity or limited by the prevailing orthodoxy of
> appropriate female behavior. (Fregoso 1995b, 320)

The integrity of the household as a private economic unit is thus the
basis for foregrounding women as sexual property and/or dependent.
Control of women's sexuality generates the ideological norms for
young women, hence producing social behavior—both acquiescent and
transgressive.

In the section following the title of the video, as the young women
stand along the wall, MG states, "We got love fo' some muthafuckas.
But other muthafuckas don't get shit up in this muthafucka." Signing
with her hands the two gangs that she is a member of, her hand pushes
away as if blocking any impact upon her body. Her body and language
speak two messages at once: on the one hand, they assert that she is not
to be messed with and will not be beaten by a rival; on the other hand,
they express her sexual control of her body. While the larger society
labels her as sexually available, she refuses the designation. Thus, the
street identity does not represent promiscuity, but choice and control
over their sexuality. This control is also expressed at other moments in
the video.

In the "Poetry" section, the young women present themes of love in
heterosexual relations. In the first poem, one of the girls speaks about

love as the completion of herself through the addition of the male. Her poem expresses the dominant ideology of heterosexuality and demonstrates the structure of gendered relations. A second poem, however, veers from the typical depiction of love relationships. Having lived and loved, the young woman chronicles her progress; she has learned there are "two parts of a guy." She moves on, not staying in a situation of unrequited love, telling a story of maturity, of experience, and of learning. "Too bad it took me all that/To open my eyes/Now, I could see/I could love better than you." The poem speaks to the young woman's independence and her attempt to commemorate her passage to wholeness, to individuality. The selection of this particular poem for the video—other readings were videotaped—offers yet another way of examining the young women's attempt to control their sexuality.

The gang girls' insistence on this control is further supported by Da Crew's accounts of affiliating with the Fifty-fourth Street (turf) gang. While independent, Da Crew like the other gangs of the NWA alliance created various rituals of joining. Some are "jumped in," or beaten up. In other instances, all that is required is that the prospective member hang with a clique to gain familiarity with the young women before being granted membership. Members of NWA underscore their independence, distinguishing their initiation rituals from those in which girls are "sexed in" to boy street gangs.[1] This practice has been a major focus of investigative reports by the media and by mainstream social science researchers. The young women of NWA, because of the alliance's all-girl membership, are not only able to avoid sexual initiation but also can maintain a greater sense of collective self-esteem. In their estimation, being sexed in relegates girls to the status of property. By contrast, the girls' description of being jumped in through fights offers a self-depiction of survival in the streets, participation in street codes on a par with men. This discursive construction of the self functions as an admittance to street "public life," enabling the girls to maintain control of their own sexuality. Moreover, the production of a gang member as a soldier and not a sexual object, as a fighter and not property, is the constant performance that their meanness and the menace of violence calls into play. When Da Crew connected with Fifty-fourth, the rites of initiation of getting jumped in remained. Additionally, they changed Fifty-fourth's pattern of allowing girlfriends in the gang, i.e., "sexed in" initiation—all prospective members were to be jumped into the gang. Affiliating with Fifty-fourth, the various leaders of Da Crew fought with leaders of the cliques within the territorial gang.

Consistent with sociological studies on gang cliques (J. Moore 1991; Vigil 1988; Jankowski 1991), *Homie* takes up some of the characteristics of the gang's clique, particularly the aspect of friendship. Attesting to general patterns, the young women note that new cliques develop based on the recruitment of a group of friends who join the gang together.[2] My research on the formation of the various units or cliques within each of the three gangs—Da Crew, Las Norteñas, and East Side Norteñas—suggests that the majority of the cliques (units) emerged out of friendships developed at school. However, my findings also mark the conditions and situations in which the cliques expand. In many instances, a younger sister or a cousin accompanies a girl to social events and consequently joins the clique. These relations are a consistent pattern found in the majority of the cliques. The network of familial relationships provides an interesting look at how families deal with chaperoning in today's culture.

Since the three girls' gangs organized independently of the boy street gangs in the neighborhood, the cliques present a unique look at the relations between women in Chicana culture. At a time when chaperoning by an older family member has dropped out of contemporary Chicano socialization, many parents assign younger sisters or other female relatives to accompany their daughters. This form of "chaperoning" then becomes a way in which the gang grows beyond the limited context of a group of friends joining a clique. During fieldwork, as I was attempting to understand gang structure and how the girls joined, I noticed that the girls often described incidents of chaperoning practices that brought relatives into the group.

Because Da Crew has up to six or seven cliques in Fruitvale and three others in nearby communities of Oakland, they provide a long-range understanding of organizational growth. Da Crew differentiates each of the various units or cliques of the gang as "generations." Each clique is designated as a "generation" when a group of friends enters Da Crew. In Da Crew, the chaperoning or babysitting creates new cliques as the young sister or relative moves to another school or moves to an area miles away from Fruitvale or begins to associate with peers of her age. In this instance of "hiving off" (Vigil 1988, 93), a unit of the gang emerges when a member has moved away or attends a different school from the majority of the other members. While the age difference between first- and second-generation members is between two and three years, the subsequent "generations" have minimal age difference. In describing Da Crew a member notes that the first grouping of girls was more of a social clique than a gang. The girls were childhood friends or attended the same school. When the members of the first generation married or left the area, the group shrank and seemed about to disappear. A very young member who chaperoned her first-generation sister entered high school and founded the second generation. This member said it was this new cohort that decided to take on the name of Da Crew. Like the first generation, the second generation began as a group of girls who socialized together. She notes that other girl groups were developing, but they were just social cliques. The name Da Crew made her group different from the other cliques at school.

The refounding of the group took just a few months, rather than the two-year interval often found in turf gangs.[3] When I asked why she accompanied her older sister, she said that her sister was minding her, "but, more, my mom wanted me to look out for her." Thus the young child was, in a real sense, chaperoning the older sister, providing eyes and ears for her parents. When the girls of the second, third, fourth, and fifth generations of Da Crew were asked about relatives joining, many of the girls said a younger sister or a cousin joined or that they themselves had joined after they escorted an older sister. One girl noted that she never was close to her cousin before she became interested in the gang. She said her parents allowed her to go to parties and picnics when her cousin attended the same events so she would have a chaperone. Similarly, two sisters who constantly fought at home "stopped a lot of our fighting" when they became interested in joining Da Crew. They became members of the third generation. When I asked how they stopped fighting, they reported that their mother gave them permission to go out because together they would behave and look after the other. Thus, by checking their behavior toward one another, they chaperoned each other.

Dating and kickin' it with any number of boy gang members has been depicted in sociological studies as one of the primary reasons for conflict among boy gangs. In my interviews with the young women of Oakland, many explained the fights differently, insisting upon loyalty to the broader Norteño/a allegiance and identity. Unlike territorial gangs that claim a neighborhood through landmarks such as particular residential areas, street boundaries, or parks, the gangs of NWA take a broader compatriotic identity as Norteñas.[4] Signaling their loyalty to a broader Norteño/a alliance of which the majority of Fruitvale street gangs are affiliated, the young women utilize the larger symbolic affiliation to determine their rivals, Sureños/as. The young women will date and hang with boys from a variety of neighborhood gangs, some of which are rivals, yet all of which are Norteño. The girls are mediating between otherwise geographically and organizationally distinct boy gangs. While some female gangs carry complementary names of their respective male counterpart gangs, particularly those with street notoriety, Da Crew, East Side Norteñas, and Las Norteñas identify with the fighting notoriety established in the broader rivalry between Norteños and Sureños. Claiming a concept of Norteño identity, which calls upon the confederate or compatriot network of identity, members of NWA map new sets of relations through the use of a more expansive symbolization. The three gangs express an allegiance to the broader Norteño federation and remain independent of the territorial gangs.

The girls discuss rivalries and tensions among the various Norteño turf/street gangs of Fruitvale. Such insider information works to minimize intra-Norteño rivalry. This aspect of independence from the boys' street gangs in many ways counters the notion of gangs as solely territorial. While fraught with tensions and the possibility of being labeled as "hoochies" (promiscuous women), the negotiations that secure their independence enable the young women to sustain their gang outside a territorial or turf context. This more fluid affiliation calls for continuous discussion with the various boy gangs and among themselves to secure safety and to lessen fights at parties and places of recreation.

LOYALTY AND TRUST

The issue of independence also provides a different look into the foundations of solidarity among the girl gang members. In many studies of gangs, loyalty, honor, and respect have been the primary sources investigated. In a society that marginalizes communities of color through housing segregation, lower incomes, and insufficient funds to guarantee a quality education and life chances, researchers have focused on subjective motives of defiance and opposition. While not evading the social and political structures that produce the categories of race, ethnicity, and class, I am attempting to refocus the gaze in gang studies by looking at bonds of friendship and solidarity, particularly the mutual trust expressed in girls' culture that operates on the personal level.

It is common to argue that the aggressive behavior, the fighting, is based on concepts of honor (e.g., Horowitz 1983). Such investigations focusing on honor produce paradigms of pathology and deviance for youth of color and sexual deviance and pathology for young women of color. In *Angels' Town: Chero Ways, Gang Life, and Rhetorics of the Everyday* (1997), Ralph Cintron takes a first step to reframe the syllogism of honor/violence. Arguing that respect and honor are not productive conditions and terms for explaining violence, he provides a descriptive model for interpreting the social world of Latinos in a segregated community near Chicago. He notes that the conditions arising from marginalization by the dominant society produce a situated response. Cintron offers a model of "the logics of violence/the logics of trust." The logics of violence are responses by some people to the dominant society's racist and classist denigration of their selfhood. The logics of violence particularly evident in codes of the streets operate as commonsense assumptions to construct fear and distrust. The logics of violence, according to Cintron, are founded upon a "brute cause and effect relationship in which the humiliation of someone call(s) for an equivalent humiliation of the offender" (Cintron 1997, 151). The drive for one-upmanship, winning a "higher moral ground" at the expense of another person, provides vengeance with its righteous justification. The counterbalance that also operates in street codes is the logics of trust that permits the possibility of solidarity. The logics of trust suggest the ways in which commitments and loyalties are established and re-established. Cintron's elaboration on the logics of trust provides ways to understand the dynamics of group affiliation and peer solidarity among youth gangs.

Cintron interprets the logics of violence and the logics of trust as structuring systems in which an individual acquires respect under conditions of little or no respect. Trust in the girls' culture I studied is much different from Cintron's model. Trust among men is different from trust among women. Cintron's concept of trust is set in a masculinist frame (masculinist because it is generated with the perspectives and values that derive from the embodied experience of living as male). The logics of trust include the emotional bonds enabling the girls to talk with their peer group about issues they feel they cannot talk about with adults. While the girls make an effort to hide many of their activities, many times the girls' concerns are outside their parents' experience. Or because they are viewed as incomplete adults, their concerns about friendships, boyfriends, and fights are perceived as problems that will be resolved with time. Thus, what one cannot talk about with parents finds expression in conversation among friends. Gendering the issue of trust reveals how subjective and affective levels define a difference in the girl gangs that I studied, one that contrasts with the other studies of gangs I have examined and critiqued.

In the video *Homie,* the term "love" has mostly been edited out. When the young women are speaking about joining and being "jumped in," one describes how she was beaten up three times in three rounds of proving herself for membership. One sees in the video the young women laughing, yet love is the reason for the laughter. Her remark that "love makes it all good," all worthwhile, disappeared in the editing. "You can't talk about love when we're talking about gangs" was the response of one young woman during the filming. Yet love is an operative word among gang members. Bloods, Crips, Norteños, and Sureños talk about love as the cement that bonds their membership. While loyalty to the gang can and does resemble a type of allegiance to a nation or the contractual obligation to an organization, loyalty in the sphere of love requires a different investigation—particularly in an all-girl gang.

Homie renders girls' culture through the gang network. In the streets "down there," the girls are being mugged. There is the constant vigilance of watching one's own back, the fear of the urban space as a place where danger can come at any time. The "logics of trust," to use Cintron's models, means "looking out for your partner," covering your friend's back. The gang becomes a place not only of recreation and pleasure, but the place of safety and trust—trust earned as a subjective feeling one gives to another. In the rituals of gang membership, being jumped in begins the process of evaluation and judgment that forms the bonds of trust, earned through backing each other up and through loyalty to the gang. However, other mechanisms are operative. What augments trust? What are its stipulations and demands?

Another look at Allison Anders' film *Mi Vida Loca* may illustrate the love and trust that develop among girls, at least among the girls of NWA. Anders' film tells the story of young Chicana gang members in a way that renders the style, stance, posture, gestures, mannerisms, and speech of homegirls who live in the Echo Park district of Los Angeles. While there have been various critiques (well summarized by Rosa Linda Fregoso, 1995a, 1995b, 1999), Anders captures on film for the first time the female solidarity of girls in gangs. The film opens by narrating a lifelong friendship between two girls who end up fighting when they both become pregnant by the same boy. The girls bring guns to a vacant lot to settle their rivalry, but the sound of gunfire stops the showdown, thus opening the story to other narrations of female bonding and friendship. In one episode, an older member ultimately calls all the girls to meet and settle the dispute between the two. The girls find out that the boy who cheated on both girls was murdered by a drug addict. The meeting also takes up the support for the children and getting past the dispute between the two main characters. Anders' story provides a strong opening to show that girls are not just victims. However, Anders gives the impression that what ruins the solidarity between women is men. She assumes an organic unity that is "natural" in women—either biologically or inherently in feminine culture. Thus, her film fails to portray the day-to-day work of maintaining and building solidarity—it doesn't happen in one meeting with one enlightened person. Love is an everyday practice.

As we saw in an earlier chapter, the young women I worked with were adamant that the fights between girls in gangs do not stem from jealousy or rivalry over boyfriends. Rejecting Anders' vision, they offered other reasons for fights, typically explaining that at times someone might slight them through gossip or pit two friends against one another—reasons with no relation to boys. In the video, the young women clarify that sometimes they just feel like fighting. In these moments of feeling bad, the girls describe a random eruption of anger. When explaining their attitudes and thoughts right before a fight, a few of the girls express their aggression as a result of mistreatment in the family, at school, or just how "people" treat them. TR says that when she is not in a mood to fight and someone calls her out, she thinks of all the bad things that have happened to her. Consequently, she becomes angry and fights with fury toward the girl or boy who instigated the fight. Such calculated anger, the girls note, comes usually when they do not "feel like fighting." On other occasions, someone bumps into a girl or looks at her as if she were "nothing." This explanation reproduces a masculinist ideology in which the gaze enacts a structural hierarchy. The cult of masculinity centers on physical prowess and contempt for effeminacy (weakness naturalized as in the "superiority" of men over women). One looks at another and attempts to win dominance. These aspects of fighting are issues of honor and respect that circulate not only in subcultures but in dominant ideology as well.

Disagreeing with Anders on jealousy as the motive in the plot, TC, a member of Da Crew, remarks that intragroup rivalry comes from different sources. Grounded by her experience of what it takes to build and unite the gang, TC asserts that the first young woman in *Mi Vida Loca* "wasn't hangin' anymore." If the young woman isn't kickin' it, that is, reconstructing, renegotiating, and actively working on friendship and bonding, TC asks then how does one know whether the girl is still in the gang or will back one up. Kickin' it with the homegirls is the active participation of building friendship. Confinement to the domestic sphere distances and possibly jeopardizes the relationship. Hangin' is simultaneously a manifestation of loyalty and a way to ensure fealty. The majority of the girls, in fact, have only limited hours of spare time between school and home. Many maintain domestic responsibilities—babysitting, housekeeping chores for the family, and cooking dinner. Moreover, while I rarely heard any of the girls excuse themselves from hangin' to go home and study, I knew many of them did. When I saw the girls in the evening at their homes, the girls spent most of the time on the phone. The leaders particularly needed to keep the group cohesive and therefore worked on the relationships among its members. I noticed, too, that many of the leaders of the gangs had pagers as well as call waiting. Often as I attempted to interview them at their homes, I felt I was in the office of a Hollywood producer, watching them flip and switch calls between girls to settle disputes, arrange meetings, and clarify rumors across different cliques. To TC's mind, friends should spend time with each other. Therefore, to neglect a friend is an insult or an act of disloyalty. Negotiation of time, then, becomes a primary effort requiring girls to understand each other's restrictions, to find time when they can talk and build intimacy. While trust is one component of gang solidarity, the idea of intimacy is a greater force uniting the network.

PREDICATING LOVE: ROMANTIC FRIENDSHIP

Since the streets are filled with danger, trust is a universal tenet of all gangs, male or female. Members build friendships based on the kinds of intimacies and secrets they can entrust only to a peer. Since, as María put it, friends "can talk about things that you can't talk about with your moms and family," the peer group's confidentiality operates in a sphere outside domestic space. In this context, the relationships are rather like late-eighteenth-century and early-nineteenth-century romantic friendships between women (Faderman 1981; Smith Rosenberg 1996). Such relations challenge the sexual normativity, often enforced by psychologists and social scientists, which has pushed romantic friendships into the category of deviancy or implied homosexuality. Indeed, today the designation of "romantic friendships" is seldom used for examining relations between women and the development of intimacy among adolescent females. A more current term is the notion of "homosociality."

Homosociality in literary studies has offered a complex reading of relationships between men in contexts where the formation of the heterosexual couple is the tantamount obligation for patriarchy. In her analysis of the sources of homosociality, *Between Men: English Literature and Male Homosocial Desire* (1985), Eve Kosofsky Sedgwick points out the difficulty of extending the concept to both male and female relationships. Sedgwick argues that male homosociality is about male power and authority, whereas a discussion of female homosociality is best addressed along a continuum of the forms of women's attention to women: the bond of mother and daughter, the bond of sister and sister, women's networking and active promotion of the interests of women, women loving women, and lesbianism. She asserts that women's bonds are not as "pointedly dichotomized" against homosexuality as in the arrangement among males (Sedgwick 1985, 2–5). Because male homosociality is about male power and authority, an examination of woman-to-woman relationships reveals a difference from the male homosocial bonds that pattern compulsive heterosexual scripts. Romantic friendship offers an appropriate paradigm for the relations between the young women I worked with in Oakland.

Developing a history of women's relationships from a pre-Freudian era to the present post-Freudian era, Lillian Faderman analyzes discourses about women's relationships in *Surpassing the Love of Men: Romantic Friendship and Love between Women from the Renaissance to the Present* (1981). While many of her texts are drawn from the aristocracy and emerging middle class, she nonetheless follows societal and institutional changes that shifted the meanings of passionate love between women. Marking the moment in the nineteenth century when medical science became the dominant institution defining human practices, Faderman argues that intimate friendships between women were not socially disparaged and that acts of intimacy and declarations of love were not considered homosexual before Freud. "Openly expressed love for the most part ceased after World War I," and same-sex love attained an outlaw status (Faderman 1981, 20). While passionate love in the Romantic era was socially condoned, she notes that the practice continued in the development of Victorian sentiment. Sensibility, faithfulness, and devotion were virtues thought to prepare women for marriage. Women's devotion to one another served men's interest and therefore was permitted, even at times after marriage. Because divorce was impossible, society tolerated these friendships. During the nineteenth century, shifts in relationships between men and women were reflected in the proliferation of homosocial (all-male) societies and spaces which excluded women. The salons of the eighteenth century, in which women could engage in intellectual and political debate, were no longer central in the development of the bourgeois public sphere. Alienated from public life, according to Faderman, middle-class women found comfort with other women in forms of romantic friendship that were permitted since they did no harm to the fabric of "normal" society.

A century later, in a very different social world, romantic female friendship aptly describes the final scene of the video *Homie* in which the young women describe elements of their close-knit relationship. As a manifestation of this friendship they run and skip up the park stairs. In the previous chapter, the structural analysis of the video, I presented a possible interpretation in which the movement up the stairs registers a third space, an imaginary utopia outside the social and economic conditions of a marginalized community. Deepening this interpretation of their mobility, I am proposing that the video's final section, "Poetry," evokes this interstitial site of cultural production. The girls' way of life in gangs consists not only of resistance and delinquency but of the strategies by which through their friendships they confront, accommodate, or evade constructed social roles.

Declaring love for each other via the masculinist structure of the gang regulates the type of romantic friendship that youth, both male and female, can participate in. The structure provides for homosocial bonding in the period of adolescence, a time marked by the turmoil of sexual exploration and romantic coupling. Homosociality in the gang provides freedom from the social expectations of marriage, as it lessens the apprehension and uneasiness of the gendered social roles of courtship and engagement. The heterosexual union is postponed. A dominant cultural script (heterosexual and middle-class) specifies appropriate sexual goals, objects, and relationships that serve as guides for the performance of proper roles. Socialization experience within the family (re)produces the patterns. The husband-wife relationship, as the normative outcome, is portrayed as one of mutual dependence: he will protect her from others, and she in turn will preserve the love in family interaction and the strength of the family. This cultural script impinges directly on the judgment and perception of the individual. As the adolescent enters into peer relations, the family norms are tempered, and adolescence becomes a tug of war between peer and adult norms. It is a period of negotiating conflicting roles about freedom, responsibility, and sexual activity.

Recent economic trends have inverted the salience of peer relations among urban youth. As Shirley Brice Heath and Milbrey W. McLaughlin (1993) have elaborated, for young men in a post-Fordist economy, the approved sex role as provider has contracted. Without access to decent or skilled jobs, young men have few available ways to imagine their gendered selves in work. As the constructed roles of masculinity and work (i.e., men responsible over domains farther from the household or communal center, women responsible for bearing and rearing children, preparing food, and maintaining the household) erode, Heath and McLaughlin note that young men's peer associations often take on greater importance than their domestic roles.

The reduction of adequately paying jobs impinges upon gender roles in the economic shift. In this regard, Heath and McLaughlin found two trends developing. "To find security the young seek arbitrary and risky courses of action and relationships. . . . For example, female gangs as independent units of violence rather than as appendages to male gangs emerged in some cities in the late 1980s. . . . Male gangs had long provided bonding opportunities for young boys, as well as occasional economic support. Now, females wanted their own secure group and more of the financial take for themselves" (Heath and McLaughlin 1993, 28).[5] Further, the authors note that at a very young age girls living in impoverished areas recognize and experience the lack of balance in the social-sexual division of labor between men and women, such that early socialization reveals gender hierarchies. Finally, Heath and McLaughlin found that young women have adapted the norms of gender roles into which they were socialized as a way to adjust to the higher unemployment in the restructured economy. Heath and McLaughlin's revelation on the dual response to the economic crisis as a gendered response—independence and at the same time acquiescence—marks a shift in the transition to womanhood in a restructured economy.

Reconciling their emerging sense of themselves as sexual beings with their social relationships and patterns of friendship, "females often looked to pregnancy and motherhood as a way out of difficult, lonely, or abusive home situations. Finding favor with males and becoming pregnant could bring approval to females from their peers as well as provide favored negotiating positions in schools, welfare agencies, and bureaucratic institutions. As individuals responsible for nurturing an infant, young women could extract greater sympathy from societal institutions than could males, who often found themselves distrusted and feared" (Heath and McLaughlin, 30).

While pregnancy may provide a more stable sense of gender identity, most young mothers found that their new status brought little relief from isolation, and they also confronted new problems or obstacles. "Males, generally relegated by welfare regulations to absence or to work at two jobs, often drew more from continued male peer associations than from life as a father and a breadwinner" (ibid). Many of the young women who had established closeknit groups through street organizations often felt abandoned once babies arrived. Fathers disappeared, and former friends rarely hung out once the day-to-day details of child care altered the new mothers' routines.

Because young women in gangs find love in a masculinist structure that is built around homosocial bonding and power among males (Sedgwick 1985), their peer group works at developing identity and intimacy in a world of physical and symbolic violence. The gang as a place of love seems antithetical to conventional definitions. Moreover, as it operates in the gang, love functions differently from loyalty. Loyalty is to the group and therefore carries the connotation of allegiance to a community or nation. Nationhood has the goal of homogenizing disparate individual wills, and it tends to instill dedication through obligation.[6] It produces rights and privileges that carry duties and obligations, thus compelling the individual to loyalty. The gang compels obligation through the benefits, leisure, and pleasure provided to its members. In particular, two studies of Midwestern gangs (Cintron 1997; Hagedorn 1988) examine the principle of obligation in which the concept of nation is a descriptive term for the solidarity found in street organizations. Similarly, Jankowski (1991) testifies to the relationship of obligation and benefits. While the concepts of nation and obligation are useful in understanding how gangs function, they do not get at the way the gang is imagined—through love. Love maps new sets of relations between members. Loyalty to the gang, like loyalty to the nation, is generally assumed to be a public act, while love is relegated to the private or domestic realm. In practice, both conceptions—of the gang as nation (obligation and publicity) and as a place of love (passion or emotion in the libidinal economy of the private)—are operative. Love provides sustenance for survival and, in effect, love empowers. Love also designates and separates. In the video the girls express that they "got love for" some but not for others. Love chooses who is the in group and the out group. Love is both public and private!

The gang organization operates under the (public) codes of allegiance, loyalty, and trust. At the same time, the girls create a culture of love through their solidarity. We have seen that romantic friendship between women, while it empowers and provides sustenance for survival, is relegated to abnormality in contemporary society. Because the young women are transgressing social codes enforced by the dominant society, by Chicano culture, and by the boys' gang culture, there is continual policing of the boundaries of love. Because of its anti-authoritarian feature, being opposed to parental control and accepted roles of behavior, lesbianism would seem to fit into the group's style of solidarity. But even though the gang is imagined as a place of peer acceptance, many girls' gangs actively watch out for homosexual behavior and have specific rules to discourage lesbians from joining. Because lesbian-baiting can be a way in which the girls are marginalized in the street space, the girls police "inappropriate love" so as not to be misunderstood, to be read as lesbian. While the three girls' gangs of NWA maintained a rule against lesbian membership, Da Crew made an exception for TC, who proved herself in fights with rivals, recruited members, and founded the fourth generation, the largest clique. The gang changed the rule because she proved herself an able fighter and leader. Moreover, in the terms of intimate romantic friendship that I have been attempting to describe, TC has a secret—a secret life that she shares with her peers—and is accepted by her peers. TC's lesbianism is the secret "that you can't talk about with your mom." Thus, since her sexual identity is outlawed in dominant society, the gang can back her up when she is denounced by family and by the community at large. TC's membership changed the way the girls learned tolerance. The leadership, in particular, learned to argue for difference. There were times when some of the girls would argue over TC bringing a date to the parties or whether TC should be kissing her girlfriend at parties. MG in one conversation asked the girls: "How do you think she feels when you're making out when we're all together?" While the debates may not have reached consensus and did not produce eloquence, TC's membership placed the subject on the table, and the girls openly debated their opinions. While some accepted TC's sexuality, others tolerated her while defending sexual difference. For the girl gangs, independent and apart from the boys, operating at the margins of society, the culture of love makes possible an acceptance and open discussion that dominant public spheres cannot afford.

MAKING GIRLS' CULTURE

As Angela McRobbie observes in "The Culture of Working-Class Girls" (1991), girls' lives are more highly structured than those of their male peers. In spite of all their acting up and time on the streets, girls are more closely monitored by parents, schools, and the community at large. Most significantly for my discussion, she finds that girls create a "culture based on each other, rather than on doing things together" (Mc-

Robbie 1991, 37). When the girls of Fruitvale create a culture based on each other, the activity of kickin' it or hangin' becomes the central focus of cultural production. The fights, drugs, and parties that would mark a culture of "doing things together" are few and far between. Friendship is the mediating link. Discussing the origin of their gangs, the girls report a pattern of groups of friends "just hangin' together." Then, as they begin to do things—like meeting at the park, going to parties, attracting more boys from the neighborhood—the girls begin to develop more structured activities which bind them. While the more formalized structure of a gang emerges with fights, the way the girls relate to each other expresses the primary production of the group in trust and intimacy. A few of the girls in their devotion to one another tattoo the names of their best friends on their ankles or legs. Another feature of the production of culture based on each other is the girls' choice of drugs. Their drug of choice is crank (speed), which they use when staying at one another's homes, awake all night talking. While at other times they use marijuana (a more meditative drug), crank is a favored group activity. Given the cultural acceptance of pajama parties for girls, the all-nighters are relatively unsupervised binges of shared thoughts, feelings, and intimacies. Such activities are the active production of friendship. Unlike marijuana gatherings, the time spent talking is clearly remembered the next day. Unlike cocaine, which is a drug used more at the individual level when a person needs a lift to take on a task, crank provides a stimulus for deepening relations and is enjoyed as a collective celebration of "just us." While the girls sporadically experiment with hallucinogens, they note loss of control as a reason for its limited use. The girls also attend raves, but few experiment with ecstasy, which can have hallucinogenic side effects. On one occasion during my research, the girls taped one of their all-nighters on speed. (They did this without my knowledge and presented me with the tape.) Sharing pain, trials, and tribulations, the girls felt that what they were sharing would be somehow important to my work. What was evident was the intimate information about their families and experiences that they exchanged during these all-nighters.

Another way of producing a culture whose object is friendship can be seen in collective poetry writing. During school, the girls carry around wide binder notebooks. The notebooks are filled not with homework and lessons but with poetry. The girls write at home, on the bus, or at school and then hand the notebooks to friends who edit, rewrite, and suggest revisions for the poems. Sometimes the suggestions pertain to meter or rhyme. Revisions are often to sharpen the emotional tenor and develop the voice of the writer. For example, in the video MG's poem is the result of numerous collective revisions. At various times she stumbles over the words or loses the meter because of the changes. Attempting to recall the emotional mood of moving on to another love and forgetting the past, she reads:

> People told me to forget about you
> But I was too stubborn to listen
> But you constantly played your part
> That is why I sit here with . . .
> . . . Naw, that ain't why. . . .
> You gave me a broken heart

"People," her friends, urge her to move on. However, "That is why I sit here with . . ." refers to the feeling she had at the time toward her friends who dismissed her love for the boy, thereby disregarding her pain. The second ellipsis, ". . . Naw, that ain't why," then moves back to the source of anger and pain, the boy. When she wrote the poem her friends reminded her of the anger toward them, not the boy, thus the shift of why she sits with a broken heart is registered. Additionally, the ellipsis contravenes the couplet where "heart" would follow "part." Fracturing the rhyme emphasizes her break from illusory love. She continues and abruptly chortles "ha!" in the middle of her recitation:

> But now I notice there could be other guys
> like the one I'm liking now
> Hopefully, he'll be the one taking your place ("ha!")
> And the love I gave to you
> I'm forgetting
> But just remember he'll be receiving more than you ever expected

When the poem was written, the advice from friends was to bring in the exact feeling she had at the time for the new love. MG's "ha!" is spontaneous, however, and it produces a double meaning. It both marks a moving on and a not moving on, as if to ask, "How did I ever believe in this?" Poetry for the girls is a dialogical form and a source for maintaining friendship. Both VR and MG insist that these personal writings are ways they keep the group cohesive rather than fighting among themselves. There are other instances when the collective writing is acknowledged. The NEL Centro de Juventud publishes a monthly photocopied or mimeographed newsletter, and staff members solicit poems from youth. Sometimes a poem is co-authored. Sometimes at the beginning or end of a poem the writer recognizes the people who contributed to the drafting, editing, and revising. Moreover, even though a poem may be about heterosexual love, many of the poems are dedicated to girlfriends. In some instances the dedication acknowledges the friend's support through talking about love or helping process the relationship.

While the gang is a public network carving out space in the institution of the street, the girls simultaneously produce a culture based on each other, a deliberately focused public intimacy that brings out of the private sphere modes of support and emotional reliance that define the gang experience. My stress on romantic friendship is not meant to claim that the girl gang and its solidarity is especially progressive, revolutionary, or inherently feminist. I am trying to highlight usually invisible specific cultural practices for achieving solidarity. If the gang is to meet the needs of its members, it must be a place of reduced tension. The gang, as described by the young women, is a place of developing peer acknowledgement, identity, and group cohesiveness. The young women through their vernacular poetics express feelings about the gang as a place of love in a world where their communities are disparaged and marginalized through economic exploitation, racism, and segregation. Romantic friendship is the culture they have made for themselves.

Another way of achieving solidarity that is "familial" in a nonprivate sense deserves mention, if only in a suggestive vein. The young women of the gang, informed by female relations in Chicana/o culture, sometimes seem to be reinventing the tradition of comadrazgo as a premarital and preparental form of solidarity. Comadrazgo is a way that women continue ties of friendship and intimacy within a patriarchal structure. In its traditional context comadrazgo as socially constructed is linked with the private realm of the home and organized as an adaptation to men's power, emphasizing compliance, nurturance, and empathy as virtues. While it may appear as an oppositional form, traditional comadrazgo—due to its constrictive heterosexual function and definition within the domestic sphere—operates as a form of containment within a gender regime.

However, other forms of feminine experience are possible. Comadrazgo, in its popular usage, refers to friendship between women who have children, and thus the affiliation is between the godparents or through the friendship that is publicly recognized as a witness of matrimony. Two significant factors have affected the system of comadrazgo, one historical and the other structural. One factor is the development of the Chicano movement that advocated a nativist return to both the Mexican culture and indigenous roots. Reclamation of identity produced revisionist histories in which "hidden histories" of experiences contested and challenged acculturation and assimilation ideals of citizenship. (The experience of spinsters, lesbians, unionists, prostitutes, locas, rebels, maiden aunts, manual workers, midwives, brujas, and curanderas became sites for investigating and recovering marginalized forms of femininity, female experience, and social networks.) Public and private forms of compadrazgo/comadrazgo were reworked into stronger support networks. Going beyond the fictive kinship relations that the church tradition instructed—i.e., through sponsorship in baptism and as witness to marriage—traditions of reciprocity through friendship (comadrazgo de amistad), through the custom of buying a child's first earrings for piercing (comadrazgo de aretes), and other forms were revived. These retrieved customs flourished as resistant practices or combined forms of compliance and resistance in the new identity politics of pride. The second factor of change occurs within the traditional family structure. Chicano families underwent massive cultural and economic changes as the rest of the U.S. population experienced urbanization and industrialization in the post–World War II period. Chicanos had a high proportion of female-headed households, contrary to sociological descriptions and self-concepts of the Chicano community. Divorce rates almost doubled in the 1970s among Chicanos, although they still were not as high as among African Americans or European Americans; for people of Spanish origin the ratio was 118 per 1,000 in 1982, whereas in 1970 the ratio was 61 per 1,000 (Mirandé 1985, 160). The divorce rate increased dramatically for all groups, including Hispanics. Additionally, gender roles were changing. "A younger generation not only challenged their traditional roles, seeking egalitarian relations in the family and in the overall society, but census figures revealed a higher proportion of single women among Mexican Americans. Thirty-four percent of all women of Mexican origin 14 years and over were single— never married" (ibid.). Comadrazgo in this changed context took on new political salience for women's survival. Transformation in the practice and understanding of comadrazgo occurs, no longer qualified by the institutions of marriage and family. Chicanas, married and unmarried, with children and without children, with male or female partners, remade the tradition as a form of emotional support.

The gang girls' culture based on each other can be seen as a deliberately focused public comadrazgo that brings out of the private sphere modes of support and emotional reliance. The heterosexual nuclear family and its domestic ideology is the expected social role, yet it remains in the future during this period of adolescence. The heterosexual script—love, marriage, and children—is a script which the girls do not challenge or resist. Their talk about love and boyfriends is about ful-filling a heterosexual scenario. Many times the girls would talk about their future relationships through children. A girl would promise to name her daughter after a best friend. Even though none of the girls was pregnant at the time, the talk of naming a child after a best friend or one of the leaders of the gang was a way of rendering one's commitment. Borrowing comadrazgo as a form for creating girls' culture in the gang then takes up much more of their time and effort. The extended kinship lines formed through godparenting are not yet part of the girls' lives, since most of them have not had children. Thus it is a prematernal ado-lescent comadrazgo. The girls in the gang re-create this form of feminine Chicana solidarity within a ubiquitously male, patriarchal, masculinist culture of the gang. The logic of trust is a personal commitment in a sphere of danger and aggression. However, in employing this as a sur-vival tactic in patriarchy, the girls are translating a form of solidarity characteristic of the domestic sphere into a new public space. Negotiat-ing friendship and compassion in a gang setting, the logic of trust illus-trates a product of feminine culture. In the terms of the girl gangs, fe-male social bonding, then, is an interstitial or liminal space before the actualization of the gendered "compulsive heterosexual" (Rich 1986) social roles. Without the materiality of children, comadrazgo is resitu-ated among the young women. The social bonding produced by inti-macy and trust found in comadrazgo is transformed to enable physical and emotional survival in the public sphere.

RECIPROCAL CONSTRUCTIONS

Pondering this chapter and my interpretation of the girls' video, I have had to think about what I learned from the young women and once again reflect upon their authority in our ethnographic relationship. The trust that developed between me and the young women was brought about because of my familiarity with their forms of solidarity. However, familiarity blinded. The girls' friendship was so familiar that I over-looked it during the time I spent in the field; it could not emerge as a "topic." Having come from a large family with five sisters and having attended a girls Catholic high school, I did not attend to the significance of their comradeship and sodality (emotional and spiritual support). While my comfort with the forms of behavior, manners, and comport-ment of their network made it easier for me to be accepted, it was only when it was made explicit in their video that I could see it. The continuing relation between our two texts registers the dialogics of the ethnographic encounter. *Homie* is a performance of identity and culture. Rendering their culture of romantic friendship, the video externalized Chicana culture and helped make visible what was most everyday and quite commonplace to me. Through the ethnographic encounter the girls were developing a self-awareness and consciousness of their power to influence representation. They were beginning to articulate their lives to a broader audience. While the world of the gangs has codes of language and behavior, the articulation of its meaning for them began with my interviews and progressed to various sites of public discourse. The video, *It's a Homie Thang!*, manifests the reflexive process in which the girls begin to author themselves.

Lila Abu-Lughod in "Writing against Culture" (1991) asks: "What happens when the 'other' that the anthropologist is studying is simultaneously constructed as, at least partially, a Self?" (140). She suggests that we interrogate issues of positionality, audience, and power that are "inherent in the distinctions of self and other" (ibid.). When we apply the split writing subject to the researched subject, we find that the "informant" goes through a similar process of othering. Adopting a speaking (authorial) subject position, they construct a self through the interview process: they see themselves in the other—the researcher. Since "self" is always a construction, the questions of who you are and of what you do, the imperative to explain yourself, is determined by audience. Abu-Lughod notes there is "never a natural or found entity . . . the process of creating a self through opposition to an other always entails the violence of repressing or ignoring other forms of difference" (ibid.). Because girls in gangs are subjects of political debate by police, news media, politicians, and community organizations and researched as subjects for movies as well as for sociological studies (and even my anthropological study), emotions and feelings become emergent points of consciousness. These emergent points of becoming are where speech may not fully articulate, where utterance indicates the impending articulation. The gaze enacts the self-consciousness so they can speak about their lives and at the same time entails a violence. In the following chapter, I trek the developing self-awareness as the girls proceed to interpret their knowledge to different publics in face-to-face interaction.

CROSS-SITES FOR CROSS-TALKS

In principle, assumptions that were previously exempt from contestation
will now have to be publicly argued out. In general, the proliferation of
subaltern counter publics means a widening of discursive contestation, a
good thing in stratified societies.   NANCY FRASER, 1992

New ethnographic practices have emerged from social movements for
decolonization, the intensification of American imperialism, and the
growth of civil rights struggles in the United States. The impact of social
movements nationally and internationally upon academic practices was
met by calls for a more committed anthropology. The attempt to use
classical forms of ethnography for new research programs raised conceptual issues—problematizing the relation of power to knowledge and
the institutionalization of knowledge. According to Renato Rosaldo in
Culture and Truth: The Remaking of Social Analysis (1989), theory
building in classical ethnography focused on ritual, featuring a struc-
tural-functionalist approach which supported universalist accounts of
culture. Problematizing the emphasis on structure, Rosaldo notes that
ethnographies were unable to account for the open-ended human processes in the informal settings of everyday life that occur outside the
circumscribed sphere of formal ritual. Because culture is an open and
"porous array of intersections where distinct processes crisscross from
within and beyond its borders" (Rosaldo 1989, 20), Rosaldo argues for
a focus on the intersections of cultural borderlands. Imagined as a crossroads, these spaces prioritize movement through space(s) that offer cultures progression or potentiality. Ethnography as a form of social analysis, according to Rosaldo, should explore the interplay of discrete factors
as they unfold within specific situations. Ethnography would, additionally, centralize the aspirations and demands of groups deemed marginal
by the dominant culture. To effectively reflect this changing content,
Rosaldo proposes a methodology in which attention is turned from general explanatory laws to cases and their interpretation. Rosaldo's pro-
cessual analysis emphasizes that culture requires study from a number
of perspectives, but it does not suggest that perspectives can necessarily be added together into a unified summation. Proffering an extended
case-study methodology that includes narrative, Rosaldo notes that such

methodology enables readers to follow a group of people through a series of incidents.

Offering a further critique of spatial paradigms that set apart and circumscribe people and cultures, Kirin Narayan argues that an "ideology of authenticity" undergirds the notion of native/other. "The term is linked to place. 'Natives' are incarcerated in bounded geographical spaces, immobile and untouched yet paradoxically available to the mobile outsider" (Narayan 1993, 24).[1] Because social science has tended to privilege bounded sociocultural arenas with marked centers and outer edges, conventional studies of gangs place their subjects in a fixed location, a "turf" or a "'hood." The rubric of place emphasizes following gang members to street corners and club hangouts where the action is. Youth, however, are mobile. They move about in their neighborhoods and communities; and the subjects of my study not only move from home to school to malls, stores, and record shops, but they also move to social service centers, clinics, and hospitals. Interacting with state and community institutions, youth "inhabit" various discursive realms. Moreover, youth are not, or not necessarily, separated from the social movements that have marked the second half of the twentieth century. Discourses on class, race, gender, and sexuality arising from social change of the late sixties continue to prevail, particularly in communities like Oakland.

In "An Ethnographer's Tale" I provided an initial critique of ethnographic authority, particularly the power of the ethnographer to represent. I began with a "tale" of fieldwork in order to highlight the selection process, the construction of texts, in order to highlight the problems of representation in writing about the subjects of our research. In this chapter I will again focus on the problems of representation, but here by actuating Rosaldo's and Narayan's critiques of place. Thus I argue against fixing youth in gangs solely to turf, a strategy that disconnects youth from the diverse sites of the Latino/a community and that separates them from interaction with a broader public sphere.[2]

While sociological studies examine institutions such as the family, education, and the criminal justice system, I examine discursive fields as sites where representation of gangs and girls in gangs are invoked and contested. Whether they are on street corners, at recreational centers, or in social clubhouses, youth are not only cognizant of the discourses on gangs but are co-discursive participants in the construction of the gang and its image.[3] This chapter, therefore, follows the young women of Oakland through various sites of interaction. Recording their movement—

between cultural centers like the NEL Centro and various institutions and conferences—this chapter recognizes a sociopolitical agency in travel across the outer edges of the gang subculture to the "borderlands" of interactive spheres. By examining the girls' participation at sites where gangs are under discussion and investigation, I move out of the rigid patterns that isolate gang youth from the discursive arenas where policy is shaped through representation. While these case studies are not typical for youth involved in gang life, I nonetheless select these exchanges in order to suggest the potential of counter or subaltern public spheres (Fraser 1989, 1992). In the cases selected, the Latina adolescents interact with various sectors of community and academy. I focus on the elements that produce the spaces in which the youth speak, on the nature of the events in which they intervene. Ethnography as a method of social analysis (Rosaldo 1989) provides a critical examination of place and subject positions within discourses of power. In these cross-sites the girls encounter situations in which they get to represent themselves as gang members in different ways. Additionally, these public sites of discourse give the girls a new kind of knowledge about their own participation in gangs. Rosaldo (1989) advises that ethnography should consider that an understanding of change, conflict, and social processes is strengthened with the reporting of the various phases of interaction. Thus, as I take up his invitation to study the moments when subjects "are more than willing to talk back," I utilize Chéla Sandoval's (2000) analytical model to situate the expressions of resistance and/or accommodation that the girls exercise within each of the public places where they speak. These "methodologies of the oppressed" define the strategies employed by marginalized communities and are implicit in my narrative descriptions.

SIGNIFYIN' GANGS
Case Study 1

On September 27, 1993, the Latino Police Officers Association sponsored a three-day conference to discuss Latino gangs in the city of Oakland. At its inception the group debated whether the conference should be limited to police officers or whether it should also include social service agencies and community advocacy organizations. Sergeant Delgadillo, who organized the conference, particularly wanted community and academic input in order to gain a wider perspective on gangs. Participating early in the conference planning was the administrator of the

NEL Centro de Juventud, Rosalinda Palacios. From the outset she had a difficult time with the conference planning committee because of her outspoken views on police conduct. She recommended broadening the planning committee and the range of speakers for the conference workshops and plenary sessions. Additionally, she advocated the participation of youth at the conference. In the end, this idea was narrowed down to only those youths working for community and social service agencies. Conflicts over planning continued up to the day of the conference. Gaining a small victory, Palacios informed the Centro that youth could attend a special evening session to view the documentary *Lives in Hazard*. The documentary would be previewed in a special evening program featuring the actor Danny de la Paz. The documentary follows the lives of the community youth who appeared in Edward James Olmos' film *American Me*.

Youth participation, however, was still an issue that conference planners contested—all the way up to the evening the documentary was to be premiered. Several of the peer counselors and I brought carloads of youth. When we assembled in the patio of the Sheraton Airport Hotel, a group of police officers attending the conference informed us that the meeting with de la Paz was closed to the public. The senior peer counselor of NEL argued with the police that the youth of the Centro were invited. Getting only a negative response, the senior peer counselor went to look for Palacios to find out what had happened. Left waiting after hoping to speak with one of the actors of the film, the youth of the Centro became disgruntled and swarmed around some of the conference participants, complaining. After a short while, Lieutenant Mestas of the Latino Police Officers Association came out of the hotel to speak to the group. He explained that they could not see the documentary because de la Paz was concerned about copyright. Additionally he explained that the film had not been rated for violence and language, a restriction that was greeted with laughter and derision. Mestas then said that only eighteen-year-olds would be admitted. This produced more shouting. One of the young women, FN, responded by demanding that de la Paz come out to the hotel patio to speak with the youth who had been waiting for him. Mestas replied that de la Paz was unavailable, since he had not yet arrived. As more complaints arose, Mestas then responded that the Latino police officers' group had decided more than two weeks back that youth could not participate in any part of the conference. He apologized for the breakdown in communications.

Throughout the planning for the conference, Palacios gave me regular updates on difficulties with the committee. When Mestas turned us away, I assumed that the police finally achieved their original aim: no community people, no youth, no dialogue. As we were returning to the cars and vans, very upset with our exclusion, the Centro's administrator came charging out of the hotel and confronted the lieutenant. A youth laughed and said, "Rosalinda's gonna give them shit now." Another said, "She can't give them shit. They're full of shit already." When Palacios called us back, she informed us that the youth could attend the evening session. The young people began to woof and cheer and performed a lot of bad attitude to the mostly male conferees who lingered at the hotel lobby windows. Victory produced a noisy entrance through the hotel lobby and to the conference hall. We finally settled on one side of the conference hall. Many of the youth sat at the back tables. Because at that time my relationship to the Latina teenagers was only through the discussion group held once a week, I felt that I would be intruding in their camaraderie to sit among them. So I went to the front of the hall where the majority of the conference participants were assembled. I turned on my tape recorder, hoping to capture the opinions of policemen and social service workers about gangs.

After the documentary was screened, Danny de la Paz gave an update on what people from the neighborhood who participated in the film *American Me* were now doing. Informing everyone that the intent of the documentary would be to create dialogue among youth to deter gang violence, he announced that it would be screened at junior high schools, high schools, and juvenile detention centers. The discussion began with questions from the audience, mostly made up of police officers, social and juvenile service workers, and community service workers. People discussed how they felt about the documentary, what they liked or did not like about it. Many commented on the lack of self-esteem among the youth of the documentary; others projected this problem upon youth in general.

Amidst the discussion someone asked for the response of the youth who were attending this section of the conference. One young woman, EV, stood up to talk about the truthfulness of the documentary: "Every character I seen reminded me of somebody that has been there or will be there. We see it here in Oakland every day. In a school year, I went to, what, thirty funerals, just friends dying every day. It's just hard, I mean maybe you know this." Speaking about her own commitment and plans for the future, she urged adults to look compassionately on the youth of today to guarantee a future for them. This was applauded roundly.

Discussion then continued on the making of the documentary, with updates on the lives of the people in the film. Responding to a question on his background, de la Paz talked about his "White boy" identity in the city of Whittier. He grew up in a Southern California suburb where there were no gangs and which was just beginning to change from predominantly White to Chicano. "I realized that I was Chicano [with the making of the film *Boulevard Nights*], that I had an incredible history to be very, very proud of, that I had an identity that I didn't know of before, because when I was in school all I knew was the Eurocentric Anglo teachings, the books, the songs, everything. They never taught me about my culture. I heard 'dirty Mexican' jokes. I remember being young and seeing the division of two colors in the middle of my fingers and wanting to erase the darker side because that's how I grew up. Now I dedicate my entire career, my entire future, everything I do to give opportunities to every Chicano. To bring the gente up. To change the serious problem we have with self-esteem that young people have that don't really believe in themselves. Like Father Boyle said, the future is not very compelling to them. They don't see their future. The present isn't very compelling either. Like [some of] you said, they don't care . . . won't get out of harm's way. That's the way it is: *mi vida loca*."

De la Paz's characterization of nihilism among youth later became controversial when two groups at the conference lined up in opposition to each other. The debate began after one of the police officers identified a youngster as a problem. Walking up to a boy seated among the youth brought to the conference by the NEL Centro de Juventud, the police officer laid his hand on the boy's shoulder and spoke to de la Paz. "I'm on this side of the room, and I see this kid writing on the table, tearing the furniture up." The laughter of the audience encourages him. "He's writing gang graffiti. How do I reach him? What do I say to him? . . . What will it take? Getting shot?"

The boy lowered his upper body, touching the table, yet the man's hands remained on him. Then the youth hid his face into the fold of his arms, no longer horsing around with the youth around him. I felt his complete embarrassment.

De la Paz responded by reminding people of the lack of opportunities for youth. "I can tell you that from the time that they are born, they know that there is nothing for them in society. They are not appreciated; they are not loved; they are not cared for, nor respected, not because there are no parents around, but on a social level, sociological; the much bigger picture: they don't feel that they are part of the system. They don't feel that they're included. They feel that they are at the margins of society, and they know it. Not intellectually—they know it from inside, at a gut level. And that's the problem. By the time a kid is ten years old, he's been growing up with this on his mind. It creates a lot of problems for him. A lot of problems. Reaching [out] is very difficult for him . . . for her."

At this point one of the young women of Fruitvale, DV, got up and pointed out the difficulty of leaving the gang once one was a member. Interrupting her, another police officer began to talk about the need to "leave the barrio." DV raised her voice and asked, "Have you ever been in a gang?" The cop continued to talk about his cousins and friends. She interrupted again, "Have you . . . ?" He replied that he had been in a gang and had stab wounds to prove it, and he continued to talk. DV then shouted, her voice trembling, "Tell us how to get out! How'd you get out?"

"The lucky thing about it is I had somebody to help. . . ."

"Luck!?" She spit out the word, "See? Not everybody is lucky."

"Hey, it's not luck. You didn't let me finish. You gotta listen. . . ." There was light applause from the conference participants. Many wagged their heads at DV and the group of youth who were now making more noise.

"No. No. You don't know about getting out." The youth around her applauded.

The man then decided to change his argument to emphasize that it is up to individuals to make up their minds and get out. One clear voice asserted, "It ain't like that!"

"You asked me. Let me finish," interjected the police officer. Turning to de la Paz and then the general audience, he pleaded. "You see, you don't listen. You asked a question and I'd like to answer."

The conference was in a hubbub of discussion, and it was difficult to hear what DV was saying. She kept attempting to speak. The police officer spoke over her, telling his story of being a former gang member. Once again "luck" and "getting out of the barrio" were heard through the commotion. Then a new phrase, "responsibility for yourself," emerged as he turned to speak to DV and the group of young women at the back of the room. Another young woman, FN, then chimed in against the police officer's narration of self-motivation and bootstrap individualism. She shouted: "Even when you try to get out of the gang, you can't turn away from your partners. . . ." The police officer responded, "People control their own destiny. I had a skill; I could fight;

and a police officer took me and got me into wrestling. I won the state championship wrestling. . . ." The girls began to hoot at him. FN shook her head, stating, "It ain't like that. We got homies." There was applause from the immediate audience around her. A participant in the conference then began to criticize the policeman who singled out the young man. "You embarrassed him. You said everything bad about him. . . . You demoralized him." To which FN then shouted, "Anyway, what do you care what he was doing?"

During the officer's speech, the youth began to laugh and shout out remarks. There was a general commotion among the conferees. The Latina youth were cheering their friends, as each raised her voice, unrecognized by de la Paz, who attempted to maintain order, urging particularly the youth to hold on, wait their turn. Visibly, many were upset; many were shaking their heads and waving their hands, waving off the remarks by the police.

A bit of order was restored when a young man from a community service organization stood up to speak. However, the room divided once again as he took up FN's complaint against the policeman's handling of the youth who was writing on the table.

"This man, he, he . . . what you just did was . . . You dehumanized . . . humiliated . . . [the youngster]. Maybe he was bored; maybe what we've been saying hasn't interested him. You're an authority, in a position of authority, and you do this to him?" When the policeman responded that he knew the youth, the community service worker retorted, "I know him better than you because I'm him."

Once again, people shouted to be recognized to speak to the assembly. At the same time the teenagers began to shout and clamor about the conduct of the policeman toward the youth. Amid this were appeals from the conferees for order and unity. Yet as each conferee took the floor to speak on the incident, the Latina adolescents rarely were quiet; they would disrupt continually with cheers or scoffing.

Ending the evening's session of the conference, de la Paz urged the theme: "You can be what you want to be." Many of the young women from the Centro immediately left the hall, going outside to the patio to smoke cigarettes and expressing their anger with the police and other adults who would not let them speak. A few adults gathered around the youth, attempting to express solidarity. Now having the space outside the conference, the girls elaborated on the difficulty of leaving the gang and were particularly critical of the idea of "leaving the barrio."

The discourse of the meeting was organized around two different positions in popular discourse on gangs. On one side, social structures seemed so dominant that the youth had no agency, and on the other, individual choice was the sole form of "rising above" the gang. In a sense, the depiction of youth as having no choices and that of having individual choice do not necessarily represent two opposite positions. Instead we can conceive them as flip sides of the same coin. Whenever the issue of leaving the gang is raised, the personal journey is emphasized, leading to a bootstrap discourse. The concept of lifting oneself out of the barrio as a strategy for social change recognizes structural factors such as race and class. But only through individual effort can one overcome or prevail over the structures which marginalize. When the policeman looks at a young man writing on the table, he asks, "How can I reach him?" Beneath the question is the idea that the boy is a victim, deaf to any appeal, ignorant of choices, and in need of rescue but capable of being awakened to his individual freedom of choice. The appeal also implies that the person has passively accepted a victim position. Similarly, the other side of the coin is couched in the discourse of youth as victims of society, having no agency other than delinquency. While de la Paz and others seem to hold a structural rationale for gangs, they nonetheless, like the policeman, also produce the discourses of victimization occluding agency. Assertions that youth "don't see other places," "don't get around, "don't even know San Francisco or Berkeley," or "don't know anything outside the barrio" reproduce the victim discourse.

Between these two factions, the youth argued a middle ground. On the one hand, the concept of choice becomes problematic for the youth as they struggle to show they reject the idea that a successful individual must move out of the barrio. In the girls' understanding of the debate, the term "personal responsibility" equals individualism and therefore equals the betrayal of one's friends (one's homies). Because the identity of the youth is framed within a collective relationship, any threat to their fragile identity is a betrayal. On the other hand, just as the policeman recognizes de la Paz's discourse of hopelessness, the girls recognize that the discourse of systematic oppression occludes choice and agency for youth. When the policeman accuses de la Paz of making demoralizing statements without offering hope, it is interesting to observe that the girls did not in fact directly cheer de la Paz, but rather effect a more strategic intervention. They use his discussion as a legitimizing point of entry into this public sphere.

Overall, what the girls were responding to was their objectification in this sphere of public discourse, a space in which their presence was unwillingly accepted and their voices only ambivalently accepted. The contrariness and rancor of the girls were particularly unacceptable, and attempts to restore order predominated in the interaction. The girls' shouting and heckling as well as their interruption of speakers recognized by de la Paz assaulted the decorum of rational communication. When the police officer selected the young man as an example, he asked, "How can I reach him?" While the officer's tone was sympathetic and paternal, he did not address the boy himself. He spoke of the youth in the third person as if he were only an object for discourse. And similarly, even the conferees who criticized the policeman also spoke of the youth in the third person as if he were not there. None of these speakers recognized that the plenary session was a portion of the conference arranged as a time for exchange. FN's response, however, took up the boy's subject position and spoke from that standpoint. Shouting "Anyway, what do you care what he was doing?" she did not speak of the boy as victim but as a person who may or may not have been writing on the table or tearing up the furniture. His intentions were his affair and should be ignored, since conferences exemplify the occasion "to talk," not to police. Her shouted response expressed frustration with the regulation and control of the girls' discourse that continued throughout the conference. "Anyway" expressed her, and the boy's, subject position—indifference to authority.

The girls' reaction to this objectification can be seen as a negotiation for reality (Kingsolver 1992; Rosen 1984). As the girls asserted a gang identity, it provided them with a legitimate reason for entry and participation in the conference. Ironically, the conference was about gangs, yet planners refused to allow gang members to participate (in spite of all of Palacios' work). It was only through their collective contestation that they were finally allowed to attend. At this site of cross-talk, the girls very ably read and placed the conferees. Recognizing the power advantages not just of the police but of the social service workers, they mapped the conferees along lines of social status. In this way they utilized the discourse of the social service and community workers to gain a space to enter the discussion. The performed identity, of "gang member," provided a way they could assert their distinctiveness, fashioning themselves to negotiate with the public gathered at the conference. Placing primacy on their gang identity accentuated and made visible the unequal power relations. By fixing their identity as gang-bangers, they enacted a position from which to speak. Negotiating for reality is about contestation where consensus—the ideal of the liberal public sphere—

is not necessarily an objective goal. And so the girls utilized the fixed, even stereotyped, image of the gang member—raucous, rebellious, and dangerous—to protest the reigning discourse of the meeting, which in its structural and individualist modes relegated them to the status of victim.

Case Study 2

At the National Association for Chicano/Chicana Studies (NACCS) regional conference held in April 1994 at the University of California at Santa Cruz, I took seven Chicana teenagers to participate in a workshop. A graduate student from Berkeley, Angela Gallegos, and I had arranged a conference panel in which I would present a report on the NWA gang structure and organization and the young women would offer a slide show. The NACCS conference was titled "Building for Our Future: Immigration, Migrants, and Homegirls." Looking at the conference agenda and the title of Rosa Linda Fregoso's speech in the plenary—"La Vida Dura of La Vida Loca: Home Girls on Film"—the Centro's youth began to laugh. One commented, "Homegirl is spelled wrong. It's one word, and she's spelled it with two words." Another told me, "You better tell your teacher to check her spelling; she don't know how to spell." I opened my conference booklet to see what was going on. Then they began to kid each other that they were never home anyway but in the streets, so they didn't know why they or anyone used the term. I told them that maybe "my teacher" had intentionally written the word wrong to question the word "home," just as they were now playing with the word. (I don't know how to describe their faces—incredulous?)

Entering quietly, since the plenary already had begun, the teens sat in the front row because all the back and middle seats were occupied. Throughout Fregoso's speech they politely listened. Fregoso looked at the street space as a site for Chicana youth to contest the gendered roles which relegate young women to the home. In addition, she analyzed films in which the Chicana, especially the gang girl, was portrayed, interpreting and challenging the representations of Hollywood-produced films. She recognized the life, the hard life, that comes with a street identity for young women in gangs. Throughout her speech the youth from Fruitvale were attentive, nodding at various parts of her speech. When Fregoso showed film clips of various Hollywood images of Chicana gang members, the girls laughed and sneered, nudging elbows during some of the scenes. I was struck by the girls' engagement with Fregoso's presentation. Something was different about their behavior at this particular counter public sphere. Somehow, among the older college professors and students, a space opened up for the Chicana youth. Fregoso's presentation acknowledged the gang as a genuine social space of identity construction and local knowledge.[4] Thus, not only were the young women allowed to be at the conference, i.e., physically to move from one locale to another, but also a conceptual space was elaborated where the meaning of representation was opened to them.

When the workshop began, people hurried to the classroom, the room quickly became crowded, chairs were pulled in from other rooms, people lined the walls, and many sat in the back aisles. The room was filled with women. Gallegos began with a presentation on the meager research on Chicana adolescents. She noted that when Chicana youth are studied, it is usually through a comparison between boys and girls. If comparative models are few, there are many more studies, Gallegos asserted, that focus on the Chicana adolescent's body—reproduction—thus reducing health-related social issues to the paradigm of a deviant body. I then presented my report. Nervous, because of the girls' presence, I discussed the gang structure and organization of three of the girl gangs found in Fruitvale. I attempted to provide a gendered analysis, underlining the strong bonds of friendship that they developed. The girls listened attentively, watching me and at times looking around at the people gathered in the workshop. At one particular moment of my report, they began to laugh. It was when I was attempting to describe power relations in fieldwork, particularly the push and pull over my research topic. While my report included extensive quotes from the discussions we held at the NEL Centro de Juventud, by and large it compared the girls' statements to information drawn from other gang studies, particularly by Joan Moore (1978, 1991), Horowitz (1983), and Jankowski (1991).

My presentation was followed by the panelist Norma Mendoza-Denton. She began to set up differences between the ethnic-social identities of the two major gang groupings in the Southwest, Norteños and Sureños. The young women I worked with began to disagree. Characterizing the Sureñas as more Mexican and Norteñas as more assimilated, she noted that fights were not struggles around turf. She emphasized that the disputes reflect a deep conflict over identity politics. Issues of Mexicanness—who is the real Mexican?—and representation—who can call themselves Mexican?—define gangs not solely around territory, but around ideology. As she began to identify styles of dress—Norteñas wear vertical ponytails, and Sureñas wear their hair down in a feathered style—one of the teenagers illustrated her own very different hairstyle. Recognizing that conditions in gangs allow variation and individuality, Mendoza-Denton began to address popular dance style. Then as Mendoza-Denton delineated the kind of dancing that differentiated the groupings—Sureñas danced banda and Norteñas danced hip-hop—a couple of girls inserted rejoinders.

"Some of us can't dance it that well, so we don't."

"My cousin dances banda and everything."

Mendoza-Denton acknowledged the statements, nodding her head, and went on with her report: "Even when they dance they throw their signs. . . ." When she twisted and curved her hands and fingers to illustrate how the gang signed, one of the girls responded, "You got it the wrong way." The girl then nimbly adjusted hands and fingers to sign not the rival Sureña hand sign but her own gang. The girls all slyly laughed under their breath.

However, it was when Mendoza-Denton took up posture and gaze that all the Chicana teens began to speak out. Emphasizing the performative act—"the way one walks and talks, the way you look at each other"—as interactive, Mendoza-Denton continued, "People have told me how Norteñas act, how they have a different gaze. What they said is Norteñas look up and down. Sureñas look people straight in the eye."

"Oh, shiiiit."

"That's a hella lie."

"What they tell you?"

"They just trying to look good."

Amid the general laughter, Mendoza-Denton asked if this wasn't true.

"They don't even look up."

"They look at the floor."

"The ones we know, they won't even look at us. They stay looking at the floor. We can't say all of them. Just the ones we know."

"A girl, yesterday when I picked up my pa'tna, was looking at me, and I looked at her straight in the eye and asked, 'Wha'z up?' and she just looked straight down to the ground."

Agreeing that she was generalizing, Mendoza-Denton went on to explain that language differences and code switching nonetheless were features of both Norteña and Sureña groups. Since adolescence is a social process of identity formation, the Chicana and Mexicana youth establish identity in relation and opposition to the dominant Euro-American culture. Therefore, both, though rivals, shared a similar social project.

Wanting to avoid debate, she turned to symbolic drawings in letters from the youth that she was studying. Again as she began to identify Norteña symbols, the youth clarified their origins. When Mendoza-Denton held up a drawing of two masks, one of the girls stated:

"Smile Now, Cry Later."

Mendoza-Denton: "The symbol of Tragedy and Comedy."

Another girl: "No, it's the oldies song, 'Smile Now, Cry Later.'"

Mendoza-Denton: "It's in their lives. . . ."

Mendoza-Denton asked the girls to hold their comments. But they continued to comment through the rest of her speech.

After the reports, the young Chicanas presented their slide show, "Our Lives," accompanied by the song "Friends" that articulates various problems and situations of friendship. The photos were gathered from shoe boxes, albums, and photos from their bedroom walls. The slides depicted the girls at parties, picnics, recreation centers, the NEL Centro de Juventud, at information tables for community and college events, and at Cinco de Mayo and Diez y seis de Septiembre celebrations of Mexican heritage. There were sets of photos of girls gathering at baby showers, photos of girls in formal dress with dates in suits and tuxedos, studio photos of couples, and photos of two and three women with a child. There were three slides of girls at graduation. The range of situations provided information far removed from dominant media images of girls in gangs adopting aggressive postures for a news camera. Moreover, the majority of the photos were of two or more girls, not the solitary figure, the passive victim, found in "art" photos. (The few photos of solitary figures were usually studio photos, commemorating a graduation or quinceñera.) The slides were a celebration of friendship—the camaraderie of the girls' solidarity network. At the end of the show, each of the teens got up and faced the workshop attendees to introduce herself.

Because the panel presentations had run overtime, there was no time for questions or discussion. After the workshop, many people surrounded them with questions, and the young women were the center of attraction. They willingly and eagerly participated in the small groups that gathered.

Disagreeing with the authoritative interpretations and presenting a slide show which depicted the youth in an unusually wide range of activities—parties, picnics, conferences—was certainly an instance of subjects "talking back." This elaboration on social life—the range of everyday practices and special events—clearly detailed the significance of the social network about gang life. The intervention had a twofold effect. On the one hand, the girls were correcting the representations of sympathetic ethnographers like Mendoza-Denton and me. On the other, the slides were a direct challenge to visual representations made by dominant media. Their corrections were also a negotiation in seeking equal participation with a manifestly sympathetic audience. The experience further amplified the young Chicanas' realization that they could provide other images of themselves in broader domains.

This site of cross-talk provides a different entry point on the discourse of gangs. Primarily concerned with representations of Chicana youth in films and sociological studies, the featured speaker and the workshop presenters provided new ways of thinking about gangs' everyday practices. The opening session by Rosa Linda Fregoso established the situated knowledge of girls in gangs and girls familiar with street life. Presenting pachucas, cholas, and "home girls" as producers of knowledge, Fregoso's address at the plenary not only welcomed the girls from Oakland but acknowledged them as co-discursive partners in knowledge production. Similarly, Gallegos' report, which urged a reconceptualization of Latina youth beyond the reproductive body, acknowledged the girls whose lives are more complex than biological determination. While the girls contested Mendoza-Denton throughout her presentation, it was a kind of jubilant co-discursivity—not oppositional to the main thrust of her report: the production of culture. Additionally, Fregoso's presentation produced excitement for the workshop, and it was crowded even before it began. The majority of the workshop attendees were women, with only two or three men.

The centrality of Chicana youth, the conference focus on "home girls," Fregoso's examination of representational practices and discourse about the subjectivities of Chicana youth, the presentation by the panelists of the workshop, and the enthusiasm of Latina professors and students concatenated. All of these engagements and critiques resulted in a "mutually constructed moment of play" (Foley 1990).[5] Whether the disruption was "approved" or not, it was nonetheless "allowed" since the focus was homegirls. In this academic sphere of students and professors, the girls utilized their identity as gang members to claim a position to speak. Moreover, gender provided an additional way in which the girls linked with participants. The very presence of the girls adjusted the general image of gangs as not only for boys. There was an expectation to view the girls' slide show, even a possibility to hear what they had to say. Overall, the girls' discursive practice, interruption, and horseplay marked difference and at the same time sought interaction. The girls fashioned a strategic identity more complex than simply that of gang member.[6]

Foley's concept of "mutual play" can be used to consider the girls' slide show. When Gallegos and I first suggested the slide show to the girls, we proposed the topic "social network." By displaying a number of activities documenting girls in school, at the park, with children, dating, graduating, we were hoping to move representations of Latina youth away from the plane of deviancy. While the girls translated our term "social network" to "friends," the photos nonetheless predominantly conveyed their gang identity. To a person unfamiliar with gangs, the photos may only convey the culture of friendship through recreation and pleasure. However, the majority of the photos signified their Norteño affiliation, wearing their colors (red), signifying their gang (DC, ESN, LN), their alliance (NWA), or affiliation (Fourteen or N) through hand signals. If one is familiar with gang culture, the signs can be decoded. Additionally, many of the photos had writing that identified the person's nickname and gang affiliation in Old English script that is not easily readable. Thus, even though Gallegos and I attempted to take out the prominence of gang identity, the girls nonetheless asserted this identity through their selection of photos. Mutual play allows the girls to provide a varied representation of Chicana youth and affirm, without contradiction, their gang identity—not solely the performance of the bad-ass, tough street persona.

I believe that one other element contributed to the girls' "talking back." This was my report. Nowhere in my presentation did they interrupt—and there were plenty of times that they could have chimed in to correct me. As Teresa de Lauretis (1989) has pointed out, there can be violence in representational practices. The act of terror in representation is lodged in the fact that the powerful define the "others." I believe the girls acted up not only to correct but because they experienced a form of alienation during my presentation. As an ethnographer, a "translator," or go-between at the workshop, my role was to inform the conferees about the culture of the girls' gang. Mark Whitaker (1996) notes the epistemological problem of representation for critical ethnographers. He acknowledges the fact that many of our representations are decontextualizing, lifting expressions out of context in order to represent a "culture." Events, concepts, or beliefs that make sense to participants get reconceptualized when the ethnographer attempts to make them understandable to a different audience. Thus, the problem of translation was a practical reality at this academic cross-site. The girls heard my translation of their organization, their solidarity, their lives, when I took up the subject position of go-between for an academic, albeit predominantly Chicana, audience. The girls were caught between my translation and an audience that was not part of their local group—experiencing a fracturing of their contextualized local knowledge.

The fracturing, moreover, was a continual experience from the moment of participation in the conference. Alienation—"Is that me?"—and recognition—"That's me!"—produced a performance of asserting their identity as gang member. The space of mutual play allowed the girls to disrupt, to contest the workshop, and to present their slide show with its double meaning. The mobility and fluidity of their various subject positions and at the same time the assertion of their gang identity was fashioned by the conceptions and ideals of a particular type of counter public sphere. While the space at NACCS sanctioned their voice, they, however, had no prepared speech, only a slide show that interrupted the academic language that filled the conference. While the conference encouraged their voice, it did so in a form that alienated them from their own experience. Therefore they insisted on an outsider's voice, taunting and scoffing. They took up the subject position of gang member, asserting that "you already have an idea of who and what we are," but in order to claim a speech and style of representation they were familiar with. From this unincorporated position, dialogue could begin.

Case Study 3

By the end of my first year of field research in Oakland, the summer of 1994, fights with rival gangs had reached new levels. One member of Da Crew, TC, had been shot during a drive-by—a bullet went into her thigh. With her was the brother of a close friend who was shot twice and nearly lost his life. The code of taking care of things on their own terms prevailed, and members refused to report the assailants to the police. In a different incident, another member of Da Crew, QG, had a gun pointed at her while her friend, MG, was beaten with a bottle and had her face slashed by a rival gang member. One of the young women, MG, after receiving emergency treatment at the hospital, went to Alta Vista Clinic for follow-up care.[7]

A local outpatient clinic of county health care, Alta Vista primarily provides services to youth and is a satellite of La Clínica de la Raza, also located in Fruitvale. La Clínica de la Raza has its origins in the free clinics of the sixties and early seventies, focusing on the health concerns of the Chicano community and balancing the need for governmental funds with a goal of community control of health services. Youth are referred to the Alta Vista Clinic, which provides general checkups and counseling services. The majority of Alta Vista's clientele, however, are pregnant teenagers seeking prenatal and postnatal care.

Having been a patient at Alta Vista after a car accident in 1989, MG regularly visited the clinic, seeing the attending doctor for various problems brought on from the accident. However, when she came in for the follow-up after the attack with a broken bottle, her doctor began to ask questions about her gang membership. Concerned about this other aspect of health, Dr. Jainen Supersade asked whether MG and members of the discussion group would be willing to make a presentation to the clinic staff. At the next Centro meeting, MG proposed that a group attend to make a presentation about girls in gangs. The group was reluctant. TC asked, "What we supposed to say?" MG assured them that they would talk about gangs, informing the clinic staff about gang life. Sensing their reluctance, MG suggested that the session with the clinic could begin with their video, It's a Homie Thang! Since the video focused on gangs, explaining why youth joined and providing information on the reasons for fights among youth gang members, MG convinced them that the presentation would not be difficult. The video, in her estimate, would get the discussion going with the health care providers: "That way, all the regular questions are covered, and we can then really get into the important stuff."

In July 1994, four youth who were in the discussion group I led at the Centro participated in a presentation to the clinic's staff. Additionally, a new member of Da Crew, who was African American, and DV's brother attended. The conversation began with the presentation of the video the discussion group had produced. In this site, the teen adolescents were the authorities, speaking as experts on their lives to the clinic's staff. MG began with the history of her gang, Da Crew, noting that the first clique was a group of friends who hung around with boys from the FruitVale gang (a longtime gang in the area). "Back then, everyone would call them FruitVale bitches, and we didn't like that, so we called ourselves Da Crew." The initial questions came primarily from Dr. Supersade— questions about the purpose of the video, the intended audience, and clarification of terms that the teens used. Most of the predominantly Chicano/Latino staff politely listened. Early in the meeting the teenagers took up the problem of leaving the gang. This looked as if ground rules were being laid out so that the discussion would not revert to easy answers for their lives. Speaking about the intended audience of the video, DV directly addressed the key issue:

> People don't know how it is . . . the way we see it. Because they're older. We think differently, we're young, you know. They think it's easy, or whatever, to get out of this thing, saying, "It is easy for you to get out. You can get out any time." But, see, you're still gonna have problems. It's not like nobody is gonna mess with you anymore. You still can't walk in certain parts of town without looking over your back. And our parents think it's easy. We just want to let them know how we feel, how we see it.

Many of the staff members were quiet.

> SUPERSADE: I hear the word getting "jumped in" and "jumped out." Is it . . .
>
> MG: Well, different gangs, they do it different ways. Like we do it, we have first one on one, then you get jumped [by a group], and then you fight the leaders [of the various generations]. Other gangs, you walk the line, and they beat you. We do it different, everybody do it different.
>
> SUPERSADE: Jumping out?
>
> MG: Jumping out, you just beat the fuck out of them.
>
> SUPERSADE: Who beats who?
>
> MG: Everybody, somebody starts it, then everybody jumps in.
>
> SUPERSADE: Once they're jumped out, you leave them alone?
>
> MG: It depends why they got out. Like if they messed us up, we go back looking for them. But if they just want to get out, well then bye, whatever.
>
> DV: The ones that have kids, they just stay home. They don't come out and hang with us anymore. They stay home with their babies. They get out of it.
>
> SUPERSADE: But they're still in?
>
> DV: Yeah.

Midway through the hour, a young woman of the staff said that she had been a member of a gang while very young. Going over which grouping she belonged to, she then told about a recent incident when some adolescent females had attempted to fight with her because she had been wearing a red bandanna. This began an exchange among the staff members. Many comments focused on the need for unity of La Raza and complained about the violence among Mexicano/Chicano youth. In particular, staff members were distressed that the violence spurred others to look down on the Latino community.

STAFF MEMBER: You see, back then, when I was in it, we, the Raza, the Chicanos, we helped each other. We had car clubs. We had parties. But now each street is killing each other. And we should be united instead of La Raza killing each other.

Responding that she herself was no longer a gang member because of the violence, DV said:

My pa'tna got shot up and I had to go to court, and all this is from guys. A lot of the girls talk a lot, roll by saying things, but we end up boxing with the guys. There was a party up in the nineties, and all the guys came out yelling "Norte! Norte!" when we got there. They threw forties [beer bottles] at us and were cornering us. These are guys. That's why I'm getting out.

STAFF MEMBER: You see, no other Raza is going to help us. It's only us. Back then we had Thirty-eighth, Sixties, Forty-second; sure we used to fight, but we also had our car clubs. And now I see people killing each other. We used to go to the [Fresno] car show, everybody used to be united. People look down on us.

Dr. Supersade asked whether they used weapons, and MG responded: "We don't. We box. But others do. They use guns."

STAFF MEMBER: And you haven't quit?
MG: I'm calmed down now, but I'm still in. 'Cause I'm [known] MG from DC.

The questions once again turned to pregnancy.

STAFF MEMBER: I'm curious, because the people we see here who are pregnant, I don't think I see a lot of women in gangs who get pregnant. . . . Do women who are in gangs get pregnant less than women who are not in gangs, or . . . what do you . . .

The girls responded that there wasn't any difference.

DV: It could be that they're just not saying that they belong [to a gang].

Only one male staff person attended the meeting, and he asked about gang codes.

STAFF MEMBER (MALE): So, in a way, it seems that if you have a baby . . . you don't get messed with. . . .

MG: They do, if you're somewhere at the wrong place. . . .

STAFF MEMBER: But there seems to be a code of respect, that if you get pregnant, then it might be a way of . . .

MG: No. It's more like when you have a baby, you just stay home. They can't go out partying like they used to. That's why you don't get messed with. But if you go out and they might see you, they might fuck you up.

STAFF: And if you're with a baby, would they do that?

DV: It depends on the person and how they might be.

LK: Like we wouldn't fight nobody if they had a baby with them. Because that's disrespecting . . . their baby didn't do nothing, you know.

MG: One of the girls that jumped me had three kids.

DV: If you got a baby, it don't make a difference. Like the girl who jumped MG. She has three kids and she rolls by in her car yelling, with her kids. Her kids were in the car when MG was knifed with the bottle, and her pa'tna held a gun to QG's head.

Another staff member then asked about an incident at the park.

STAFF MEMBER: At the Cinco de Mayo at San Antonio park, wasn't there a minor riot afterwards?

DV: We were there. . . .

LK: That was us. . . .

MG: No, this is what happened. I mean, that was us, but we didn't have no riot. Because they kicked us out. There were some girls from MPL [a rival gang]. There was about five of them, and they told security that we was messing with them. So they kicked us out. And then after it was over, they were riding around, and we were just sitting at the corner. There were fifteen or twenty of us. They drive around yelling "wha'z up, wha'z up" and this and that. And there was fifteen or twenty-five of us, and we started walking over to the car. They left. They are punks. . . .

DV: 'Til they have the guys [with them] . . .

Throughout the discussion the young women attempted to point out differences between their gang and rival gangs. The girls mapped out various turf gangs of Fruitvale and Oakland and attempted to clarify the difference between Norteños and Sureños.[8]

Distressed by the regional and local antagonisms that produced violence among Chicano youth, the staff members decried the false divisions and became critical of gangs. Staff members urged a need for unity in the face of the overwhelming racism confronting the Latino community. The youth responded by emphasizing the codes of respect that operate in their group versus rival groups. Raising the particulars of how their group operates, DV charged that rivals have picked fights with members of Da Crew when they were with their parents or the rivals had children with them. She added:

Some people call up our house and yell at our parents, and they have nothing to do with this. They have no respect.

Then abruptly a staff member asked, "Do you believe in God? LK did not miss a beat and answered "Yes."

DV: I don't really think about it.
STAFF MEMBER: Do you believe your gang is more powerful than God?
MG: Naw, that ain't it. That ain't what it's about. . . .
STAFF MEMBER: There are some people that think so.
MG: That's stupid.

While everyone agreed that respect was of importance, there were nonetheless sharp differences between the youth and the clinic staff. Not finding any resolution, the topic of respect segued to some practical concerns of the clinic staff—their attempt to discourage graffiti on the office's walls and equipment. While some of the teens suggested blank sheets of paper (as in the NEL Centro), they nonetheless noted that "you can't stop someone from tagging." Others noted that for some youth it's a matter of disrespect, while for others it's to express themselves, "like art."

Dr. Supersade then thanked the girls for their participation and asked if the girls had any questions for the staff. While I was expecting embarrassed or uneasy silence or wiggling in their chairs, MG quickly responded.

MG: Like what you, how you consider a gang-banger?
STAFF MEMBER: Is a gang-banger different from a gang?
MG: It's a person in a gang.
SUPERSADE: I had a very bad view of gangs. A couple of years ago I heard somebody talk about gangs, that they were just friends and

started off for just support. A lot of families are, I guess you'd say, broken, and they need support. That's how they start, they need support and just hang around. . . . The thing I still am uncomfortable with is the violence. I see the reason [of getting together], but . . .

STAFF MEMBER: Just like when I was growing up, we had cliques like you. But it's different.

DV: A lot of people see it as "Gangs, oh, they're bad." Or "They're troublemakers." But it's not like that. They judge us. People, like when we go into stores, they just stare at us and follow us around. . . . It's like they judge us.

LK: We're normal people, it's just that it's a bunch of us, kickin' it.

MG: Most likely it's the way you dress. You dress different, you ain't all pretty and stuff. They spot you with the quick [right away] and say, "She did it."

DV: Sometimes I go to the store and people think something. Like I'm Mexican . . .

STAFF MEMBER: It's because you're Mexican. It happens in jobs, too.

STAFF MEMBER: That's why we should all stick together.

STAFF MEMBER: That's true.

STAFF MEMBER: So you guys heard [the younger staff member who was formerly in a gang]. They used to do something positive. Do you think you could do something positive, like something they did?

MG: That'll never happen.

STAFF MEMBER: Like you could help everybody to go to school . . .

DV: Shoot, we don't go to school ourselves. . . .

The girls started to laugh and joke with each other as to how serious they were about school.

STAFF MEMBER: That's the thing that some of us can understand, the idea of wanting to be together, for the support. But it's the negative stuff, the violence. If you're hanging out together, why does the violence have to come into it? There's lots of cliques. Lots of cliques. Why encourage the violence to continue or even be a part of it? Or not wanting to encourage each other to do something more positive?

The girls looked at each other with questioning looks. No one volunteered to answer until finally DV began to talk about possibly returning to school and graduating.

DV: For me and MG, it was hard for us in school. All our friends, we were all together. We'd cut school together, mess up all together.

There was just a bunch of us. Then we started at [another school], and there's just five of us. We just go to classes. Before, we'd cut out, start riots.

As the meeting was coming to an end and people were quietly leaving one by one, the lack of resolution and agreement produced an uneasy mood in the room. Recognizing that the meeting should formally close, Dr. Supersade asked for any last remarks. While I had participated in the discussion throughout, I attempted to summarize the girls' information—the variety of gangs, the diversity within a gang, the rivalry between gangs. I also raised the problem of the increasing harassment and physical attacks on the female gang members by boys from rival gangs. While this had begun to emerge as a topic during my interviews with the girls, I noticed throughout the girls' presentation with the staff how many times these incidents were raised. No matter what the topic, the girls would introduce an incident in which boys were beating them up. I particularly asked the clinic staff to cue into these types of problems, as most studies have not addressed the issue of boys beating up girls as a specific practice among gangs. Some staff members commented that they only heard of gang rapes to initiate girls into gangs. And most had heard of this through the media. I felt that the staff members were reticent to discuss this aspect of gang violence, since it was never addressed throughout the discussion.

After the meeting one woman in response to my intervention asked whether I felt this was a possible backlash against girl gangs by male-dominated groups. However, we did not have a chance to discuss this, since the girls wanted to leave. I noticed that none of the staff tried to engage the girls in a more informal discussion. They moved around the girls as they went to their offices or discussed lunch. The girls huddled by the door and waited for me.

The girls by this time had become much more experienced with speaking, having intervened at the police and NACCS conferences as well as at the premier of Allison Anders' *Mi Vida Loca*. They had also produced their video and had been interviewed by two newspapers and a public radio program in San Francisco about their gang, while also spending countless hours answering my questions. They strategically began the discussion with clinic staff by raising the obstacles to leaving the gang, and they consistently emphasized that not all gangs are the same. The girls particularly stressed differences in initiation rituals and use of weapons, and they insisted that not all girl gangs are attached to boys' gangs. Additionally, they made it clear that there were no honorable codes of conduct that all gangs upheld. Pregnancy, while marking a change of status, did not necessarily mean leaving the gang. All of these points were counter-discursive critiques of prevailing images.

At the clinic, the girls asserted their gang identity in order to highlight a different health problem—physical violence against girls in gangs. The local epistemology, the everyday discursive and interpretive practices of the clinic, had a set system about gender—a discourse that placed priority on the reproductive body of the teenager. The girls had to engage with, and attempt to overcome, the staff's set ideas about teenage girls. By prioritizing their identity as gang members, the girls sought to fashion a different representation of girls. However, it was not easy to "fix" that identity, since the clinic staff was reading in other subjectivities, particularly of race/ethnicity. The collective (gang) identity that gave the girls a way to exclude other subject positions was repeatedly being challenged: "We're all Raza." When the girls attempted to define the rivalry between Norteñas and Sureñas, they raised language use. True, they were not as eloquent as Norma Mendoza-Denton, whose presentation at the NACCS regional conference recognized gang specificities through ethnic and national identification in order to unravel the violent rivalry found among the gangs. However, the young women were still attempting to describe and explain these differences in their own words. So they provided the staff with the names of the rival gangs and gave as much information as they knew how to, to help the staff understand the ideological differences between Norte and Sur.[9]

In all sympathy with the clinic staff, I admit that the information was not clearly evident. However, there were moments when the girls fell silent, particularly as the staff members returned to the question "Why the violence?" The question did not produce an interactive exchange. Rather, the question was put together in a counseling framework: Why do you participate in violence? What can you do about it? When MG attempted to differentiate the gangs—some box and others use weapons—a staff member asked, "And you haven't quit?" It is a question that is more from a counseling session than a remark that would help her elaborate other differences in gangs. The girls' authority as experts on gangs is thus taken away from them, and they are positioned as clients of the clinic. The girls were attempting to bring new knowledge— the battered body, not the reproductive body—to the clinic. But silence reigned, disturbing any easy answer for unity along the lines of race/ethnicity.

NEGOTIATIONS IN COUNTER PUBLIC SPHERES

The tension and tolerance reflected in the case studies convey some of the problems of intragroup relations and understandings of race, politics, and social justice in the post–civil rights era. These different discussions are framed by media representations of gangs and by popular notions of past sociological concepts about gangs.[10] Currently the perception of gangs and violence within the Latino community has come to be understood as either an issue of individual awareness or of a failed broader social solidarity. While these attitudes may reflect exhaustion or a lack of progressive solutions, this view is shaped by broader discourses of the Reagan-Bush backlash against the democratic gains of the civil rights struggle.[11] Contemporary counter publics must contend with these developments as they work to affect state policies, whether as a caucus within the state (police) or as pressure groups within state service agencies or education (clinic or academy). The multiple spaces of interaction discussed above offer compelling examples of democratic participation and discourse in the public sphere.

Habermas' *The Structural Transformation of the Public Sphere: An Inquiry into a Category of Bourgeois Society* (1994) investigates political participation and the consolidation of citizenship rights in early modern Europe. Conceived as a particular form in which private citizens gathered to hold the state accountable to "publicity," the ideal public sphere was White, male, and propertied. Feminists and critical race theorists have elaborated Habermas' basic concept, contending that there were (and are) multiple public spheres which contest, compete with, and oppose the official organized body of public opinion. These subaltern or counter public spheres, as Nancy Fraser has defined them, contest the exclusionary norms of the official bourgeois public sphere, elaborating alternative styles of political behavior and alternative norms of public speech (N. Fraser 1989, 1992). In her essay "Feminism, the Public Sphere, Media, and Democracy" (1993), Lisa McLaughlin explains that counter public spheres have both internal and external functions. "On the one hand, they are places for withdrawal into specific oppositional identity, and on the other, they have a 'public' character, directing oppositional claims and agitational activities outward . . . to wider publics" (McLaughlin 1993, 600).[12] This double function exactly describes the inward and outward movement of gang affiliation and performance I have been tracing. Examination of speeches at the cross-sites offers a way of understanding how specific power arrangements shape the discursive spaces. The various conferences and meetings at which the girls intervened perform the dual functions of a counter public whose social groups interpret their needs, invent their identities, and collectively formulate their political commitments.

At the various sites, the girls intruded into the counter public spheres. While their speech was informal, it was often pointed. They also brought in a raucous noise outside the decorum and conventions of the bourgeois public sphere, i.e., of the polite exposition of principles and reason for civic deliberation. Whether through shouting or intended silence, the disagreement the young women enact is a method of intervening in the patterns of objectification in the world (Sandoval 2000). The girls at these cross-sites challenge their objectification. As counter public spheres, the sites provide a possibility for change, movement from one way of imagining gang members toward a different way of conceptualizing them. Within these counter public spheres, the girls' participation, cooperation, and contention are acts of decoding and transcoding, translation and criticism (Sandoval 2000). By highlighting these discursive engagements for ethnographic examination, I am hoping to problematize those "pure" sites which are generally considered the typical expression of gang activity and life. What happens at these "untypical" moments of interaction and engagement between the various publics found in the Chicana/o community can be seen as forms of cultural encounter. In those moments of "cultural contact," the girls struggle to gain authority and to become co-discursive partners in the production of knowledge.

While the police conference would seem the most hostile to interactive communication, it must be historically situated. The organizing of minority police officers in special caucuses and organizations is an outcome of the civil rights movements. While it was an attempt to end nepotism and discriminatory hiring practices, the call for affirmative action included the need for officers who had an experiential knowledge of the various communities of the segregated inner cities. Attempting to lower the rate of police violence, the influx of minority officers highlighted racist practices within the police force, both discursive and extra-discursive in nature. Minority caucuses and associations were directed toward reform within the police, both in personnel and police-community relations. The conference in Oakland, even with the limitations of inadequate representation of youth, exemplifies the desires of the civil rights struggles—police from communities of color and concerned for their communities. The Latino police officers organization attempted to influence policy in police-community relations at a time when the government and voters seemed fixated on more prisons. Thus, while the police may be regarded as an arm of the state, the recruitment of minority police has produced special caucuses for equal rights which reveal the liberal democratic intent of such groups as the Latino Police Officers Association.

The dynamic of argument that ensued at the conference could be seen as the antagonism between the youth of the Chicano community and the overall police force. However, the boldness that the young women asserted conveys a dual reaction of people of color to minority police officers. On the one hand, the general thought is that the minority police are in the community for public relations purposes with no real intention of rectifying injustices. They are only there for showcasing. This may have been a part of why the adolescents were so bold, because they were speaking to token representatives of the police department. On the other hand, the Latino Police Officers have opened a smaller precinct house in the community of Fruitvale to strengthen Latino police officer relations with the predominantly Latino community. Many of the leading members of the association are present, taking the heat at community meetings on police misconduct. Most of the cases have involved Euro-American police officers beating Chicano youth.

Youth as members of the Latino community are conscious of the variety of discourses regarding police-community relations. A complex view of the police is evidenced in my discussions with the girls' parents. While the various families reflect a multitude of different opinions about the police, the majority of the parents of the young women with whom I worked are law-abiding residents and citizens who will work with police in neighborhood disturbances. This cooperation goes against the stereotype of hostile minorities that the police confront. Their parents are another source of attitudes and knowledge toward police. The young women are able to draw from life experiences and community notions of the police to gauge their audiences' reception of their intervention.

Overall, the youth spoke about gangs in general terms, without specifying particular differences of gender or age and without drawing the distinctions between rival gangs. Speaking on behalf of all gang members, their subject positions flattened differences in order to renegotiate the police officers' misconceptions. Initially, the girls spoke to the conference members as if everyone was a police officer, but they quickly grasped the goal of affecting public policy. A moral and political discourse on victims of poverty or broken families was evident in the terms the officers used: "mixed up," "lack of confidence," "picking yourself up," and "bettering yourselves." Such phrases convey a sympathetic or socially conscious understanding of the constraints of barrio life. The Latino police officers brought the conference together in an attempt to influence city policy toward gangs—a liberal rather than repressive policy. Moreover, the conference, the words and actions of the police and social service workers, reveal the subject positions of ethnic minorities within and in relation to the state, which I will further unravel in a comparison of the discussions at the Alta Vista Clinic and police conference to the other venues.

The presentation of the video and the discussion at the Alta Vista Clinic provides a frame for analysis of the variety of service organizations and advocacy groups within the Chicano community. Legislation and funds for adolescent females are primarily focused on the problem of teen pregnancy and teenage motherhood. Social service agencies like the clinic attempt to educate young women about sex, birth control, prenatal care, and child-rearing for young mothers. At the same time, as they battle for funds they confront debates that racialize teen pregnancy as a social problem within the Chicano and African American communities. On other fronts, the clinic is shackled by legislation denying adolescents information about abortion and by public pressure to limit information on safe sex and birth control. Social research and social policy overwhelmingly focus on the "uncontrolled female sexuality" of teenage girls of color.[13] The national discourse of the nuclear family operates to define the social category of female adolescence at its reproductive level and to channel funds toward controlling the sexual behavior of young females. Caught at the intersection, social agencies like the Alta Vista Clinic operate in a restricted field of possibilities.

Likewise, counseling service is focused on the intimate space of the family, reflecting the public discourse that situates social problems in the private sphere. Feature stories in the dominant media present problems as the result of the breakdown of the nuclear family structure. This concept runs through media stories from teen pregnancy to gang families to the feminization of poverty. Thus, social policy develops through the dominant understanding that the private sphere and the nuclear family are normative, closing off any reformulation of policy that could depathologize teen sexuality. In spite of liberal contestation, public policy continues patterns of gender subordination and racial and class stratification. The insistence on accountability at the level of the individual and the individual family unit reduces social struggle to a fight for dwindling funds and constrains a focus on empowerment at the social level.

Given the national situation, the staff members of the clinic, in my es-

timate, were caught off guard by the discussion of gangs and in particular of young women in gangs. The main concern for the clinic members
was the violence among Latino youth. This became problematic for the
girls in various ways. The discussion reproduced a recurrent split within
cultural nationalist concepts of community. The prevalent adage and
mood of the discussion, "We are all Raza," reveals two views about
gangs in the Chicano community. One view would valorize the gang
member as a future barrio warrior and celebrate the codes of honor and
the culture of solidarity the gang could bring once it reached the goal
of nationalist consciousness. The assumption underlying this concept
is that youth have an obligation to be radical. The other sentiment of
"We are all Raza" reflects pessimism for a younger generation without
the ideals and values of traditional Mexican culture. Both reflect generational difference in the Chicano community. The difference may register a fear that the dominant system is just too strong and thus the
struggle returns to individual endeavors by the most dedicated. In all instances, the once-radical administrators become paradoxically conser-
vative. Overwhelmed by the problems of today's youth, the pessimistic
outlook and romanticized vision perform a depoliticizing function.[14]

Other features of this interaction became apparent to me. The young
women had thought they would be able to "really get into the important
stuff" as they had in the discussion at NACCS (and at the other places
where they discussed gangs with a sympathetic audience). Perhaps they
hoped to have a discussion of the identity differences between Norteños
and Sureños. The social space of the clinic as a counter public sphere of
exchange perplexed the youth. Most of the girls were quiet, producing
an indifference toward and low level of engagement with the clinic staff.
The tone of the girls' answers seemed to reflect acquiescence, delivering
what the teenagers thought the adults wanted to hear. Rather than the
rambunctious exchanges the young women had participated in before,
the meeting's ambience was muted and the girls' interest in the discussion was low. Many stared at the carpet designs and clinic walls; generally their demeanor seemed as if they had drifted into a daydream. It was
striking to note, too, that the young women stated that they had quit the
gang or were trying to leave the gang behind. Yet the previous day they
had met and selected a new leader of Da Crew. Then they were enmeshed
in animated discussions about the viability of their organization to sustain its reputation for toughness among friends and rivals.

Upon reflection, the conduct of the girls illustrates two important
points about the social production of the spaces where the Latina youth

spoke at the police conference and the clinic. In each, the topic of leaving the gang became dominant in the conversation. In both spaces the authority figures—police and health workers—were bent toward service and only remotely associated with political mobilization or activism. The micro-level discursive interaction was shaped by the wider institutional power to contain political activities and maintain public discourse within administrative and governmental institutions. Within this sphere, the processes of debate and the formation of oppositional identities was limited. The girls' "public transcript," that of wanting to get out of the gang, was shaped by the power exercised within these institutions. Within these constraints the adolescent women shaped their appeal to the expectations of the audiences. Their different speeches reveal the complexities of pubic and hidden transcripts that reflect power relations in discursive fields.

James Scott in *Domination and the Arts of Resistance: Hidden Transcripts* (1990) finds that confrontations between the powerful and powerless are filled with deception—where the powerless may feign deference as a public role, the act may in fact reveal resistance. Remarking upon the parallel discursive arena of the powerless, the hidden transcript, those excluded from dominant discourses invent and circulate counter discourses so as to formulate oppositional interpretations of their identities, interests, and needs. Within these enclaves, the hidden transcript produced with an audience of peers is a setting where speeches are rehearsed. Thus, what may appear spontaneous is part of imaginary speeches made to an audience of peers about what one would say, if given the chance, to the powerful. Scott's findings suggest that the rehearsal and speech preparation would be a part of the hidden transcript of the youth; their response to pressures from parents, schools, and society to leave the gang is enumerated in the social subculture among peers. The response to dominant society's "Just say no" slogan is rehearsed at those relatively isolated sites away from surveillance by authority figures. The discourse within the enclave enumerates the reasons why one cannot leave the gang, the problems one will face alone. Among peers they can agonize why it is impossible to leave the gang, and they are able to express their anger toward parents and authority without fear of repercussions. The transcript from the enclave is received unevenly at the various sites of public interaction. The speeches become part of heated debates with authorities.

At the police conference and the clinic, the youth now get to say the speech that has been produced in their shielded ring of peers. Assuming the dominant "get out of gangs" discourse will prevail at the cross-sites, the teens develop a strategic response. At several of the public meetings, I noticed different girls claiming that they were no longer in a gang. However, as soon as they announced that they were no longer in the gang, they would quickly argue that it was impossible for other gang members to leave, citing any number of obstacles that make leaving the gang impossible for the majority of youth. The claim that one is no longer a gang member is lodged in order to reveal the hidden transcript rehearsed in the enclave of peers. For example, at the police officers' meeting, DV does not identify whether she is a gang member. At this cross-site, ambiguity produces strife and a certain amount of hostility. However, at the clinic, she claims that she is no longer in the gang. The tactic she is using is to appeal to what the audience wants to hear. Had she claimed that she left the gang at the police conference, maybe a different engagement would have ensued.

Subsequently, in various exchanges after the police officers' conference, many of the girls opened with the statement that they were no longer gang members. What is interesting is that, for the people who come together to discuss solutions, there is a desire to hear youth express that gangs are "not good." When youth open with this statement, the common ground is established. The youth directly aligns herself with her audience's desire. She can then assume a voice of experience that the audience is willing to hear. And at the same time, she attains a measure of power and authority in the public discourse through her denial of gang membership. (She also shields herself from any future harassment from police and social service workers who would penalize her for being a gang member.) In the act of renunciation, she can make public the hidden transcript of the peer group. The rationalizations of why one cannot leave—to turn away from confidantes and sympathizers found in the gang and to turn away from partners who have come to one's defense—is now able to enter the public domain. The girls attended these meetings hoping to state why they could not simply leave the gang—to counter public outcry against their support network. They are there to assert their gang identity as a legitimate social choice in response to the hegemonic motto: Just say no to gangs. However, in these public policy meetings, they cannot just speak from their gang position, finding that they must hedge their challenge with a claim that they are no longer gang members. Additionally, the claim opens up the floor to the rest of her peers, who are then permitted to reveal their ideas about gang membership.

By the time the girls attended the meeting with staff at Alta Vista Clinic, they were much more familiar with their recitation of "defending homies" and the difficulty of leaving the gang. Ready for their presentation, a different engagement ensued. At the health center, the girls came in as authorities to present a different type of health issue that should have been of concern to the staff. But what happened in this discursive space was that the rhetoric of Chicanismo was privileged, and therefore difference was elided. The girls were frustrated, unable to sustain their initial authority and unable to register their social difference. The clinic became a problematic space. The rhetoric of nationalism draws upon interconnections to produce commonality and solidarity for social justice. However, the seemingly egalitarian discourse of nationalism denies the recognition of difference and fractures the exchange. The girls were, in the end, silenced.

At the cross-site of the clinic, the girls were unable to deconstruct and utilize the rhetorics of the dominant discourse to their advantage (Sandoval 2000). On the one hand, the girls entered as experts on gangs requiring a different form of engagement, one to which the girls were not accustomed (no interruptions, shouting, or horseplay). They were more in the habit of speaking from a subjective position about the subjective world through the more unruly practices of intervention to dominant discourse.[15] As experts in this particular public sphere, the girls are in a position that requires a different mode of communication—to present facts objectively. On the other hand, despite their expertise, their positionality was challenged by the nationalist discourse. The nationalist ideology presumes sameness as an inherent premise of unity, thus any threat to the unity of the body politic is suppressed. While the staff at the clinic attempted to create solidarity by appealing to common understanding and interests, the nationalist discourse located the girls outside of the Chicano *imagined* community (i.e., why the violence among Raza, we are all Chicanos, why wage war with each other). Therefore, silence prevailed. While the staff's appeal toward the greater commonality of Chicanidad had a democratic purpose, this cross-site as a counter public sphere of exchange to develop public policy failed to develop. The premise of the visit—to explore the issue of why girls are joining gangs, participating in aggressive behavior, and violence as a social "health concern"—was impeded by the staff's ready solution. The clinic, I believe, lost out on the reason the girls were there—to raise a different health issue and to expand the staff's vision of health care service beyond pregnancy and teen sex. Since teen pregnancy and teen sexual activity are contained in pathological paradigms, the criminalization of gangs prevailed. The combined ideologies of "reform" and the nationalist discourse take away from the meaning that the gang members have in their lives and flatten out difference. The need for unity and solidarity in the process of lobbying for social change is an important strategy. But to utilize this strategy at points where we need to understand and discuss a problem, within the group or the collective, differences must be accepted. Only then, perhaps, can solutions emerge.

I will add here that the discursive sites of the police conference and the clinic are particular types of counter public spheres.[16] Augmenting Nancy Fraser's conception of counter or subaltern public spheres, Catherine Squires (1999) systematizes a finer set of distinctions for the types of public spheres that may be relevant. She designates additional types of public spheres which operate: (1) enclave, (2) oscillating, (3) counter or subaltern, and (4) parallel or ideal. Describing the various types of spheres that subordinated groups produce, Squires locates historical conditions in which the state or dominant grouping extends democracy or regulates discourse. The enclave develops as a recourse for groups when the possibility of speech is limited. The oscillating sphere is marked by the less oppressive regulations of the state, yet there are still legal and social obstacles for the group. In this sphere, participants produce an imagined community through shared opinions; community-building is a goal. The counter or subaltern public is usually illustrated through the feminist and civil rights movement; issues previously shielded from contestation are now publicly argued, deliberated across a range of discursive arenas and publics. The last type in Squire's estimate is the parallel or ideal public sphere. As discourse is broadened by opportunities for speech and debate, this sphere becomes more institutionalized. (The prime example of parallel spheres is manifested in single-issue coalition-building.) Situated in the state apparatus, the people who come together with particular interests to intervene in the state by the nature of their occupation or profession, i.e., the police and clinic staff, form a particular kind of "public." While the discourse is set within liberal democracy producing particular interests, identities, and needs, there are discursive and ministration limitations due to the nature of the state. These spheres are different from NACCS, where Chicanos/as "colonize" particular institutions to change discursive representation and have a different relation to the state. The different public(s)—one that is subordinate in its capacity to function independently or in opposition, and the other that colonizes to controvert—nonetheless disclose the democratic potential of counter public spheres.

At the NACCS site, like the other case studies in which attendees were predominantly Chicanas/os, a different type of counter public operates. In this particular counter public sphere, issues which address the wider institutional and power structures are publicly argued and debated. Thus the girls are not limited by the constructions based on their bodies and reproduction as, for example, at the clinic where the discursive practices—administrative goals and agenda—limit how to discuss Latina teens. Similarly, at the Latino police conference, the young women intervened by disrupting the normative assumptions of knowledge, by producing their stories to contest the "bootstrap" ideology operating in this sphere. Because the police are situated within the state with a particular form of power, the ideology of individual uplift takes dominance; thus the girls illustrate the collective network that the gang produces and their unwillingness to submit to the power of individualist ideology. In the other types of counter public spheres, the issues of identity and interests and needs predominate in order to formulate and counter hegemonic apparatuses of dominant powers. In these, unlike in the enclave or oscillating forms, issues are subject to political struggle. The goals and ideologies of these spheres are to compensate for the representation in media or to compensate for the omission of subaltern discourse in the media. These spheres facilitate activism. Opaque linguistic play and performance of deference, the dynamics of hidden transcript, are not imperative in these spaces. Additionally, difference is recognized and accepted as part of the proceeding, as well as subject to the discussion.[17]

At the NACCS regional conference, the young Chicanas were able to construct a different kind of narrative and explanation of themselves. The presentation by Norma Mendoza-Denton on language distinctions between Norteña and Sureña gangs followed Angela Gallegos' (1994) feminist analysis of the status of young women of the Chicano community and of related scholastic research. The majority of the workshop attendees were Chicanas, and during the slide show presentation the audience laughed at the points in which the Centro's youth had plotted satire in their slides. The familiarization with girls' culture, an experiential commonality, produced a different power differential for interaction and intervention. Given the presentations by Rosa Linda Fregoso and by Mendoza-Denton, the girls were not positioned to have to explain their behavior. While they had arrived at the conference with great trepidation, they quickly felt the invitational ambience and were excited to present their slide show. Because they did not have to speak on behalf of all gangs, they were able to speak at a different level of information: to speak to particular cultures within gangs. Mendoza-Denton's analysis did not prioritize language as the structuring of behavior but focused on language choice as agency for ethnic identity. Addressing the particular styles among Norteñas rather than focusing on the gang codes of behavior allowed the young women to perform agency, enacting the diversity of their subculture. Moreover, their voices bore authority because the goals of NACCS as a sphere for intellectual debate and exchange prioritize experiential and local knowledge for social analysis on behalf of the Chicano/a community.

The NACCS conference opened up a space for the young women to speak. Yet, at this crossroad, the girls were developing a self-awareness and consciousness of their power to impact upon representation. They were beginning to articulate their lives to a broader audience. While the world of the gangs has codes of language and behavior, the articulation of its meaning for them began with my interviews and progressed to the various sites of public discourse. The feminist ideology operating in Fregoso's presentation and the NACCS conference registered the conjuncture of spaces where their worldview of female solidarity, a lifeway of their gang membership, converges with feminist projects and practices. In this counter public sphere, the interweaving of feminist discourse with the experiential knowledge of their lives is understood.

The ways in which the young women confronted the differences they found at each of the sites involved recognizing key words that participants used. Detecting those who were sympathetic, using the narrative that was expected of them ("I left the gang"), the girls recognized the specific power relations in each of the sites. Utilizing available discourses, the girls attempted to gain equal ground for participation, to authorize themselves, gain authority, and unbalance power relations. Overall they contested patterns of objectification, where others speak about youth in the third person as if the girls weren't there. The "methodology of the oppressed" (Sandoval 2000) highlights the problem of representation that the girls encounter at each of the settings. Re-presentation then works to get at how the girls perceived their positionality in these sites and offers a way to engage in discussion, i.e., at the clinic to go beyond the basics—somehow to position themselves as gang members and attempt to reach another level of discourse. For the girls the issue before them was respect. Because their lives are filled with a daily struggle for respect and recognition, the girls similarly expect and fight for their valued identities, for self-worth, in the sites of public discourse.[18] The politics of representation are imbued in a recognition of their identity. Therefore, when the girls hoped to have a discussion in which "all the regular questions are covered and we can then really get into the important stuff," to get at the way people perceive them is to address their exclusion from participation in the social community.[19] Their presence at the sites begins to shift concepts of representation. As a primary motive for participation, representation is both challenged and acquiesced. The girls mobilize their gang identity and the dominant concepts of gangs in order to engage or intervene in the discussion. While the various sites may allow the girls to speak, other sites with other purposes will silence them, leaving the girls to stutter or stammer their own perplexing subjectivity and positionality. Their strategies of representation are to utilize what adults and authorities want to see and hear, in order to turn attention to what the issues are for them and how they conceive of the problems they confront.

THE POTENTIAL OF COUNTER PUBLIC SPHERES

These case studies have provided a basis to examine those spaces in which identity is produced through representational systems—discursive systems. Discursive systems produce objects to study and represent; representational systems are not solely media, news, television, film, and photography. They include social science literature and popular notions of normative behavior. Through discourse—on gangs, girls in gangs, and generally female adolescents—subjects are produced. Foucault's (1980) rendering of the different modes by which human beings are made subjects and the forms of power that make individual subjects allows us to examine how one's own identity and a conscious self-knowledge develop through discursive regimes. While the subject is subject to someone else's control, the operation of power/knowledge brings about the possibility for the subject to speak. Because discourse defines and categorizes attributes, individuals can subject themselves to meaning, power, and regulation. The subject is the bearer of particular discursive knowledge that produces a "place for the subject" to speak. What is more, these discursive systems yield categories of knowledge that give meaning to the actions and experiences of the subjects. Though they are identified or categorized, individuals take meaning and combine and tie together their own experience, which produces a position in which to speak. Nonetheless, this always involves a relationship to power. Agency in these case studies is manifested through the ways in which the girls took the meanings of others who identified them in order to refuse the objectification. My choice of case studies once again emphasizes the subjective selection and construction of narrative. It is the translation that is the role of the ethnographer. By choosing these sites of discourse, I attempted to problematize the messy field of representation, where stereotype and type are an oppositional binary. Where the two become mirror images, the differences between them become the all-bad and the all-good, from deviance to victims, and thus we don't effectively change the representations. The problematic of representation lies in a discursive field, in discourse, ideology, and the limitations to represent gangs and particularly girls in gangs.

Rosaldo's guideline for case studies emphasizes the examination of social drama. Yet, he asks whether there necessarily will be turning points and a climax to every narrative. Since stories describe and shape human conduct, will the stories by the ethnographer and the informant necessarily share the same form? Will they agree on the events and issues that constitute the social drama's chain of events? Will they agree on the central incidents? Through these ethnographic questions, Rosaldo re-emphasizes the interactive role between the researcher and the researched subjects. From my field journal in the spring of 1993, I consider the relation between the ethnographer and the subjects a dialogical relation. The process of interview sets up a self-reflective consciousness for the girls. I think after the NACCS regional conference in Northern California and the girls' participation with the director of *Mi Vida Loca,* combined with the video project, a space was created, but not quite a geographical space. In many ways it was a territorial space, that is, the rights of the girls to occupy the space, to speak. The speaking to inform the public was a different or additional development, enhancing the primary dialogical relationship between ethnographer and informants.

I wrote down my hopes in my journal—that the girls through their speaking about the gang experience could somehow begin to identify what the problems are, to identify why they fight; that they would deliberate as to why the slogan "We are all Raza, brown" doesn't work to stop the violence; that they can begin to speak about the Norte/Sur differences and thus help end the violence with which they live. Still, the "solution" lies with the researchers and makers of social policy. Ultimately, we must change the discursive field in order to hear them. What languages, what differences we are able to sustain in our inquiries will provide the examination with more fruitful data for interpretation and analysis. By registering difference and sustaining it through inquiry and analysis, maybe we will break from the homogenizing effect of studying gangs as male and also break from the nationalist rejoinder that flattens differences in social identity. Can we begin to elaborate on the rivalries, beyond turf, and make a contribution to sociological models and proffer social policy?

Through the case studies, I have constructed a narrative in order to disrupt the conventional "turf" studies of gangs. By highlighting the discursive spaces of the various agencies and people who make up the breadth of the Chicana/o counter public sphere, I consciously hope to reorganize knowledge production—the way we come to know about gangs. Through the use of case studies, I attempt to resituate the girls within various discursive sites in order to think of a different kind of subject. By shifting them from the sites of turf, I consciously reconstruct the girls: from gang subjects to civil subjects. Turf is not the only site from which they can speak, where they gain subjecthood. At each of the sites, the spaces construct the subject, just as a conventional study of gangs would use turf to construct the subject. Their participation in forums like the Latino police conference, NACCS, the clinic, and the premier of *Mi Vida Loca* as well as the Women of Color Film Festival are also spaces which construct the subject. Yet, each of the sites "creates" different kinds of subjects who speak about their lives. The sites in which they are interpreted can construct them differently, particularly from models that fix gangs in turf. My political project through the use of case studies is to disturb the "gang subject." Locating the youth at different sites, it is hoped, will provoke us to think of them as civil and social subjects. At each of the sites, different audiences assembled according to particular interests and objectives.

Thus the self, constituted through the encounter, was a feature of the kinds of interaction that the youth utilized in these public places. The dialogical relationship between ethnographer and subjects amplified into a variety of discursive fields in which gangs were not only the subject but brought the subjects to speak. The girls were speaking not only to the ethnographer but to others, forming a wider network among ethnographer, girls, and others. From a dialogical process of self-consciousness or self-reflectivity a larger process emerged, elements of which are recognizable from du Gay and Hall's model of the processes of representation, identity, production, consumption, and regulation that make up the "circuit of culture" (du Gay et al. 1997). The girls wanted to talk—to the media, to the clinic staff, to others. This shift enhanced their terrain, an expansive struggle to re-present the gang. The issue was not just self-representation but access to media and control of discursive situations.

The multiplication of sites of representation marks the postmodern moment—the proliferation and plethora of simulations. Postmodernity also consists of the process of self-inscription and indigenous, subaltern self-documentation—making ethnographers marginal, even dispensable. As I have followed the girls through their struggles to articulate a worldview, I recognize their speech and texts as auto-ethnography. And perhaps my interpretation and analysis could be called a kind of post-auto-ethnography. While it is fun to muse about a term for my text, I confront a different question raised by the politics of representation. Since ethnography is about the politics and power of representation, can ethnography—to paraphrase Habermas—construct a space which is adequate to the task of democracy and political action? The linear progression of my ethnography moves from a study that began with audience reception to a study of girls in gangs to a study of the girls' representational practices. The previous case studies have brought me back to the girls' audiences. The task of the public sphere, if we are to include youth, is to assure their voices through a self-reflective turn—constantly asking: Are we listening, and how can we listen better?

DIALOGUING DIFFERENCES

[W]e have a hard time accepting and celebrating differences. Why? I think it is because we are immersed in a society where "sameness" is venerated as the most desirable quality.   PAPUSA MOLINA

An experience following my fieldwork reconfirmed the open-ended and productive nature of the girls' cross-talk in diverse public arenas. In conclusion, I present the last site where the girls and I participated in a public meeting. My elaboration is not to suggest that this site is the ideal public sphere but to emphasize the variety of dialogues needed with youth. In effect, we need one, two, many public spheres where acknowledging difference as the essential element of democracy allows for a greater variety of subject positions to become articulated and elaborated. Limiting interpretation and analysis, I believe, permits a continuing, open-ended relation between myself and the reader but, more important, accentuates the continuing dialogics of the ethnographic encounter.

After a year and a half in Oakland, I returned to Santa Cruz to survey my data and develop an analysis. My field research at this point occurred every two weeks—meeting the young women at the Centro, visiting their homes, and dropping by the hangouts where they gathered. Upon returning to UC Santa Cruz, I was an active member of the Research Cluster for the Study of Women of Color in Conflict and Collaboration (informally called WoC). One of the research cluster's working groups was the WoC Film Festival group, whose project was the examination of resistant and oppositional practices of representation by women of color. That year's festival was "Subversive Geographies: Out of Bounds," a title that seemed, in many ways, to evoke my research. Although I was a newcomer in the working group, its members soon became interested in the girls' video, *It's a Homie Thang!* The girls and I were invited to participate in the festival.

I phoned a core group of girls to set up a meeting to discuss the invitation. At the meeting, about twelve signed up to attend the festival. My excitement about their participation, the use of the video, and the prospect of a sympathetic audience excited them as well. The festival could be a place, in my estimate, for talking about girls in gangs. The encounter at the clinic had been such a letdown for the girls that I hoped the festival would provide a counter site. Gender and gender roles would become a primary way of exploring images of gangs and the conventional views of teenage girls that are dominated by issues of reproduction. Those who participated in the discussion at the Alta Vista Clinic were the most excited about attending the festival.

On the day of the festival, however, only three girls attended. One reason for the low turnout was that I had to pick them up very early on Saturday morning to get to Santa Cruz on time. In many cases, parents went to wake up the girls only to find that they wanted to stay home because it was not a school day, and it was raining. MG, my most constant companion at the various sites, was ill. And while she was willing to put off her doctor's appointment, her mother steadfastly insisted to both MG and me that she could not attend the film festival. Of the three who came, TC and QG had consistently participated in the discussion groups and were central subjects in my research. LT had rarely participated, though I knew her from various gatherings I attended during field research. Additionally, LT was not a member of any of the three girl gangs. She identified herself as a tagger, one of a crew of preteen boys and girls who participated in graffiti art associated with the various neighborhood gangs found in Fruitvale.

Without MG, FN, DV, SG, and María, the peer counselor, who had spoken out at the previous sites, the girls were nervous about their public performance. When we arrived at the site of the festival, QG began to talk about going back home. I became angry because I couldn't just drive back in the rain over the winding Highway 17; this wasn't Oakland, where I could just jump in the car and zoom her back home. Our group divided, LT siding with QG and TC siding with me. I kept insisting that the talk would be well received and that if QC wanted, she could just sit there on the stage and not say anything. TC and LT then informed me that they would not speak either. I then revealed to them that I was just as nervous as they were. In the audience were not only my peers but colleagues about whom I felt nervous because of their intellectual abilities. I characterized them as "really so smart, sometimes I don't even understand what they're saying." This got a laugh from them. Then I told them that I was also nervous because a couple of my teachers were there. "You know? I've been talking to them about you, and they've been pretty good. But, it's like just talking, this is the first time they're goin' to hear what I got to say . . . like a presentation." This drew immediate sympathy, and QG said, "Okay, what are we going to talk about?" We organized the presentation. I would start with my analysis of magazine photos I had collected depicting girls in gangs. The video would follow, and the girls would then speak. I would ask questions about the video and attempt to make the setting as much as possible like the discussion group. Then we would open up for questions from the audience. I detected that while the girls remained nervous about speaking in public, their manner changed. They began to take control of their nervousness by controlling the space. They went outside to smoke, teased each other, and talked loudly. Upon returning to the auditorium, they went up the stairs to the back of the audience to view the films before our presentation. Attempting to dominate the space, from the heights, they could look down upon the audience—like being in the back of a classroom or the back of the bus. They created a sense of safety and marked their outsiderness. They reaffirmed this position by waiting until after my presentation and the video screening before coming down the noisy wooden steps to take a place on the stage.

When we were all gathered, TC ducked behind the table and loudly stated, "I'm not here." While we nervously laughed, QG held the festival program book in front of her face so that she would not have to look at the audience. LT turned to TC, and they spoke to each other while I attempted to create a discussion setting that we were used to. There were other motions and movements that accentuated their nervousness. However, in many ways these were performances of shyness, attempts to control nervousness, because everything was audible and visible. The performances drew sympathy from the audience and worked to put the girls at ease and finally in control of the space.

Beginning nervously, I asked the girls what happened to the rest of the girls. TC softly explained why some couldn't make it. I explained to the audience that the possibility of a lot of questions about the video might have deterred some of the girls, and then I expressed appreciation to TC, QG, and LT for showing up. The audience broke out in loud applause, and the girls smiled, slightly embarrassed by the response. I then began asking about various parts of the video, particularly the opening "language" section in which the girls curse and swear at each other. TC and QG softly explained that this was meant "to show how we are. The way we always talk . . . That way, you'd know . . . how we are." Rather than stay on the subject longer, I moved to the section entitled "Herstory." Again the girls looked to one another to see who would speak, then QG lightly hit TC with the program book to encourage her. TC responded from under the table, "I told you, I'm not here." During the first few minutes, I kept rubbing the back of my neck while QG kept wringing the program book into a tight wand. TC would crouch under the table, and LT would only direct her gaze at me or one of the other girls.

KM: I think it was McCrae [Parker], who taught you about making the video and taught the editing, but who thought of that, "Her story" . . . ?

TC: Yeah.

KM: It didn't sound right? You're used to history . . . but it's about girl gangs, so "her" works . . . ?

QG: We just thought it would say how we are.

TC: It's about us, about showing us. I don't know. . . .

Her hands flew in front of her face. Then as she looked at LT and QG she shook her head as if to say "this is going all wrong." Then as I was attempting to have them explain who "we" and "us" were, TC interrupted, "Wait a minute. . . . What you think about the video?" Her hands waved in the air as if erasing my question, and then she looked directly at the audience, directing her question to them. There was a surprised laughter and joyous applause by the audience.

One of the filmmakers volunteered a question from the audience, asking how long it took to make the video and if the girls were thinking of another project. The girls volunteered one-word answers, and I volunteered answers about the video production, i.e., two months of camera training, script productions, and process, editing by the girls with the technical advice from the video instructor. Then I talked about a project that we were considering: a "memory book" fashioned after two popular youth magazines, *Low Rider* and *Teen Angel*. As I participated, providing some answers, the girls relaxed. Somehow as my subject position shifted, from interrogator to interrogated, the girls began to provide additional comments, and the nervous twitching, hiding behind program books, and blank stares decreased.

When a young White man in the audience asked if the video met their wishes and whether they had full control of the project, the girls were attentive to the question, nodding their heads as they understood its intent. But as he continued—"It seems to me that you're talking about getting a voice, about self-esteem. . . . This is the foundation for the world you live in. . . . so is it . . . ? Do you know what I mean?"—the girls looked at me to translate. I supplemented. "If you do another video what would you leave out or try to include? We talked about fights and initiation?" to which the girls responded in the affirmative. Then TC and QG began to elaborate.

TC began to explain, "We'd get more of what we do, like, to know how we down. But, some girls say 'I'm down' but then . . ." QG continued, "It's just talk. DC is hella deep, but some girls [don't get it]." TC followed up, "Like before, we ruled the school. We beat people but we also made the walkouts. It was all different before. It's now, in DC, some girls fight over a guy. That's not what DC's about." She looked directly to the audience and every once in a while turned to QG for confirmation of the events that were changing her gang. QG responded, "Yeah, all these little girls makin' problems." TC then elaborated, "If you in DC, you a homegirl. . . . That's not what DC is about, fighting over guys. If in DC you have some funk with some fools, well, go ahead. Now, little girls see other foolish folks and yell 'DC' and then run. . . . That's not down. Being down for your gang [isn't happening anymore]. That's being a punk. You can't be in the gang just so people can know you. Just to be popular. It can't be like that. Being in a gang ain't no joke. Because me and her [QG's] brother, we have a lot in common. We run together, been through a hella shit. We got shot. I wish he was here, then . . . maybe . . . we'd get into it."

This provoked a different set of questions from the audience concerning how different DC was from other gangs. QG responded that their gang boxed, "not like other gangs. We fight with fists, box, but those other gangs . . . We've proved ourselves. We down . . . for a fight . . . but . . ." On the one hand, the girls distinguished their gang from other gangs by affirming that they use fists, not guns. On the other hand, the speakers distinguished themselves from younger members and newer cliques. The girls who yell and run or join to be popular are actually bringing down the gang because of their unwillingness to fight, expressing disloyalty to the gang's image. Since Da Crew has proved itself, built a reputation on the members' fighting capability, "boxing," it becomes a way of distinguishing the other gangs as "punks" because they use guns. The girls then began to discuss how other girls in gangs were cowardly, calling upon the boys to protect and defend them. TC articulated this difference. "We don't go to Ninety-eighth [Street]. We don't cross there. We don't get along. If we do, they cuss at us. But over there, the guys be jumping the girls. The girls over there, they need their guys to fight. They fight girls! Nothin' but pussies. We hooked up with Fifty-fourth [Street gang]. They guys. They don't go out and hit girls. If they got funk with some bitch, they call us. You see, homies got love. We got love for some muthafuckas . . . like we said [referring to the video] but others . . ."

An audience member then asked about news stories and movies about gangs and what the girls thought. QG and TC noted that many of the films have problems. TC stated, "They just don't understand . . . make mistakes . . . " adding sarcastically that people will "walk away saying, 'Wow! that's a gang?' That's not a gang." QG argued, "They go overboard." An audience member asked, "What movie?" to which QG replied, "*Mi Vida Loca.* They fight over a guy, that's not what . . . it's not like that." TC piped in, "I just don't like that kind of shit. . . . You can't be in a gang and do that shit. . . . A dude ain't worth it, you know?" The audience applauded loudly and laughed heartily. TC added, "Give me a girl, and I say give me a hug." While she made this comment as if an aside, it was loud enough and directed at one part of the audience so that there was loud laughter and applause.

During the first part of the discussion, I had been looking out at the auditorium and recognizing speakers. But as questions continued, turning to the structure and organization of the gang, LT, who had been very quiet, suddenly sat forward and recognized the next speaker from the audience. Laughter and applause encouraged her. Questions continued: What were the differences between the younger or more recent cliques and the older cliques? How does one mature out of the gang? When does one leave the gang? TC noted that some left the gang because "they got old. Some got babies; they mamas." QG noted, "I don't make trouble anymore. I kick it . . . but with only some folks. I'm down, but I'm not going to get in trouble." TC added, "I'm not down for everybody [referring to the video]. Only [for those who] kicked it back in the day. Now days," she shook her head as a veteran of the gang, "I don't understand them myself."

Then an audience member spoke directly to TC. Noting that the girls' video showed girls in gangs as particularly different from what news stories show, she asked, "You talked about doing another film. And all three of you said it would be different or you'd change it. Have you thought about doing something about homophobia in gangs? Because, I mean, a film about young women in a gang . . . one or two of them would bound to be lesbian or bi [bisexual]. . . . That's what I think when there's a group of . . . Not to put you on the spot . . . but how is it for you? in the group . . . ?"

TC: How my homegirls feel about me?

AUDIENCE MEMBER: Yeah, how would you talk about it on film?

TC: I'm gonna tell you how I did with my homegirls. One day we had a meeting. And I wasn't even going to tell 'em, just keep it to myself. We used to all kick it on Forty-first. They had a meeting, they said they didn't want lesbians in DC or else they would get jumped out. And I let myself out, like you say it. I told MG, 'I don't know how you gonna take it.' I told MG, 'You could jump me out, you know, do like you guys say.' She didn't want to believe me. But I said, "Yeah, it's true. I'm lesbian.' She goes, 'Hey, we ain't going to kick you out for that. Hey, that's you.' I respect that, you know. All my homegirls, they ain't got a problem with that.

TC was at ease when she recounted her coming-out story. She looked at the woman who asked the question and directed her comments to the general audience. QG and LT nodded their heads, listening attentively and agreeing, particularly on the issue of respect. TC then noted, "Actually, they play with me like that. Say 'Yeah, baby!' and shit like that. My homegirls and homeboys treat me with respect. And in fact, sometime treat me like a boy, and I ain't." The audience's laughter in response to TC's comment created a bond. The laughter rang of recognition—how sexuality is misread or misunderstood by heterosexuals. When the audience member asked, "Would you do a video about this?" TC responded affirmatively, and QG added, "Yeah, that's how we are. We have feelings too [referring to the video]." TC concluded, "You gotta give respect. . . . People then respect you."

Questions then moved on to issues of loyalty and family. The girls clarified that the reason the video was only about the gang and did not include family members was because many parents disapproved of their membership. In response to another question about family and loyalty, the girls commented that loyalty was learned from the family and extended to the gang. And once again they noted that while loyalty to the gang was important, loyalty to individual gang members was built on respect and conditioned by the particular reason a person joined.

At this cross-site, while general questions about gangs predominated, the questions also registered difference. What do you girls do in your gang? The gendered questions enabled the girls to draw upon their specific experiences in gangs. Stereotypes of girl gang members as sexual property or as "maladjusted tomboys" were brought out. The girls were able to elaborate that they were not recruited into the gang through pressure or coercion but that their membership developed from regular friendship groups in the neighborhood. They explained that most members of their gang came from the same neighborhood, the same schools, and were friends before they formally joined as a clique. They also demonstrated that girls in gangs engaged in the same behavior as the boys, drinking, fighting, and partying. Noting that they were not sexed into the Fifty-fourth Street gang but jumped in [beaten up], the girls underlined what their gang membership meant: that friendships were of utmost importance to them. Having babies in their estimate would take them out of the everyday practice of the gang. The practice of "kickin' it" (which includes drinking, smoking, fighting, participation in petty theft, truancy, and violating curfew) took on gendered significance as a temporary resistance to the social convention of becoming wives and mothers. Pregnancy was described as "getting old," and having children meant drawing away from the intimacy and solidarity of gang life.

At the WoC Film Festival the girls were able to express that being in the gang gives them status and a sense of belonging. The gang, beyond illegal activities, provided recreation, parties and picnics, going to dances. And when members have cars, the girls spend their time rollin' (cruising). Due to lack of resources, jobs, and spending money from parents, the gang offers a social outlet. "Kickin' it" demonstrates a makeshift strategy to fill time, a solution to the boredom in their lives in the low-income community of Fruitvale, which has few recreational centers for youth and where nothing to do and nowhere to go is the order of the day. Conventional expressions of masculinity such as drinking, fighting, and petty theft offer ways to break the boredom. But the girls of DC also express their differences from masculine street behavior.

WoC's gendered space provided the girls an opportunity for a gendered response. While news media have noted an upswing of girls in gangs and that more girls are using guns, the girls attempted to speak about this as well. "They" use guns; "we" don't. The escalation of violence was a major concern for the girls. TC had been shot, QG had a gun pointed to her head, boys were beating them up. In just a few short years, these gang members—ages fifteen and sixteen—had begun speaking like adults, saying "things had gotten too far." While the aggressive behavior and troublemaking that the girls engaged in would seem to violate traditional notions of femininity, they draw a line at the use of guns as the way to show strength. In their estimate, girls who use weapons are cowards, "acting like a guy." Using guns betrays a need to reach for something outside themselves, to gain courage. Weapons do away with other forms of behavior such as boxing, which in their judgment is neither masculine nor feminine. Such fighting provides safety from being mugged. Moreover, the girls noted that the most common reason for fighting was to preserve their reputation for toughness and consequently to maintain loyalty to the group. Fights usually arose over the issues of integrity or loyalty, that is, public reputation. The gang, as they saw it, provided them with opportunities to learn traditional male skills so they could defend themselves against attacks on their gang's righteousness. However, when guns were involved or when boys were called on to fight girls, this was a clear lack of integrity.

At the WoC Film Festival, issues of gender became topics of easy cross-talk. I had hoped this would be the case. But I had not anticipated the emergence of sexuality and TC's specific interaction with the audience. While TC had participated in the other sites of discourse discussed in earlier chapters, assumptions of sameness obscured her difference. TC's style of baggy pants and large T-shirt disguised her body much like the other girls. Yet, the clothing falls differently on her, presenting straight planes, fashioning her thin, small body into a somewhat angular and gangling physique. Aside from her hairstyle—a short buzzed cut or, when longer, slicked and combed straight back—her comportment and mannerisms are markedly different. Her stride imitates the gang boys' style. When standing, her shoulders roll in, caving her chest, not in embarrassment of her breasts, but a curling of the shoulders, a hunch prepared for anything that will happen, a cool style. Yet, in every site, while people sometimes mistook TC for a boy then heard her speak as a girl, they would nonetheless evade her sexuality, perhaps too afraid to ask. On stage at the festival, TC began with her head under the table. But she soon began to "read" the audience, take their language, and enlist them to reach a different level of understanding (Sandoval 2000). Her asides were directed to women dressed in a masculine or butch style. And her insistence that one shouldn't fight over a guy brought everyone to applause and agreement. TC's remarks on "having babies, being mamas" marked the independence of Da Crew—how the gang socialized girls to be independent and assertive and to take risks. The audience's response affirmed that this independence would be crucial for a future in which the flexibility in social and gender roles demonstrated by the girls could provide survival strategies in a dangerous, changing world.

FREQUENTLY ASKED QUESTIONS

The dilemmas of representation have directed this project in order to represent and depict the young women of Oakland in spaces other than the clandestine geographies of the streets and clubhouses. The challenge for ethnography is to allot authority to the voices of the people one works with and to interpret and analyze their words and actions without taking their agency, that is, usurp their authority. My concern has been to acknowledge their voices as authorities of their lives. My project has brought their words from the field to a broader public sphere.

Still, a perplexing issue arises—the power I have as a researcher taints the post-fieldwork phases of writing and public presentations when I present accounts about the girls. Struggling to present and represent myself in the field and in this ethnography has produced various dilemmas, contradictions, and ambiguities for me. "Insider" and feminist critiques have warned against any essentialist solidarity with informants and emphasize the diversity within such categories as class, race, ethnicity, color, and status as points of engagement in which we enter the field of research. I offer that the knowledge I have of gangs emerges from two very different ways of knowing.

On the one hand, I spent two years with Chicana youth in gangs. However, this does not make me a gang expert. The girls' organizations and types of membership, along with the particular politics of Oakland, produced some very uncommon events in the activities of the gangs. On the other hand, most of my knowledge is from social science texts about gangs. Nonetheless, when positioned as an authority, I often bend to it. That is, I find myself answering the most frequently asked questions, when I am aware that what I should do is answer and cite what others found and concluded about gangs. My answers are likely to come from the pages of Joan Moore, James Diego Vigil, Anne Campbell, Norma Mendoza-Denton, Martin Sanchez Jankowski, Malcolm Klein, and others. Thus, if I can be positioned as an expert, it is as one who has consumed a variety of studies about gangs and gang members.

What I have discovered in this long chain of knowledge production is that young women are rarely interviewed, and thus the particular features of girl gang membership remain hidden, and why the gang is meaningful to them as young women is overlooked.

In a confessional mode, I as an ethnographer developed questions based on previously written studies. How was their gang organized? What were the origins of their gang? What is the source of gang rivalry? What do they feel when they are fighting? What are their relations to the boy gangs in the neighborhood? I did not develop particular questions or hypotheses to examine difference. Many times I did not find a very different answer from the studies already written about gangs in general.

But as the field project expanded into the various spheres of debates and dialogues about gangs with gang members, my project unfolded—not to define or explain gangs, but to rethink how we represent gangs and in what settings and locations we choose to provide thick description. I found that *place* can determine how one develops a narrative and shapes description. When making presentations, I have used two visual sources (*It's a Homie Thang!* and slides of photos from various media sources) in order to problematize the depiction of gangs, gang members, and girls in gangs. The images stir up various questions about gangs. In this section, I offer the reader just a slice of the interaction between myself and various audiences, additionally referring to the literature about gangs and girls in gangs that one may wish to pursue.

Question: Are the girls part of a boys' gang?

They are from three of four all-girl gangs from Fruitvale, an area of Oakland. At the time of her study, Joan Moore (1978) noted that independent girls' gang were infrequent and that earlier girl gangs usually had a two-year longevity. Also, the dating patterns allowed the young women to date boys from the various street gangs of a community or neighborhood. Boys' turf gangs had greater longevity, and a couple of gangs in East Los Angeles have existed since World War II. Moore found that many of the girl groups began as cliques of friends from school or a neighborhood, and the boys usually named the group. Eventually the clique became recognized as a gang grouping.

Question: I'm from Oakland, and even though I'm White, I was protected by Chicanas in gangs. We were friends. A lot of the girls got pregnant and dropped out of school. Did you focus on this?

I did not focus on teen pregnancy, primarily because it seems that most literature on Chicana youth is focused on their bodies as deviant bodies. Additionally, I was very interested in Angela Gallegos' presentation at the NACCS regional conference (1994) analyzing the literature on Chicana/Latina adolescents found in the Chicano database at the UC campuses. She notes that in the few studies about Chicana youth, the prominent categories pertain to issues of reproduction, fertility, contraception, sexuality. Studies on identity and self-construction emphasize female self-perception in relation to their male counterparts. Studies focusing on social problems such as substance use and abuse, high school dropout rate, and gang culture comprise the majority of the studies for both male and female Latino adolescents. Few of the studies focus on Chicana adolescents in education, sports, and literature. Gallegos concludes that, overwhelmingly, the literature constructs Chicana identity with reference to their sexual and biological functions. Overall, the studies (mostly of boys) frame the youth of the Chicano community in a criminal or deviant mode—as addicts, gang-bangers, and dropouts.

I began the fieldwork focusing on audience reception. I hoped to have a general or more diverse population of Latina youth. I did not want to do a study of gangs, and I resisted such a study in the beginning because it seemed that the focus on gangs took up the majority of studies about the Latino community. Similarly, the studies of young women focused on their bodies—issues of the body and reproduction. I found that my informants placed great stakes in the gang and the friendship of their peer group. They discussed sex and birth control and argued about abortion. They have such high stakes in the gang that getting pregnant meant moving out of the gang—not kickin' it. Their investment of protecting each other—"backing up"—meant that in the end they didn't want to get pregnant. Many of the girls took precautions, because the gang was their primary peer group. And they did not want to miss out on the fun of "hangin'." (See Corrigan's study of British youth culture in "Doing Nothing," 1991; see Heath and McLaughlin 1993.)

I do want to make clear that I am not opposed to studies about teen pregnancy. I am attempting to figure how we research a group, what questions we ask that continue to place young Latinas in paradigms of pathology or deviance. Attempting to represent the group differently requires that we situate our studies, our questions, and our analysis through a different filter. Layering problems of past representation, then an analysis of representation, and an additional critical eye to one's own representation becomes a conundrum. I am not suggesting this as a required method of research and writing. It is the requirement I have made for myself.

Question: When was the video *It's a Homie Thang!* aired? And what did the girls think about the video? Did you study their responses? Did you conduct audience reception interviews?

It aired on a local Oakland cable station in the summer of 1994. We did not know the exact date, so we didn't have a gathering to discuss it. QG, while flipping channels, discovered it. She saw it on television with her mother. QG had no qualms about watching it with her family. Knowing about QG's gang involvement, her mom felt that it was an important video because it addressed girls in gangs and showed the girls responding to the stereotypes. When completing the video, the girls viewed it in the discussion group that I held at the NEL Centro de Juventud. I heard mixed responses—not on the content but on the "performances" and how they looked. Many of the girls did not see the video on television. Many hid their involvement with the video because their parents either did not know about their gang membership or the girls had told their parents that they were no longer involved. As a result they worried about it airing again. The discussion died down. I couldn't force a conversation about this, and the girls changed the subject.

Question: Do you still see the girls?

That's a very political question. I have kept contact with them throughout the writing process. Because my endeavor proposes to interrogate representation, I hoped to represent them in a way that would honor and recognize their experiences and at the same time interpret their words. I took drafts of two chapters—to find out their reaction. They primarily examined whether and where they appeared in my text; they especially liked it when I quoted them directly. We have kept in touch by phone and sometimes bump into each other at various places in Oakland.

I think it's a good question because it addresses the hierarchy of the research relationship, of power. It's difficult to address because I have to think about my position in life and what lives the girls have now. I don't think we had an equal relationship, not just because of age but because I was aware of my position as a graduate student. After writing up the study, I would get a pretty good job. It is a kind of cannibalization because I take their knowledge and experience, chew on it, and issue my study. I get a Ph.D., become an "expert" with all the privileges, and they get very little. Other types of projects, like an action-research project, would engage researcher and informants in joint activity for a social, economic, or policy goal. Yet neither did the girls nor the Centro invite me to help them in a participatory project or assign me a specific task. While our discussions empowered them to articulate their lives, the interaction was brief. Perhaps I can view myself as a counselor—to imagine a fair exchange. When the girls discussed problems, I couldn't tell them what they should do. Instead, I tried to figure out how to ask questions, hoping there would be a balance, that my questions would be a form of counseling. When leaving the field, ending the concentrated day-to-day interaction with the girls, I felt some form of reciprocity. Leaving the field registers power differentials for everyone. We got together at the Centro, and I attempted to bring closure to the group. The girls resisted. We talked about getting together again, and then they asked if my study would ever be a book. I figured it would take me a couple of years to write the study. I explained that I would first have to write the dissertation, then rewrite it for a book. Then QG looked at me, asking, "Three or four years?" As she said this, a look of disbelief and wonderment came into her eyes. I could see that she had a moment of clarity. "Three or four years . . . I never even thought about that . . . that far. I can't even think that far." For me, her clarity marked what the girls had been unable to do during all of our discussions—think of the future. The future could never be a factor in discussing their lives; the topics had to be immediate. When QG and the other girls started to think about being sixteen or twenty, they became somber. Generally, the future rarely informs teenagers' ideas or conceptions of life. And for low-income youth of color, the future did not measure in because of the limited opportunities that they have and because of the lives they lead. If some form of reciprocity occurred, then I think it was at that moment, when they thought about the future.

Question: What happened to the gangs? Are they still around?

The three girl gangs have now all dissolved. East Side Norteñas (ESN) dissolved during the first months of field research. As the video indicated, some of the young women had left Las Norteñas (LN) because of disagreements. LN still functioned with very few members; I interviewed primarily former members of LN. Da Crew had an eight-year existence. Two years after I left the field, DC broke up. Some of the girls joined boy street gangs through their girl clique cohorts. QG had dropped out of junior high school and returned. That's gutsy, to me, to return to junior high, when she was older than the other students. Another, FN, went on to attend community college. Two others went to Job Corps.

Question: The gang is like a second family, but through friendship. Did you study the families?

Yes, but I chose to write about the girls in different types of spaces. However, I sometimes found myself as a mediator between the girls and their parents. A problem of fieldwork for an insider, in this sense part of the racial-ethnic class of the community under study, causes a dilemma. When you are in the field doing interviews and researching girls in gangs, observing teenage behavior, particularly aggressive and transgressive behavior, you find yourself in a variety of roles and find that people utilize a variety of terms to describe you. Many times the girls introduced me as a counselor. At times, the young women asked me to meet with them and their parents to work out some issues and problems they faced. I was in a peculiar role, trying to bring two parties together and at the same time a confidante, not in a position to tell all to the parents.

Writing is a process of selection. While I structured my text to talk about participation in the public sphere, many areas are not addressed. Authorial selection erases the support the girls had around them, whom they went to for support and counsel. My narrative does not mention the fathers who also attempt to reconstruct their roles and functions within the patriarchal tradition and endeavor nonetheless to provide better male role models for their daughters. In a number of instances when I was asked to mediate between parents and their daughters, the girls' fathers pitched right in to help and support their daughters. In a few instances, I observed the fathers talking to the young women in a much different way than my generation of female adolescents experienced. I don't know how to describe this difference. At best I can only describe it in the following way: they talked to their daughters as if they were boys. This male type of camaraderie, understanding the lure and thrill of the streets and public, struck me as the emergence of the new Chicano father. While the youth told me of their fathers' interventions in arguments between mothers and daughters, I found their fathers attempting to work out the problems of a public persona. While I am not attempting to represent a utopian sphere of domestic contentment, I do want to mark the emergent appearance of a different set of relations between fathers and daughters in the Latino community.

Even though I have immediate knowledge of the families, I decided not to focus on the families because of my own feelings of uneasiness and my own hesitations on the paradigms of the culture of poverty. I did not want to reproduce this depiction, because while some of the girls came from difficult home lives, others were asserting their independence through their participation in the gang. I found concerned parents and others who did not know about the girls' involvement in gangs. So I did not want to fix families and the community in a depiction where they have no agency. The community confronts political, economic, and social problems—issues of power—and I did not want to let the economic situation be the final word on the variety of ways in which people struggle to survive in both the formal and informal economies.

I want to comment on the idea of the gang as "family." This idea became popular through the media. Most researchers on gangs understand that "family" is a metaphor to describe the type of solidarity among peers in public space—trust in others to "watch your back." For the girls I worked with, it's interesting that they used the simile "like family." The young women transgress many of the social expectations of what young Latinas are supposed to act like in public space. Transgressing these expected behaviors, the second family describes their network. The media's depiction of the gang as a substitute or surrogate family follows the culture of poverty model or even takes a concept of William Julius Wilson (1987) regarding the development of an underclass—in dysfunctional families they construct this other family. Sound-bite explanations do not explain the variety of reasons kids join gangs. For some, the gang is family; for others, gang membership means fun, recreation, belonging, protection, and so on (Vigil 1983; J. Moore 1991; Cintron 1997). However, there are many role models in the community.

Question: There are a lot of drive-by shootings that we hear about, a lot of youth dying. Were any youth, male or female, killed during your field research?

No, not killed, probably because the girls distinguished their gang as different from the guy gangs. Carl S. Taylor (1993) also offers a typology of gangs. Some gangs deal drugs, and some protect the dealers, turf gangs, scavengers, and taggers; some are stoners (recreational drug use groupings). Moore and Vigil (1987) found that a significant characteristic of Chicano gangs is that they are fighting gangs. This involves fist-fights and the use of bats, chains, knives, and guns. The young women I worked with distinguished their gangs in that they did not use guns. They characterized the use of guns as a guy thing. They fought, using bats sometimes, but usually they used their fists.

When I first entered the field, most of the girls claimed that a lot of their friends had been killed in drive-by shootings. However, as I continued to ask, I found that they either heard of a death or did not directly know the person murdered. In one incident, TC and the brother of another gang member were injured in a drive-by. The girls discussed payback, but the leaders of the gangs had to find out if they needed to retaliate. They thought it didn't involve the gang since the young man was not a member of any of the gangs. Also, since TC had been in some personal antagonisms at that time, the leaders had to find out if the shooting was gang-related or a personal vendetta. Jankowski (1991) explains that gangs, as organizations, have to maintain peace in order to fulfill the needs of their members. Reckless warring then has to be averted, and leaders will decide when and under what conditions the gang will retaliate. Vigil (1983) also notes that if a member is too loco, gets into scruffs constantly, then the gang will not take all occasions as a threat to the gang organization. NWA had to take into account what was going on with TC. In another incident, MG and QG were assaulted by members of a rival gang. QG had a gun pointed at her head while a girl knifed MG. The girls wanted to retaliate, and they discussed using guns. Rational heads prevailed, and the girls' parents convinced the girls to press charges. The rival girls were jailed and sentenced. After that incident, the fights accelerated. However, I did not hear any more discussions of guns, although I did see bats and a few brass knuckles after the assault. Incidentally, no one used automatic weapons, Uzis, AKs, MACs, or other assault weapons. (On the stereotype of gangs and assault weapons see McCorkle and Miethe 2002.)

Question: Many Chicano and Chicana youth have no support from teachers, and the schools are failing them. Is there a relationship between joining gangs and dropping out?

Not all of the girls dropped out. Many of them did graduate or went on to get their GED or enrolled in continuation school. Angela Valenzuela's (1999) study of Mexicano and Chicano youth at a Houston, Texas, high school would be informative. She explains how "schooling" is different from the Chicano and Mexicano concept of "educación" and how mechanical lessons, teaching to test, and lack of caring contribute to the high dropout rate. So, schools failing Chicano/Mexicano youth do not have a direct relationship to gangs. The girls I worked with dropped out of school for various reasons. One young woman liked to get high, so she had problems of attendance and keeping up with assignments. She had a poor school record. As a consequence, she did not want to stay in school. Another young woman returned to community college. During my interviews with her, she just cut through a lot of the questions I circled around. She had a lot of encouragement from teachers and counselors, but she dropped out as she became more involved in the affairs of the gang. (Managing a gang entails a lot of personnel work to attend to in order to keep the group cohesive.) When we take up the particular persons, the reasons vary. Another girl, TC, left school because she self-identified as lesbian. She came out at a very young age—at twelve. The kids at her school fought her daily because they wouldn't accept her public sexuality. She attempted to get into another school, which the majority of the gang girls attended. However, the bureaucracy of filling out papers and needing parental approval discouraged her. Her grandmother missed work trying to get the girl transferred, but the grandmother didn't feel comfortable speaking English. She understood English, but the communication was difficult. She became frustrated with the administrative language and procedures, the bureaucracy (see Cintron 1997 regarding the language barriers for parents). Also, even though TC's grandmother made the effort, it was half-hearted. She always felt that transferring TC to the other school would entrench her in the gang. Consequently, the young woman became truant. She dropped out and made various attempts to enroll in the school that her homegirls attended to have protection.

I do want to point out that these young women participated in the Oakland school walkout by Latino students in the spring of 1992. They

demanded more Chicano teachers and Chicano studies for greater mul-
ticulturalism. Many participated in the walkout, and some of them participated in leadership roles for the walkout.

I'm always hesitant about wholesale blame—blaming teachers and
counselors—as a few members of my family are teachers and teaching
assistants. The reasons young people join gangs could be their families
or school or in some instances their own brazenness and rebellion. The
mother of one of the young women said, "Desde chiquita, era core-
juda," that the girl was always angry even as a child, implying a natural
characteristic. I try not to get into the personalities—an interpretation
and analysis of personality would be a psychological study. I attempt to
look at the investments, what they found in the gang as a social group.

Question: You said one of the girls is a lesbian. Is there homophobia among gangs? Are they anti-homosexual?

I don't think anyone has done a study on homosexuality in boy gangs or
about the homosociality found in the gang. And little is said about homosexuality in girl gangs. Generally, girl gangs and members have been
described as "tomboys" (Hanson 1964; Campbell 1991).

I have been looking at the literature that would help me to understand
homophobia and to think about girls in gangs. Sedgwick (1985) and
Butler (1990) offer ways of examining identity through the concepts of
binary opposition of self/other and performance. Since homosexuality
is constructed as other, then the construction of masculinity can become
parodic, a performance that becomes a hypermasculinity, even an aggressive masculinity, to construct the self. Adrienne Rich (1986) suggests
that we examine sexuality and homosociality among women through
the concept of the continuum. Lesbian relations make up one end along
this line, and the progression identifies forms of feminist solidarity, feminist politics, female friendship networks, sister/kinship relations, and
mother-daughter relations on the other end. This continuum offers some
beginnings to examine homophobia and the potential of lesbian-baiting
for girls in gangs. Possibly through a longitudinal study, it can be investigated to find out whether the girls remain heterosexual or identify as
lesbian after some time.

Girls who perform a masculine aggressiveness, even if in mixed gangs,
run the chance of lesbian-baiting. They have produced this homosocial
grouping and foster transgressive behavior in public space. The type of

clothing, the large shirt and baggy pants that hide the female body and subvert conventional forms of femininity, and the performance of street tough are meaningful signs. In effect, the dress style signifies that they have not been "sexed in" to the gang (joining the gang through a boyfriend or series of boyfriends or joining through group sex). The baggy clothing signifies that they are street soldiers, fighters, thus their investment in being read correctly. The-baggier-the-better concealment of the body distinguished them from "girl-girls." In their syntax, "girl-girl" constructs a succession from wannabes to sexual property. Signifying that they are in control, the girls view sleeping around—hoochies and 'ho's—as a sign of weakness and dependency on boys. The performance of an aggressive masculinity as soldier achieves respect in public space, a space dominated by boys and men.

The dominant discourse—by parents, social service workers, people in authority—labels the girls as tomboys, resulting in the tendency to lesbian-bait these kinds of groupings of girls. This is similar to the stereotyping and lesbian-baiting that happens to women in the military—other than military nurses who care for (male) soldiers.

Because of the potential for lesbian-baiting, all three of the gangs I studied had a rule not to allow lesbians into their organizations. This caused problems for TC. She recruited the fourth generation, the largest clique. Most of the young women in her clique respected her. She had proved herself by backing up her friends and other members. When the rule came down, she went to the former leader of the gang to ask about her status. She had proven herself, in the estimate of the leader. Also, the young woman had strong leadership skills, ensuring constant contact between leadership and members. DC threw out the rule, yet there were regulations about her conduct in the group. Concerned about the perception of their gang, girls constantly negotiated her membership.

Notably, as the girls proceeded through the various passages of sexual experimentation, they stipulated the young woman's conduct. I noticed a scale of progression as the girls talked about their sexual exploits—from kissing to French kissing to petting to sexual intercourse, and significantly, discussions about oral sex incited pandemonium. Similarly, TC went through her own process of experimentation. And the "straight" girls complained and grumbled. As participant observer of the group, I heard conversations among the members of Da Crew. A young woman said, "She can bring her girlfriend to the party, but I don't want to see her kissing her girlfriend." Another young woman responded, "What do you think she feels every time you're kissing a dude at the party?" The conversations occurred again when there were girls petting with their boyfriends at a party, and the young woman brought her girlfriend. While there was never clear agreement about her conduct at gatherings, both the formal and informal leadership seemed to compare her sexual experimentation to the rest of the members. However, there were other regulations.

Question: What were the regulations?

That she could not be in the gang to find a girlfriend. In effect, there was a company policy about dating within the firm. While they had no explicit policy about her participation in leadership, many did not want the lesbian label for Da Crew (DC) or for the alliance, Norteñas With Attitude (NWA). Under the usual practice, when the leader of DC stepped down, the leader of the following generation ascended. This meant that either TC or QG of the fourth generation would move up. Since QG did not want the leadership, TC should have been the new leader. In the end, the leaders of the various cliques, from the second generation to the sixth generation, decided to select someone else. I do not know if QG took part in this decision. Thus the regulation of conduct in the beginning did in fact determine policy about lesbians in the organization. So a policy on dating implicitly resulted in a policy about leadership and a qualification of one's membership.

Question: Did the girl gangs start as social peers, not gangs?

In the video, one of the girls states that East Side Norteñas started as a group of girls "hangin' together, then there was all the problems." They would go to parties or go as a group to various places (malls, parks, community activities) where fights would develop. Many felt they should defend their girlfriends. So pretty soon, their reputation began, and they identified as a gang. However, when I asked more about how they came together, I found that the basis of their friendship was their fighting reputations. The majority had been in fights before they hung out together. Even though they had not coalesced initially around fights, they had histories of fighting in grammar school. They came together as a result of their common behavior. While the clique began with the girls hanging out, the label of being a gang developed as a result of their reputation as fighters.

Question: Why did the girls join? Because of the rivalries, for protection, or were they forced to join? Or was it because of a reputation as you explained?

DC, the largest gang, had members who joined for various reasons. With larger groups there will be greater diversity (see Vigil 1988 for types of members and Jankowski 1991 and C. Taylor 1993 for types of gangs). Las Norteñas, a smaller grouping, began with a few members. Two members had boyfriends, and another had a cousin in the same boys' street gang. Since the street gang did not have girl members, LN formed but not in any official relationship to the gang. The girls dated boys from any number of gangs that identified as Norteños, the broader alliance of area gangs (see Mendoza-Denton 1999 on Norteños and Sureños). The gang began breaking up when members started dating Sureños, a rival confederacy.

At one point, before the fourth generation formed, DC nearly dissolved. There weren't enough members to sustain the gang—especially because the group had a fighting reputation to keep up (see Jankowski 1991). DC's membership shrank, and it seemed there were more and more rival groupings looking for them. Constantly watching their backs, they had a difficult time defending themselves and their reputation. The third generation went on a recruitment drive, beating up girls to join their gang. That means that if you didn't join, you would get beat up until you joined.

Question: Many of the girls seemed to have leadership potential. Is their leadership something that just happens in the gang as their friends create the circumstances for leadership? Or do they just get caught up in the gang, and therefore they have limits restricting them from other possibilities, from being leaders outside the gang?

I want to get behind that question a bit. Sometimes we think of gangs as subcultural "outlaws" or as potential revolutionaries. As an influence of the cultural nationalism and new-left politics of the sixties, these ideas became part of the informal discourse about gangs. In fact, scholars criticized Anne Campbell (1991) because she had not considered youth in gangs as "naive revolutionaries." (I believe this was the first social science study to focus primarily on girls in gangs.) However, "naive revolutionaries" implies that they have no class or race consciousness. This idea erases their agency because they know about the power relations in society.

In several discussions about my research, people have romanticized gangs as a potential guerrilla group against "the system." To think about gang youth as "rebels without causes" may be a sympathetic view, as it acknowledges a different kind of knowledge and conception of leadership and organizational skills. This conception attempts to overturn the pathology paradigm. Because they experience marginality, exclusion, racism, classism, segregation, and ageism, I believe the idea of a protorevolutionary places a burden upon the youth. We have to open the doors to their participation and implement services geared to youth. We have to amplify democracy and broaden the spheres where the youth can participate with equal voices and authority, as public citizens.

The young women I worked with were bold and had developed a large network of peer support. They had friends outside the gang. They participated in a Chicano/a high school walkout and school boycott. Some of the girls of NWA occupied leadership positions. The leader of Da Crew, a sharp and outspoken young woman, took risks in a number of spheres. She not only engaged in fistfights, but she also confronted teachers about education. She had a sharp analysis of social conditions in the Chicano/a community. She read a variety of literature—leftist newspapers and Black Muslim literature as well as the various community advocate papers—and she made trouble for authority figures. She could be a leader in multiple spheres.

Possibly in the gang the young women developed and honed their personnel skills. They negotiated so many disagreements and intervened in fights among the members. We think of girls' culture generally as talking on the phone and getting together because the peer group is central in adolescence. They utilized girls' peer group pressure to force conduct, and the gang had rules and regulations as a form of social control.

Question: Is the gang a phase, and then they "mature out" of the gang?

Generally, we think of adolescence as a "phase." We usually say, "You'll grow out of it." Adolescence is fraught with the intensity of living in the moment. To consider adolescence as a phase discredits or depreciates young people's words and their authority on what it is like to be a young person in these times, in these situations. It dismisses their sense of personhood, when these youth have invested so much of their social identity in the gang.

For some girls pregnancy allows them to leave the gang without any hard feelings. For others pregnancy and staying at home present a very limited option (Heath and McLaughlin 1993). Campbell (1991) found the girls ambivalent about the lives their mothers led, particularly their subordination to "the man in the house." The gang, therefore, may be a way of putting off the inevitable. I can understand how Campbell found ambivalence among the girls.

Joan Moore's study of the life course of Chicanas in barrio gangs (1994) found that gang membership limits the possibilities of social mobility for young women. Examining the social processes in which young women in gangs or other deviant lifestyles are stigmatized by traditional Latino culture and gender norms, Moore found that a double standard operated within the gang as well as the community. Of those girls who drank and took drugs (the activities that confer prestige on male members, but not on girls), stigmatization restricted the options for women. Additionally, the choice of mates was restricted to the milieu or to the wilder boys who initiated a more street-oriented adult lifestyle, especially if girls used heroin. Moore also found (1991) that boy gang members tended to date non-gang girls, and young men hoping to advance economically and materially did not choose girls from gangs as their marriage mates. For Moore, gang membership will limit life opportunities through both community convention and gender expectations for girls, and I agree. They are breaking socially expected norms of the family, of the Chicano community, or of what dominant society expects of young women.

We have to rethink the idea of "maturing out." It reaffirms that boys will be boys and are sowing their wild oats. The concept of "maturing out" frames adolescence within a masculine paradigm. Boys are relieved from the gang when they have responsibilities for work or raising a family. The "mature" person is moving from the peer group to accept duties and obligations. For boys this means moving to the world of work and the family. I'm not sure we can use the same idea for the girls in gangs. Pregnancy leads to isolation. Because regulated gender roles assign a young woman to the private sphere, where her primary interaction is designated to her mate and children, I'm not sure we can consider "maturing out" a positive occurrence. Even if the young woman works outside the home, her principal responsibility is to the patriarchal family. When reviewing the discussions about the original theme for a video project, teen pregnancy, the girls were concerned with the separation and isolation that occurred when girls got pregnant. They asked: "What happens to your friends when they get pregnant? Do things change? What or how do they change?" However, they had such disagreement on the issue of abortion that the they decided to change the topic to gangs.

Question: Do you feel that you affected the group?

There were many times I felt that maybe DC would not have lasted as long if I had not been in the field. The discussion group became another place for them to hang out, to tell their war stories—becoming an essential place to articulate their identity. I always feel uncomfortable on that account.

Oakland politics imparts the type of involvement in which the girls participated. The community politics that emerged there as a result of the civil rights and identity politics movement provided a wider forum for the girls to participate in the counter public sphere. The Centro's goal advocates youth issues and develops leadership among the youth.

The girls spoke at the various sites about their gang identity as the Centro fought to include the voices of youth in policy-making meetings. The Centro's program empowers the voices of youth, providing youth the forum to express their opinions and frame their own programs. As I situated my presence in the context of an activist center, a different kind of relationship between ethnographer and informants emerged.

Through interrogation, examination of what they were doing and what circumstances surrounded an incident or what they felt about an issue, a process developed in which language produced a reflexive subjectivity (Hebdige 1979). They seriously considered my questions and found different ways of providing answers to help me understand and therefore be more supportive. They were explaining to me what their gang membership meant, which produced a different conception of the self. The process of recognizing oneself in a different setting, in a different institution—not only in the family or school—disrupts one's usual sense of self, articulating their lives and worldviews.

Question: You said you asked naïve questions, and that is how the video came about?

I feel that the video produces a critique of my research. They assume my role, accentuating power differences—educational privilege and class. It also underscores the power to control the research process and agenda.

The girls take my position as a researcher who asks the same old questions about gangs. So they provide their answers. With those questions settled, they move to a new area, the issue of girls in gangs. They move to the particular, marking difference.

Question: When they asked each other questions, did they express their resistance to always being objectified? Does the video express how they felt about always being asked the same questions?

They are expressing their feelings about always being objectified, particularly in the scene when the camera shows the girls filming. Three girls were interviewed on the porch, and the next scene shows the members of the gang filming, making the film. This scene shows that they control the project. I attempt to mark this scene.

Also, the "in your face" performance attempts to disrupt objectification. They use the stereotype; they put the stereotype to their purposes. They work the stereotype to alienate and at the same time to draw in the viewer. This is a complex representation. Street-tough difference draws the inquisitive, the curious audience. Luring the viewer to the alien, they then move to more relaxed spaces, allowing the viewer to come into their world.

Question: Do the girls still get together? Or are they isolated?

After I left the field, I would drop by the Centro and the homes of the girls. About two years later I took them drafts of two chapters. María got together the girls who were my primary informants. There were some interesting dynamics. FN and QG had kids and usually talked with others by phone. They still talked with each other but were not "hangin'." For example, FN spoke with me about MG's behavior, still running around, heavy drinking, and taking drugs. Campbell notes that the social network of the gang—the need to be with each other—produces strong normative controls for the girls, particularly over sexuality (Campbell 1991). The girls of NWA did not want a reputation of being 'ho's (whores) or hoochies (promiscuous women), and on that account the peer pressure was effective.

Additionally, the everyday hangin' brought a camaraderie in which a girl can tap the shoulder of her friend and tell her to ease up. Talking things out managed issues among the girls, especially if a girl was too crazy—getting into too many fights, getting too loaded, destroying and vandalizing property, stealing, and other escapades that endangered the member and/or the gang (Vigil 1988). When these acts become too frequent or too conspicuous, it gets the attention of the police or parents and neighbors, who would further disparage the girls.

As they moved out of their various gangs, they moved out of the type of solidarity in which they could tell a friend that she's too crazy. FN's concern reflects this breakdown of the type of affection that the gang had. Interestingly, MG also felt she could not tell FN anything "to straighten her out." MG felt that FN had forgotten what things were like. FN was responsible for raising her kids and felt that MG had to grow up. They expressed that not getting together anymore had weakened the type of camaraderie to talk things out. Any intervention caused anger and frustration between them, and each felt that the other was reluctant to hear her out.

Question: How were you accepted by the group?

When I think about this, I want to laugh. While I have a romantic tale about connections as well as stories of conflict, I have to think of the girls' pragmatism. First, my research began with gang films, and they had the real story. So that initiated their response. The girls wanted the attention. They wanted to be interviewed to brag about their gangs. Second, in the beginning I called the girls each week to remind them of the discussion group. A reminder, a personal call, helps to coalesce. Many times I would leave messages with their parents, sisters, or brothers, so the discussion group became a familiar activity for their families. With an older woman calling regularly for a discussion group at the Centro, the girls began to explain to their parents that I was either a counselor or teacher. It legitimized me in the eyes of their families. And the girls used this. When a few of the girls were punished—couldn't use the phone or could not leave the house except for school—they would plead to participate in the discussion group. Attending the discussion group became the source for them to keep up with gang activities. Third, I had a car.

The use of my car happened when one of the girls, MG, was hiding out. She had been in a fight, and her rivals were watching for her. She asked me to pick her up so that she could continue to participate. Riding in a car with a middle-aged woman with salt-and-pepper hair provided safety for her. Her rivals, thank goodness, did not bother her when she rode with me. We got to know each other, and a trust developed. MG encouraged the girls to participate regularly. This started a situation in which if the girls needed a ride, they were confident that I would give them one, especially as the audience reception study changed to a study of gangs.

Then as the other areas of their gang life opened up to me, not only did the girls need to be someplace, but they wanted me to attend many of their activities. As the number of fights increased, or maybe as I became more aware of how much violence was part of their lives, my car became known by rivals. The girls would ask for rides more strategically—otherwise we would all be in danger of some assault.

Question: Do you think of yourself as a role model for the girls?

Not exactly. Primarily, because I think the girls had a lot of role models around them. As they struggled with issues like getting a job or trying to get back into school or deciding to have children, I have to admire their mothers, aunts, older sisters who gave them so many other ways of going about life. There are so many ways of surviving as well as finding other ways of taking on the challenges of life in the barrios. Certainly, Rosalinda Palacios, the Centro director, was a great role model. As a single mother who raised two children, she went to college and worked tirelessly for community causes. María, the peer counselor, influenced the girls; she chose not to be in a gang and was a great source of support.

Moreover, I am not too comfortable with the idea of "role models." I think we have come to a point of politics where we rely on the idea of role models, kind of like Bush's points of light. I think we need many role models, since in some communities the gang is the dominant subcultural group. Moore and Vigil (1993) note the tremendous number and wide range of community-based organizations of the sixties and early seventies that emerged as a result of the War on Poverty and the Chicano movement. The disappearance of these organizations in areas like Los Angeles has affected not only the services but the public culture and public discourse.

The environment has to be expanded. What we need are more community and service centers that address the needs of youth. What we need are more public discussions with the participation of youth to develop programs that are geared to serving the communities. I think we have to reinstate programs like those of the War on Poverty that brought youth as participants into decision making for community projects. When we have more institutions that are constituted from the people of our communities, we not only accelerate economic opportunities, but we expand democracy.

NOTES

Rollin' through Oaktown

1. Younis remarks that to characterize Oakland as a Black city misses the extent of the city's diversity. "The 1990 census counted 372,242 residents of Oakland, representing an increase of 9.7 percent from 1980. . . . The increase marked Oakland's first recorded population growth since World War II. . . . Indeed, from 1980 to 1990 the fastest-growing population groups were Asians and Latinos, who accounted for 14.1 percent and 13.9 percent, respectively, of Oakland's population in 1990. Other groups combined, including Native Americans, formed nearly 1 percent of the population in 1990" (Younis 1998, 224).

2. Younis further remarks upon the legacy of multiracial struggles in noting that "community organizations that advocate activism and community empowerment are most clearly cross-racial/ethnic in practice even while they may not explicitly seek to promote diversity. By addressing specific nonracial/ethnic concerns that affect communities irrespective of the race or ethnicity of their residents, such organizations identify bases for common concern and action that transcend race and ethnicity.

"In 1993 the density of community organizations produced the Fruitvale Community Collaborative (FCC), a consortium of 16 organizations, churches, schools, business and homeowners associations, and research and planning groups. FCC has recently ceased to operate as a collaborative, but it remains a testament to the critical mass of organizational efforts characterizing the area (Herranz 1995). Moreover, it was a multiracial/ethnic effort that brought Asian, African-American, Native American, and Latino organizations together. It continues today as a distinct organization" (Younis 1998, 234).

3. Examining community attitudes toward the police, Younis found that the "city has sought to improve police/community relations and has adopted community policing programs. Its image, however, is tarnished by its record of excessive force and virtually non-existent accountability processes and procedures. Indications are that conditions have deteriorated rather than improved over the past 5 years (1991–1996). It may be argued that Oakland's police force is ham-

pered by policies that are not conducive to good relations between officers and the communities they are meant to serve. In 1994 only 8.7 percent of the city's police officers resided in Oakland, compared with 34.5 percent of officers in San Francisco and 56 percent of officers in San Jose (Staats 1994). Reasons cited by police officers for residence outside the city are poor housing and schools and fear of retaliation. Besides the fact that some of the city's best-paid public employees are taking their incomes elsewhere, nonresidence could be argued to detract from sensitivity to or identification with the communities" (Younis 1998, 230–231).

4. Acuña notes that in the 1880s under President Porfirio Díaz, the Mexican elites cooperated with foreign investors to industrialize the economy. While modernization contributed to the industrialization of agriculture, mining, and transportation, it led to the demise of the communal village and loss of land for peasants and a decline in handicraft trades, consequently displacing peasants and craftsmen in villages and cities. While the national debt increased, "by 1910 foreign investors controlled 76 percent of all corporations, 95 percent of mining, 89 percent of industry, 100 percent of oil, and 96 percent of agriculture." The intensified drive was coupled with the curtailing of bourgeois freedoms, anti-labor repression, and establishing the dictatorship of Díaz (Acuña 2000, 156–163).

5. While the labor shortage ended after the war, the Bracero Program continued until 1964. According to Acuña, "The US government functioned as a labor contractor at taxpayers' expense, assuring nativists that workers would return to Mexico after they finished picking the crops. Growers did not have to worry about labor disputes. The braceros were used to glut the labor market to depress wages and were also used as strikebreakers. The US government fully cooperated with growers, allocating insufficient funds to the border patrol, ensuring a constant supply of undocumented laborers" (Acuña 2000, 287).

6. Only gradually were Blacks able to secure residence in East Oakland, which became another ghetto. In addition, residential restrictions preventing Chinese from moving out of Chinatown were in force (Younis 1998, 223).

7. Oden notes that under the leadership of an African American, Mayor Lionel Wilson, who had worked with the Chinatown community as the chairman of the local Economic Opportunity commission, Oakland entered a $100 million downtown development proposal to build commercial buildings in Chinatown. In dire need of funds, the city hastily approved the plan. However, protest emerged from the Chinese community, complaining that "(1) some of the buildings scheduled for demolition were historic monuments, (2) the citizens in the area were not fully participating, and (3) the affirmative action hiring programs had not happened" (Oden 1999, 148). Other complaints registered class differences with the city's representatives who were middle-class. Additionally, they

questioned the destination of the project's benefits, as profits would go to transnational investors rather than local Chinese businesses. Oden's narration of compromise and conflict reflects the problems of local governments that compete for local, national, and foreign investments as well as city management that prioritizes the central business districts over neighborhood development (Oden 1999, 146–153).

8. In the 1970s the development of downtown meant the construction of the Wells Fargo and Clorox buildings with connecting parking lots (Oden 1999, 134–136).

9. In her examination of the two Community Development Districts of San Antonio and Fruitvale in Oakland, California, Younis notes an income increase in the districts. "There is tremendous variation across and within Oakland's CDDs in terms of incomes and living standards. In 1990 the combined median household income in San Antonio and Fruitvale was $27,179, compared with a high of $61,066 for Oakland Hills and a low of $15,265 for West Oakland. The same median household income was reported for both CDDs in 1990. Fruitvale experienced a 32.6 percent improvement, and San Antonio experienced a 29.4 percent improvement in median household income between 1980 and 1990; these increases were substantially higher than those of the city as a whole, where median household income had increased by 17.3 percent. Yet there are notable differences within the districts. Per capita income by census tract reveals a low of $6,562 and a high of $18,176. Again, higher incomes are predictably found in the tracts adjacent to the lake and the lower hills [San Antonio CDD]. Similarly, in 1990 the percentage of persons living below the poverty line ranged from a low of 10.6 percent to a high of 40.0 percent" (Younis 1998, 227). While there is no indication of the types of jobs or whether the increase is due to combined family incomes, the increase nonetheless reflects the overall tendency of restructuring, a low-wage service sector that is non-unionized.

10. Public school enrollment for Fruitvale shows that the "Latino student population ranged from 17 to 89 percent in the district's six schools, with Latino pupils accounting for at least 55 percent of enrollment in five of the schools in 1994" (Younis 1998, 225).

11. A xenophobic response to the demographic increase of Mexican and Central American immigration, California's Proposition 187 denied state services (health, education, and welfare) to undocumented immigrants and their children.

12. While traditional manufacturing cities and states bore the brunt of impoverishment, Moore and Vigil in "Barrios in Transition" (1993) argue that the technological and service industries commensurate to the restructuring produced the global cities populated with low-paid workers in a service economy. Recognizing the economic restructuring (from manufacturing to finance capital investment) that disrupted many communities and set up conditions for the de-

velopment of an underclass, they contest the far-reaching application of Wilson's underclass model.

An Ethnographer's Tale

1. Analysis of the familiarizing motifs, writing style, and the selection of events used to construct the researcher's thesis is found in the essays collected by Clifford and Marcus (1986) and Wellman (1994). Essays by insider/indigenous researchers have further problematized the "ethnographer's tale," addressing the shifting relationship and identities of researchers (Narayan 1993; Abu-Lughod 1991) and reversing traditional arrival scenes (Panourgía 1995; Strathern 1987; Hastrup 1992).

2. Vigil (1988) distinguishes pachuco from cholo. The former were second-generation youth of Mexican immigrants of the 1930s and 1940s who wore zoot suits and developed a lifestyle for an emerging urban culture. Youth gangs of the fifties, although their style had considerably changed, continued the self-designation as pachuco. Rooting the term "cholo" to the sixties, Vigil registers the development of a more structured group organization for self-identity.

3. "Carnalismo" describes the type of solidarity found among Chicano youth gangs. As a code of brotherhood, the male-centered concept was adapted by the Chicano youth and student movement of the late sixties and was a central part of the cultural nationalist ideology.

4. Shulamit Reinharz (1983) notes that in experiential analysis, methods and methodology are combined relational perspectives to the sociology of knowledge. While Reinharz develops a rigorous and reliable method to social inquiry, I stumbled upon various aspects of her methodology. One clear point that I grasped was the suspension of preconceptions as a necessary corrective to conventional studies of gangs. While I had taken a course on gangs, I was intent on not reproducing the same kinds of representations. I had no hypothesis to prove and only hoped to avoid assuming I knew the cause of the girls' experiences.

5. I'm sure other academic folks understand this refusal to talk about movies. As intellectuals we engage texts—films and novels—through critique, while family and friends insist that we "stop analyzing" and just "enjoy" the movie and/or book. In addition, the discussion group is not a classroom where we can guide students to discuss the meaning of a film. Thus, for the girls, a movie had no relevance to real life because "it is just a movie."

6. While there are many versions of the folk tale about a ghost woman who weeps and wails along rivers or lakes, the story is usually told at night to scare children. In one version of the tale, she is a sexualized mestiza who loves a Spanish aristocrat who dumps her for a woman of his own class and race. In another

version, La Llorona is a married woman who leaves her husband and children for a soldier. When he leaves her, she kills and mutilates her children, throwing their limbs all over the earth. God punishes her and she is condemned to search the earth for her children's parts. While there are many more ways of telling the story, most have a strong lesson for young girls, to regulate their behavior. Many Chicana writers and critics have refigured La Llorona as a symbol of resistance who as a sexual subject resists patriarchy (see D. R. Pérez 2002).

7. Caló is an argot originating with the Gypsies in Spain and several Indian languages. Caló can be heard in the capital of Mexico and in other large cities of Latin American countries. In the United States, while Chicano youth have transformed the vocabulary and idioms to include many Spanglish terms, caló is still used. For example, the term "cholo" is used in Peru and Los Angeles, yet the meaning has shifted. "Cholo" in Peru is derogatory, implying that one is low-class; many indigenous Peruvians are called cholo. In Los Angeles, the meaning has been turned around, and young gang members proudly claim to be cholos.

8. Norma Mendoza-Denton (1999) successfully elaborates on ethnic/racial identity of Sureñas and Norteñas. Her research examines ideology at the level of everyday practices, thus Norte (north) and Sur (south) organize themselves around concepts and displays of cultural identity—Chicana or Mexicana background. Language, ways of dressing, and even ways of walking signify one's concept of national/cultural identity.

9. I also felt the irony of the situation: the girls were not "my people" but subjects in various research projects. Rosaldo (1989) notes that accounts of the lone ethnographer in remote places and situations are part of a mythic past.

10. I will elaborate on how these contexts relate to Habermas' (1994) classic formulation of the public sphere in another chapter. It is enough here to note that the girls' participation in these public arenas arose from a concatenation of social forces that includes the ethnographic encounter and the Centro's program for youth rights, as well as the strength of Oakland's politics, where democratic institutions arising from the civil rights and identity politics movements operate as counter or subaltern public spheres (Fraser 1989 and 1992).

11. Nutini et al. (1976) found that the kinship network of compadrazgo and co-madrazgo was not only a result of Christianization. Finding many groups in central Mexico combining both indigenous and Catholic practices, he notes that the system is more than godparenting but extended relations of reciprocity through the fictive kinship network. In the girls' gang the comadrazgo system is translated from the familial, private sphere into a public domain. Comadrazgo as practiced under the Church's doctrine has been a form of survival in patriarchy. Comadrazgo has worked as an agency of socialization when women are confined to the domestic sphere. This praxis changes, however, as moderniza-

tion affects familial relations, particularly as more women become the sole head of household support in the Chicano/a community. I examine this system and its reworkings in the chapter "Affinity and Affiliation."

12. The girls, as already noted, were involved in other research studies and participated in youth group activities at other community centers found in Fruitvale. At one center they were involved in various activities whose aim was empowerment of the Chicana/o community and as a result attended youth-oriented conferences throughout the East Bay area.

13. Concerned with spectatorship in the study of film, Laura Mulvey's essay (1989) has generated a wealth of texts on the female spectator. Audience reception studies attempt to trace reading strategies and forms of subcultural resistance, thus entailing an ethnographic turn in media studies. Studies of audiences consist of qualitative analysis surveys or intensive interviews in relation to such factors as class, gender, political affiliation, ethnicity, and age (Brunsdon and Morley 1978; Hobson 1982; Radway 1984; Bobo 1988 and 1995).

14. While ethnographic audience reception studies were celebrated for "conducting in depth studies of media audiences in natural contexts" (Newcomb 1988, 242), critiques focused on the definition and constitution of audience as "community." Implicit notions of community, defined by essential categories like gender, class, and race, tend to produce overly neat descriptions which undermine the situational position and historical context of social subjects (Bergstrom and Doanne 1990).

15. As Joan Moore has argued, "gang" studies actually turn out to be studies of boys in gangs, concentrating on one gender to the exclusion of the other. Noting that there are few studies of gang girls that omit any discussion of boys, she intimates that the neglect of gender composition of the gang is systematic and structured (J. Moore 1991, 136–138). Thus, when my study focused on the universal gang, I found either little difference in the girls' responses or disinterest in my questions.

16. In *Gender and Power* (1987), R. W. Connell conceptualizes a gender regime or gender order to describe the sexual politics within any institution. Gender regimes reflect an ideology as well as articulating distinct sexual divisions of labor and behavior. Like the family and the state, "the street," a more diffuse institution, has a division of labor, a structure of power, and a structure of cathexis in which emotional and mental energy is invested in a gender dichotomy (see chapter in this study on "Affinity and Affiliation").

17. In the chapter "Cross-Sites for Cross-Talks," I engage Habermas' concept of the public sphere augmented by critiques from Nancy Fraser (1989, 1992) and Fregoso (1995b). I particularly focus on Catherine Squires' (1999) types or

genres of spheres produced by subordinated groups. The four types are: enclave, oscillating, counter or subaltern, and the parallel or ideal public sphere.

Mediating Images

1. The next chapter, "Affinity and Affiliation," draws on the fieldwork to contextualize the video, unraveling the elements of the social relationships which are made prominent by the girls. This chapter emphasizes the anthropologist as interpreter.

2. Rina Benmayor, Rosa Torruellas, and Ana Juarbe (1997) speak to vernacular discourses among a group of Puerto Rican women who develop community and a common set of interests through their daily interactions in an educational center in Harlem, New York. Their participation in the authors' life history research, combined with a Spanish literacy program, contributed to the women's individual self-images as well as a collective affirmation of their social and cultural rights in the home, in the community, and in the larger sphere of civil society.

3. Narrative structure develops not only "characters"—the performative—but additionally elaborates a plot, in which an ascending order of scenes, events, and dialogue work toward a theme or thesis of the film.

4. Because of the change in content and form, the video instructor allowed the video to extend to twelve minutes. It aired on an Oakland cable network in the summer of 1994.

5. "Film" in this chapter refers to works produced either on film or on videotape. Similarly, "filmmaking" refers to the process in which either medium is used (Rabiger 1987).

6. The method of interpretation interrelating a film's parts is obtained from Jerry W. Leach, director and coproducer of *Trobriand Cricket: An Ingenious Response to Colonialism* (1988). Leach's primer for content analysis is useful to my interpretation.

7. The last section, "Poetry," has three scenes. In the third scene, two young women introduce the topic of recreation among them. "Kickin' It" was initially introduced in the discussion of the script for the video yet eventually was dropped as an explicit intertitle.

8. The long shot of the disguised female bodies, baggy pants, and overlarge T-shirts creates another complicated imagery. The pastoral setting, which usually designates women as a part of nature, is inconsistent with the representation of urban street tough. This oppositionality of urban and pastoral further provokes the notion of otherness.

9. Joan Moore (1978) asserts that gangs have become quasi-institutionalized in socially and economically marginalized urban areas. Extending Moore's idea, the institutional effect becomes a predominant frame for considering girls in gangs. If institutions are structures for social order in dominant society, then the gang as a quasi-institution develops codes and rules for public space, bringing about order in a field of disorder, danger, and fear.

10. The computer-generated puzzle wipe becomes a trope within the video since it is used to build each scene. Since the goal of the documentary or ethnographic film is to provide basic knowledge about a cultural grouping, the puzzle as an editing device represents the goal of the young women, to reduce the puzzlement, to inform the viewer about the logic of their actual life. While the young women are not professional filmmakers and editors, the puzzle nonetheless becomes a trope about the enigma of gangs. However, the jigsaw fitting-together of the scene suggests their authority to provide understanding about gangs, to make the picture "come together."

11. Notably in the video, the young women do not speak in Spanish, Spanglish, or caló, but speak in a dialect of urban Black youth. I have seen at least two reactions to the language performance. The young women on viewing their production were quite astounded or surprised at how much they spoke like African American urban youth. They had not realized how much of the idioms, tone, and rhythm they had incorporated in their daily speech. Another reaction has come from Chicana/o youth who live in other regions of California, not Oakland or San Francisco. They have remarked upon the speech as something not within their experience of hanging with or knowing gang youth in their barrios or colonias.

12. But, unlike the urban rap group's misogyny, the form of solidarity practiced by and among the girls refuses their denigration as sexual objects. The hypermasculine stereotype of aggressive toughness that is attributed to Black and Latino men reveals a hierarchy of gender where White middle-class masculinity sets the normative. Raced bodies are the effect of power prescribing various social relations about gender. Since the stereotype of Latinas is of submissive and dominated women—and the stereotype of girls in gangs is of sexual property—in *Homie* the girls use the gangsta' stereotype and appropriate it as a counter effect. In the chapter "Affinity and Affiliation," I will explore the performance of gender in the culture of the streets and its meaning for the girls.

13. Defining the Bakhtinian notion of the authoring process, George Yúdice notes that it "consists of the ways in which sets of individuals, marked by certain features socially recognized as common to them, negotiate and manage the heterogeneity of perspectives by which they are variously imaged, valued, and devalued, in this way or that, on the basis of class, sex, race, religion, regional provenance, and other 'subject positions'" (Yúdice 1993, 219).

Affinity and Affiliation

1. When a young woman is "sexed in" as an initiation rite, the practices vary. The term is usually understood to mean that a girl has sex with a group of boys (a train or gang bang). This is not always the case. A girl can have a boyfriend who is a gang member and therefore be sexed in as a result of their sexual relationship. In other instances, when the young woman has been kickin' it and has had several boyfriends in the same gang, she becomes a member if she has proven not to cause disagreements among the boys by baiting rivalries among them, or she proves her loyalty to the gang by not having boyfriends from rival gangs (that is, she is not a gang-hopper).

2. Framing the structural properties of Chicano youth gangs that help facilitate a youth's involvement and encourage a deeper commitment, Vigil notes that the gang's age-graded nature "ensures that there is a place for everyone, even the youngest member; it allows for gang regeneration with the inclusion of each new generation; and it additionally provides the social arena for youngsters to learn and demonstrate important gang customs among themselves" (Vigil 1988, 87).

3. Klein (1971) and J. Moore in her early study of Chicano gangs (1978) find that most gang cliques are age-graded and separate. However, among girl gangs in Los Angeles sixteen years later, Moore found that "while new male cliques started every three to five years in Hoyo Maravilla, the girls' cliques were not so clearly age-graded" (J. Moore 1991, 29).

4. Carl S. Taylor in *Girls, Gangs, Women, and Drugs* (1993) offers the following description of territorial gangs: "Territorial gangs are those which have taken positions within a particular territory and claim ownership. This ownership is collectively the gang's property, territory, or person(s). The protection, maintenance, and identification of gang ownership is the bonding force for members. . . . Territory, in general, means physical land, ground or neighborhood. This general ground may have no other significance than symbolic value. The land is worthless to the outside world. Territorial gangs can be involved in criminal activity. Yet there is no rule that crime is essential to their definition. . . . Some are not successful in their quest of moving into serious crime. Yet, they will not relinquish their neighborhood fiefdom. Their power is their control over who can and cannot enter into their 'hood.'" (C. S. Taylor 1993, 16–19).

5. See also C. S. Taylor (1993), Burris-Kitchen (1997), and Venkatesh (1998).

6. Benedict Anderson notes that "the nation is always conceived as a deep, horizontal comradeship. Ultimately, it is this *fraternity* [my emphasis] that makes it possible, over the past two centuries, for so many millions of people, not so much to kill, as willingly to die for such limited imaginings" (Anderson 1983, 16). In this patriarchal vision of community the horizontal fraternity accentuates the hierarchical arrangement in which women are designated to the private,

domestic space and excluded from the public domain. Thus, women are "protected and defended" by public citizens (i.e., men).

Cross-Sites for Cross-Talks

1. See also Appadurai (1988).

2. Angela McRobbie (1991) and other researchers on girls' culture have asked for a renewed attention to domestic relations, examining the complexities between young women and the "family." Therefore an important departure for a study of girls in gangs would be ethnographic work on the relationships of the girls both at home and in public. While my fieldwork provided opportunities to investigate these two spaces, I have focused on public spaces in order to destabilize still-dominant conceptions of the family as the "root cause" of the development of gangs. Such conceptions tend to hold youth in place. My effort here, obviously a partial approach, is to dislodge these localizing habits.

3. The co-discursive partnership can be discerned through the performance of toughness and aggression for cameras, news stories, and even social science research projects. While my point is that they are co-discursive in the construction of alien(ated) otherness, I also recognize the differential power in this co-discursive participation.

4. Basic elements of Fregoso's speech have since been published (Fregoso 1995a; 1995b; 1999). While Fregoso's presentation and subsequent essays register the gang as a place of knowledge, she also calls attention to the emotional and material support that broader social networks—like that of mothers, sisters, and other female family members—provide to youth at risk. At the regional meeting she articulated the presence of girls in the public sphere through her analysis of cinema as well as through life stories. Her explication provoked the development of my work, for which I am greatly appreciative.

5. Examining boys' smart-aleck, flippant horseplay in a South Texas school, Foley (1990) understands these disruptions as mutually constructed since the construction of a gendered hierarchy is social, outside the school. The boys' horseplay silences women in higher status positions, restoring the broader social relationship of gender that is inverted temporarily during school.

6. I am indebted to WoC member A. L. Anderson for the concept and expression of "strategic identity."

7. Both MG and QG later pressed charges on the girls who assaulted them at the urging of their parents not to continue to allow the codes of the street to rule out other choices.

8. In Norma Mendoza-Denton's presentation at the NACCS conference (1994) and her essay (1999), she examines the use of Spanish as an oppositional prac-

tice among the youth she interviewed. Most of her informants identified as Sureñas and as Mexicanas. Similarly, I found that the girls I interviewed often referred to Sureños/as as Mexicanos/as or Central Americans. Predominantly identifying themselves as Chicanas, the girls of NWA rarely spoke Spanish to each other. Although many of them spoke Spanish at home with their parents, among themselves their speech was an accented urban Ebonics. When they spoke caló, it was usually in deriding the cholo image. The use of caló, in the girls' view, was old-school, old-fashioned, or identified as Sureño/a.

9. Interestingly, staff members disregarded the issue of language differences between Norte and Sur gang members. The girls had become empowered by the discourse on language and representation, and therefore they provided important knowledge to the staff members. This power/knowledge (Foucault 1980) assisted their claim as authorities. The girls' focus on language differences took an everyday practice of the Chicano/a community out of its commonsense practice. While the staff ignored and took for granted the everyday language practices of the Chicano/a community, the girls through interrogation and as authorities at the various venues had become an intelligentsia about gang life and the Chicano/a community. They began to comprehend that everyday practices were sources for interpretation and social analysis.

10. Whether the tone is tolerant or condemning, the gang member is constructed through concepts such as dysfunctional families, cultures of poverty, cultural bifurcation, peer pressure, outlaw capitalists, or organic solidarity.

11. Steven Gregory (1994) notes that the civil rights movement not only provided a vocabulary for new identities but also produced a heterogeneous array of social networks and institutions. The seventies and eighties, through repressive measures of the state against the proliferation of counter publics, reinterpreted social issues with a language of individualism and "service," thus reshaping the social justice terrain.

12. McLaughlin's (1993) explication about the dual function of the counter public spheres offers me a way to enter the debate about gangs and subaltern public spheres—to differentiate various groupings. For example, while a gang does fulfill the first function, i.e., confirming an oppositional identity, much debate centers on whether the gang could be distinguished as a subaltern public sphere. While the gang develops social identity for marginalized youth (Vigil 1988), it is also the place for members to produce and articulate hidden texts (J. Scott 1990), i.e., to complain about authority without reprisal. However, most critics consider the criminal and antisocial activities of the gang and therefore do not place it in relation to the development of democracy. Since critics focus on the first function, the gang continues to be characterized as isolated from productive social interaction and insignificant in the theorizations of the public sphere. Because gangs are affected by the broader representations—the media, public officials, police, and community—I focus on the way in which the subal-

tern speak outward in order to provide a way of reconsidering the gang. See also Cintron (1997).

13. My thanks to WoC member Catriona Esquibel, who underlined this point as we analyzed what fears might lurk in the hearts of men and women when they consider and portray girls in gangs.

14. My critique is not solely aimed at the staff members at the clinic. I consider myself very much part of the problem in attempting to visualize a better future for youth of color.

15. Jodi Dean (1995) outlines Habermas' theory of communicative action in which proficiency and skill are regulated through gender.

16. Fraser (1989, 1992) registers two types of public spheres, one, the dominant (bourgeois, male propertied) and two, the counter or subaltern. Recognizing the stratification of society, subordinated groups excluded from dominant discourses invent and circulate counter discourses so as to formulate oppositional interpretations of their identities, interests, and needs.

17. In Habermas' theorization of the ideal public sphere, everyone enters equally; vested interests are to be put aside in order to discuss and determine the common good. Recognizing that there are class inequalities, Habermas insists that in an ideal public sphere inequalities are bracketed and should not be part of the determinations of the public gathered. However, as Nancy Fraser (1989, 1992) and Fregoso (1995a, 1995b, 1999) have insisted, exclusions based on gender, race/ethnicity, and sexuality have produced the counter or subaltern public spheres that contest the straight, White, male, bourgeois public sphere.

18. In the chapter "Mediating Images: *It's a Homie Thang!*," I elaborate on the issues of respect and recognition through an examination of their vernacular poetics that implicitly address the way in which they perceive their marginalization in society.

19. Johanna Meehan (1995) explains that the experience of disrespect can cause the identity of a subject to collapse, thus those who are violated by exclusion are denied the right to interaction.

BIBLIOGRAPHY

Abrams, M. H. 1988. *A Glossary of Literary Terms.* 5th ed. New York: Holt, Rinehart, and Winston.

Abu-Lughod, Lila. 1991. "Writing against Culture." In *Recapturing Anthropology: Working in the Present,* edited by R. Fox, 137–162. Santa Fe, N.M.: School of American Research.

Acker, Joan, Kate Barry, and Joke Esseveld. 1983. "Objectivity and Truth: Problems in Doing Feminist Research." *Women's Studies International Forum 6,* no. 4: 423–435.

Acuña, Rodolfo. 2000. *Occupied America: A History of Chicanos.* 4th ed. New York: Longman.

Agar, Michael. 1983. "Ethnography and Cognition." In *Contemporary Field Research: A Collection of Readings,* edited by R. M. Emerson, 68–77. Reissue, Prospect Heights, Ill.: Waveland Press, 1988.

Aguilar, John L. 1988. "Insider Research: An Ethnography of a Debate." In *Anthropologists at Home in North America: Methods and Issues in the Study of One's Own Society,* edited by D. A. Messerschmidt. New York: Cambridge University Press.

Almaguer, Tomás. 1994. *Racial Fault Lines: The Historical Origins of White Supremacy in California.* Berkeley: University of California Press.

Althusser, Louis. 1971. "Ideology and Ideological State Apparatuses: (Notes towards an Investigation) (January–April 1969)." In *Lenin and Philosophy and Other Essays,* translated by Ben Brewster, 174–177. New York: Monthly Review Press.

Amit-Talai, Vered. 1995. "In the Waltz of Sociability: Intimacy, Dislocation, and Friendship in a Quebec High School." In *Youth Cultures: A Cross-cultural Perspective,* edited by Vered Amit-Talai and Helena Wulff. New York: Routledge.

Anderson, Benedict. 1983. *Imagined Communities: Reflections on the Origin and Spread of Nationalism.* London: Verso.

Appadurai, Arjun. 1988. "Putting Hierarchy in Its Place." *Cultural Anthropology 3,* no. 1: 36–49.

Appadurai, Arjun, Lauren Berlant, Carol A. Breckenridge, and Manthia Diawarain, editors. 1994. Special issue, "The Black Public Sphere." *Public Culture: Society for Transnational Cultural Studies 7,* no. 1 (fall).

Asch, Timothy, John Marshall, and Peter Spier. 1973. "Ethnographic Film: Structure and Function." *Annual Review of Anthropology 2:* 179–187.

Baca-Zinn, Maxine. 1979. "Field Research in Minority Communities: Ethical, Methodological, and Political Observations by an Insider." *Social Problems* 27, no. 2: 209–219.

Baca-Zinn, Maxine, and Bonnie Thornton Dill, editors. 1994. *Women of Color in U.S. Society.* Philadelphia: Temple University Press.

Back, Les. 1993. "Gendered Participation: Masculinity and Fieldwork in a London Adolescent Community." In *Gendered Fields: Women, Men, and Ethnography,* edited by Daniel Bell, Pat Caplan, and Jahan Karin, 215–233. New York: Routledge.

Barthes, Roland. 1990. *Mythologies,* translated by Annette Lavers. New York: Noonday Press.

Baugh, John. 1983. *Black Street Speech: Its History, Structure, and Survival.* Austin: University of Texas Press.

Becker, Howard Saul. 1963. *Outsiders: Studies in the Sociology of Deviance.* London: Free Press of Glencoe.

Bejar, Ruth. 1993. *Translated Woman: Crossing the Border with Esperanza's Story.* Boston: Beacon Press.

Bell, Daniel, Pat Caplan, and Jahan Karin, editors. 1993. *Gendered Fields: Women, Men, and Ethnography.* New York: Routledge.

Benmayor, Rina, Rosa M. Torruellas, and Ana L. Juarbe. 1997. "Claiming Cultural Citizenship in East Harlem: 'Si esto puede ayudar a la comunidad mía . . .'" In *Latino Cultural Citizenship: Claiming Identity, Space, and Rights,* edited by William V. Flores and Rina Benmayor, 152–209. Boston: Beacon Press.

Berger, Peter, and Thomas Luckmann. 1966. *The Social Construction of Reality: A Treatise in the Sociology of Knowledge.* New York: Doubleday, Anchor Books.

Bergstrom, Janet, and Mary Ann Doanne. 1990. "The Female Spectator: Contexts and Directions." *Camera Obscura* 20–21: 5–27.

Bhabha, Homi. 1994. *The Location of Culture.* New York: Routledge.

Bhavnani, Kum-Kum. 1988. "Empowerment and Social Research: Some Comments." *Text* 1, no. 2: 41–50.

———. 1991. *Talking Politics: A Psychological Framing for Views from Youth in Britain.* European Monographs in Social Psychology. New York: Cambridge University Press.

Bobo, Jacqueline. 1988. "The Color Purple: Black Women as Cultural Readers." In *Female Spectators: Looking at Film and Television,* edited by Deidre Pribram. London: Verso.

———. 1995. *Black Women as Cultural Readers.* New York: Columbia University Press.

Breslauer, Jan. 1992. "Hangin' with the Homegirls: A Woman Director Has a New Take on Gangs." *Los Angeles Times,* Sunday, July 26, calendar section, 3.

Brown, Lyn Mikel. 1991. "Telling a Girl's Life: Self-Authorization as a Form of Resistance." In *Women, Girls, and Psychotherapy: Reframing Resistance,* edited by Carol Gilligan, Annie G. Rogers, and Deborah L. Tolman, 71–86. New York: Harrington Park Press.

Bruner, Edward M. 1986. "Ethnography as Narrative." In *The Anthropology of Experience,* edited by Victor W. Turner and Edward M. Bruner, 139–155. Urbana: University of Illinois Press.

Brunsdon, Charlotte, and David Morley, editors. 1978. *Everyday Television: "Nationwide."* London: British Film Institute.

Buriel, Raymond. 1984. "Integration with Traditional Mexican-American Culture and Sociocultural Adjustment." In *Chicano Psychology,* edited by Joe L. Martínez Jr. and Richard H. Mendoza, 95–130. New York: Academic Press.

Burawoy, Michael, Alice Burton, Ann Arneet Ferguson, Kathryn J. Fox, Joshua Gamson, Nadine Gartrell, Leslie Hurst, Charles Kurzman, Leslie Salzinger, Josepha Schiffman, and Shirori Ui. 1991. *Ethnography Unbound: Power and Resistance in the Modern Metropolis.* Berkeley: University of California Press.

Burris-Kitchen, Deborah. 1997. *Female Gang Participation: The Role of African-American Women in the Informal Drug Economy and Gang Activities.* Women's Studies, vol. 17. Lewiston, N.Y.: Edwin Mellen Press.

Butler, Judith. 1990. *Gender Trouble: Feminism and the Subversion of Identity.* New York, London: Routledge.

———. 1993. *Bodies That Matter: On the Discursive Limits of "Sex."* New York: Routledge

Calderón, Hector, and José David Saldívar, editors. 1991. *Criticism in the Borderlands: Studies in Chicano Literature, Culture and Ideology.* Durham, N.C.: Duke University Press.

Calhoun, Craig. 1994. *Nationalism and the Public Sphere.* Lectures and Papers in Ethnicity, no. 4. Toronto: University of Toronto Press.

———, editor. 1992. *Habermas and the Public Sphere.* 3d printing, Cambridge: Massachusetts Institute of Technology, 1994.

Campbell, Anne. 1990. "Female Participation in Gangs," In *Gangs in America,* edited by C. Ronald Huff, 163–182. Newbury Park, Calif.: Sage Publications.

———. 1991. *The Girls in the Gang.* 2d ed. Cambridge, Mass.: Blackwell Publishers.

———. 1993. *Men, Women, and Aggression.* New York: Basic Books.

Caputo, Virginia. 1995. "Anthropology's Silent 'Others': A Consideration of Some Conceptual and Methodological Issues for the Study of Youth and Children's Cultures." In *Youth Cultures: A Cross-cultural Perspective,* edited by Vered Amit-Talai and Helena Wulff, 19–42. New York: Routledge.

Carter, Erica, James Donald, and Judith Squires, editors. 1993. *Space and Place: Theories of Identity and Location.* London: Lawrence and Wishart.

Castañeda, Antonia I. 1992. "Women of Color and the Rewriting of Western History: The Discourse, Politics, and Decolonization of History." *Pacific Historical Review* 61, no. 4: 501–533.

———. 1993. "Sexual Violence in the Politics and Policies of Conquest: Amerindian Women and the Spanish Conquest of Alta California." In *Building with Our Hands: New Directions in Chicana Studies,* edited by Adela de la Torre and Beatríz Pesquera, 15–33. Berkeley: University of California Press.

Chabram, Angie. 1990. "Chicana/o Studies as Oppositional Ethnography." *Cultural Studies* 4, no. 3 (October): 228–247.

———. 1991. "Conceptualizing Chicano Critical Discourse." In *Criticism in the Borderlands: Studies in Chicano Literature, Culture and Ideology*, edited by Hector Calderón and José Saldívar, 127–148. Durham, N.C.: Duke University Press.

Chabram, Angie, Rosa Linda Fregoso, and Lawrence Grossberg, editors. 1990. Special issue, "Chicana/o Cultural Representations: Reframing Alternative Critical Discourses." *Cultural Studies* 4, no. 3 (October).

Chalfen, Richard. 1987. *Snapshot Versions of Life*. Bowling Green, Ky.: Bowling Green State University Popular Press.

———. 1991. *Turning Leaves: The Photograph Collections of Two Japanese American Families*. Albuquerque: University of New Mexico Press.

Chow, Rey. 1993. *Writing Diaspora: Tactics of Intervention in Contemporary Cultural Studies*. Bloomington: Indiana University Press.

———. 1995. *Primitive Passions: Visuality, Sexuality, Ethnography, and Contemporary Chinese Cinema*. New York: Columbia University Press.

Cintron, Ralph. 1997. *Angels' Town: Chero Ways, Gang Life, and Rhetorics of the Everyday*. Boston: Beacon Press.

Clifford, James. 1983. "On Ethnographic Authority." *Representations* 1, no. 2 (spring): 118–146.

———. 1986. "Introduction: Partial Truths." In *Writing Culture: The Poetics and Politics of Ethnography*, edited by J. Clifford and George E. Marcus. Berkeley: University of California Press.

———. 1988. *The Predicament of Culture: Twentieth-Century Ethnography, Literature, and Art*. Cambridge, Mass.: Harvard University Press.

———. 1989. "Notes on Travel and Theory." In "Traveling Theories, Traveling Theorists," special edition, edited by James Clifford and Vivek Dhareshwar. *Inscriptions* 5: 177–188.

———. 1997. *Routes: Travel and Translation in the Late Twentieth Century*. Cambridge, Mass.: Harvard University Press.

Clifford, James, and George E. Marcus, editors. 1986. *Writing Culture: The Poetics and Politics of Ethnography*. Berkeley: University of California Press.

Cloward, Richard A., and Lloyd E. Ohlin. 1960. *Delinquency and Opportunity: A Theory of Delinquent Gangs*. New York: Free Press.

Cohen, Anthony. 1992. "Self-conscious Anthropology." In *Anthropology and Autobiography*, edited by Judith Okely and Helen Callaway, 221–241. New York: Routledge.

Connell, R. W. 1987. *Gender and Power: Society, the Person, and Sexual Politics*. Stanford, Calif.: Stanford University Press.

Contreras, Maximiliano. 1982. *Crossing: A Comparative Analysis of the Mexicano, Mexican-American, and Chicano*. San Pedro, Calif.: Travel/Study Inc.

Córdova, Teresa. 1994. "Roots and Resistance: The Emergent Writings of Twenty Years of Chicana Feminist Struggle." In *Handbook of Hispanic Cultures in the United States: Sociology*, edited by Félix Padilla, 175–202. Houston: Arte Público Press.

Córdova, Teresa, Norma Cantú, Gilberto Cardenas, Juan Garcia, and Christine M. Sierra, editors. 1993. *Chicana Voices: Intersections of Class, Race, and*

Gender. Proceedings of the National Association for Chicano Studies 1984 annual conference. Albuquerque: University of New Mexico Press.

Corrigan, Paul. 1991. "Doing Nothing." In *Resistance through Rituals: Youth Subcultures in Post-war Britain,* edited by Stuart Hall and Tony Jefferson, 8th ed. Cambridge, Mass.: Harper Collins Academic.

Cosgrove, Stuart. 1989. "The Zoot Suit and Style Warfare." In *Zoot Suits and Second-hand Dresses,* edited by Angela McRobbie, 3–22. Winchester, Mass.: Unwin Hyman.

Crapanzano, Vincent. 1980. *Tuhami: Portrait of a Moroccan.* Chicago: University of Chicago Press.

Crawford, Peter Ian, and David Turton, editors. 1992. *Film as Ethnography.* New York: Manchester University Press.

Cummings, Scott, and Daniel J. Monit, editors. 1993. *Gangs: The Origins and Impact of Contemporary Youth Gangs in the United States.* SUNY Series on Urban Public Policy. Albany: State University of New York Press.

Davis, Angela Y. 1981. *Women, Race, and Class.* New York: Random House.

Davis, Mike. 1985. "Urban Renaissance and the Spirit of Postmodernism." *Left Review* 152: 106–113.

———. 2000. *Magical Urbanism: Latinos Reinvent the U.S. City.* New York: Verso.

Dean, Jodi. 1995. "Discourse in Different Voices." In *Feminists Read Habermas: Gendering the Subject of Discourse,* edited by Johanna Meehan, 205–230. New York: Routledge.

De Certeau, Michel. 1984. *The Practice of Everyday Life.* Berkeley: University of California Press.

de la Torre, Adela, and Beatríz Pesquera, editors. 1993. *Building With Our Hands: New Directions in Chicana Studies.* Berkeley: University of California Press.

de Lauretis, Teresa. 1989. "The Violence of Rhetoric: Considerations on Representation and Gender." In *The Violence of Representation: Literature and the History of Violence,* edited by Nancy Armstrong and Leonard Tennenhouse, 239–258. New York: Routledge.

del Fuego, Laura. 1989. *Maravilla.* Encino, Calif.: Floricanto Press.

Delpit, Lisa, and Joanne Kilgour Dowdy, editors. 2002. *The Skin That We Speak: Thoughts on Language and Culture in the Classroom.* New York: New Press.

Dietrich, Lisa Christine. 1996. "Coming of Age in the Barrio: Girls, Gangs, and Growing-Up." Ph.D. diss., University of California, San Diego.

Dimitrov, Georgi. 1945. *The United Front against Fascism.* 5th ed. New York: New Century Publishers.

Douglas, Mary. 1966. *Purity and Danger: An Analysis of the Concepts of Pollution and Taboo.* New York: Routledge, ARK, 1989.

du Gay, Paul, Stuart Hall, Linda Janes, Hugh Mackay, and Keith Negus. 1997. *Doing Cultural Studies: The Story of the Sony Walkman.* Culture, Media, and Identities Series, vol. 1. London: Sage Publications with Open University Press.

Duvignaud, Jean. 1970. *Change at Shebika: Report from a North African Village,* translated by Frances Frenaye. New York: Pantheon Books.

Emerson, Robert M., editor. 1988. *Contemporary Field Research: A Collection of Readings.* Prospect Heights, Ill.: Waveland Press.

Epskamp, Kees P. 1983. "Film Literacy and Importance in the Production of Instructive Films To Be Used in Third World Countries: A Paper on Applied Visual Anthropology." In *Methodology in Anthropological Filmmaking: Papers on the IUAES-Intercongress, 1981,* edited by Nico C. Bogaart and Henk W. E. R. Ketelaar, 161–175. Gottingen, Germany: Edition Herodot.

Erlanger, Howard S. 1979. "Estrangement, Machismo, and Gang Violence." *Social Science Quarterly* 60, no. 2 (September): 235–248.

Faderman, Lillian. 1981. *Surpassing the Love of Men: Romantic Friendship and Love between Women from the Renaissance to the Present.* New York: William Morrow.

Fainstein, Susan S., and Norman Fainstein. 1983. "Economic Change, National Policy, and the System of Cities." In *Restructuring the City,* edited by Susan S. Fainstein and Norman I. Fainstein, 1–26. New York: Longman.

———, editors. 1974. *Urban Political Movements.* Englewood Cliffs, N.J.: Prentice-Hall.

Fantasia, Rick. 1989. *Cultures of Solidarity: Consciousness, Action and Contemporary American Workers.* Berkeley: University of California Press.

Flores, William V., and Rina Benmayor, editors. 1997. *Latino Cultural Citizenship: Claiming Identity, Space, and Rights.* Boston: Beacon Press.

Foley, Douglas E. 1990. *Learning Capitalist Culture: Deep in the Heart of Tejas.* Philadelphia: University of Philadelphia Press.

Foucault, Michel. 1980. *Power/Knowledge: Selected Interviews and Other Writings, 1972–1977,* edited and translated by Colin Gordon, Leo Marshall, John Mephan, and Kate Soper. New York: Harvester Press.

Fraser, Nancy. 1989. *Unruly Practices: Power, Discourse, and Gender in Contemporary Social Theory.* Minneapolis: University of Minnesota Press.

———. 1992. "Rethinking the Public Sphere: A Contribution to the Critique of Actually Existing Democracy." In *Habermas and the Public Sphere,* edited by Craig Calhoun, 109–142. 3d printing, Cambridge: Massachusetts Institute of Technology, 1994.

Fraser, Steven, and Gary Gerstle, editors. 1989. *The Rise and Fall of the New Deal Order, 1930–1980.* Princeton, N.J.: Princeton University Press.

Fregoso, Rosa Linda. 1993. *The Bronze Screen: Chicana and Chicano Film Culture.* Minneapolis: University of Minnesota Press.

———. 1995a. "Hanging out with the Homegirls? Allison Anders's *Mi Vida Loca.*" *Cineaste* 36–37. http://search.epnet.com/direct.asp?an=950824629 2&db=aph

———. 1995b. "Pachucas, Cholas, and Homegirls: Taking over the Public Sphere." *California History* (fall): 316–327.

———. 1999. "Re-imagining Chicana Urban Identities in the Public Sphere, cool chuca style." In *Between Woman and Nation: Nationalisms, Transnational Feminisms, and the State,* edited by Caren Kaplan, Norma Alarcón, and Minoo Moallem. Durham, N.C.: Duke University Press.

Freire, Paulo. 1970. *Pedagogy of the Oppressed,* translated by Myra Bergman Ramos. 20th anniversary ed. New York: Continuum, 1995.

Gallegos, Angela. 1994. "A Review of Literature on Chicana/Latina Adolescents." Panel presentation at the National Association for Chicano/Chicana Studies California FOCO regional conference, University of California at Santa Cruz, April.

Geertz, Clifford. 1973. *The Interpretation of Cultures.* New York: Basic Books.

———. 1983. *Local Knowledge: Further Essays in Interpretive Anthropology.* New York: Basic Books.

Gilligan, Carol. 1992. *In a Different Voice: Psychological Theory and Women's Development.* Cambridge: Harvard University Press.

Gilroy, Paul. 1987. *Ain't No Black in the Union Jack: The Cultural Politics of Race and Nation.* London: Hutchinson.

———. 1993a. *The Black Atlantic: Modernity and Double Consciousness.* Cambridge: Harvard University Press.

———. 1993b. *Small Acts: Thoughts on the Politics of Black Cultures.* New York: Serpent's Tail.

Gitlin, Todd. 1987. *The Sixties: Years of Hope, Days of Rage.* Toronto: Bantam.

Gluck, Sherna Berger, and Daphne Patai, editors. 1991. *Women's Words: The Feminist Practice of Oral History.* New York: Routledge, Chapman and Hall.

Goffman, Erving. 1959. *The Presentation of Self in Everyday Life.* Garden City, N.Y.: Doubleday.

———. 1963. *Behavior in Public Places: Notes on the Social Organization of Gatherings.* New York: Free Press of Glencoe.

Gómez-Quinoñez, Juan. 1990. *Chicano Politics: Reality and Promise, 1940–1990.* 2d printing, Albuquerque: University of New Mexico Press, 1992.

González, Alfredo Guerra. 1981. *Mexicano/Chicano Gangs in Los Angeles: A Sociohistorical Case Study.* Ann Arbor, Mich.: University Microfilms.

González, Rafael Jesús. 1988. "Pachuco: The Birth of a Creole Language." In *Perspectives in Mexican American Studies,* edited by José R. Reyna, 75–88. Issue title "Readings in Southwestern Folklore." Tucson: University of Arizona Mexican American Studies and Research Center.

Grant, Barry Keith, and Jeannette Sloniowski, editors. 1998. *Documenting the Documentary: Close Readings of Documentary Film and Video.* Detroit: Wayne State University Press.

Grant, Linda. 1994. "Helpers, Enforcers, and Go-Betweens: Black Females in Elementary School Classrooms." In *Women of Color in U.S. Society,* edited by Maxine Baca-Zinn and Bonnie Thornton Dill, 43–64. Philadelphia: Temple University Press.

Gray, Herman. 1995. *Watching Race: Television and the Struggle for "Blackness."* Minneapolis: University of Minnesota Press.

Gregory, Steven. 1994. "Race, Identity and Political Activism: The Shifting Contours of the African American Public Sphere." *Public Culture* 7, no. 4: 47–164.

———. 1998. *Black Corona: Race and the Politics of Place in an Urban Community.* Princeton, N.J.: Princeton University Press.

Griffin, Christine. 1988. "Youth Research: Young Women and the "Gang of Lads" Model." In *European Contributions to Youth Research,* Raedarius

Books, vol. 3, edited by Jan Hazekamp, Wim Meeus, and Yolanda te Poel. Amsterdam: Free University Press, 1988.

———. 1993. *Representations of Youth: The Study of Youth and Adolescence in Britain and America.* Cambridge, Mass.: Polity Press.

Griffith, Beatrice. 1948. *American Me.* Boston: Houghton Mifflin.

Grossberg, Lawrence. 1992. *We Gotta Get out of This Place: Popular Conservatism and Postmodern Culture.* London: Routledge.

Grossberg, Lawrence, Cary Nelson, and Paula Treichler, editors. 1992. *Cultural Studies.* New York: Routledge.

Gusfield, Joseph R. 1981. *The Culture of Public Problems: Drinking-Driving and the Symbolic Order.* Chicago: University of Chicago Press.

———. 1996. *Contested Meanings: The Construction of Alcohol Problems.* Madison: University of Wisconsin Press.

Gutiérrez, Ramón A. 1991. *When Jesus Came, the Corn Mothers Went Away: Marriage, Sexuality, and Power in New Mexico, 1500–1846.* Stanford, Calif.: Stanford University Press.

Habermas, Jürgen. 1994. *The Structural Transformation of the Public Sphere: An Inquiry into a Category of Bourgeois Society,* translated by Thomas Burger with assistance of Frederick Lawrence. Cambridge: Massachusetts Institute of Technology Press.

Hagedorn, John. 1988. *People and Folks: Gangs, Crime, and the Underclass in a Rustbelt City.* Chicago: Lake View Press.

Hall, Stuart. 1980. "Encoding and Decoding." In *Culture, Media, Language,* edited by Stuart Hall, Dorothy Hobson, Andrew Lowe, and Paul Willis. 129–138. London: Hutchinson.

———. 1992. "New Ethnicities." In *'Race,' Culture, and Difference,* edited by James Donald and Ali Rattansi, 252–259. London: Sage Publications.

———, editor. 1997. *Representation: Cultural Representation and Signifying Practices.* London: Sage Publications.

Hall, Stuart, and Tony Jefferson, editors. 1975. *Resistance through Rituals: Youth Subcultures in Post-war Britain,* 8th ed. Cambridge, Mass.: Harper Collins Academic.

Hanson, Kitty. 1964. *Rebels in the Streets: The Story of New York's Girl Gangs.* Englewood Cliffs, N.J.: Prentice-Hall.

Hansot, Elisabeth. 1993. "Misperceptions of Gender and Youth: Learning Together, Learning Apart." In *Identity and Inner-city Youth: Beyond Ethnicity and Gender,* edited by Shirley Brice Heath and Milbrey W. McLaughlin. New York: Teachers College Press.

Harding, Susan. 1991. "Representing Fundamentalism: The Problem of the Repugnant Cultural Other." *Social Research* 58, no. 2 (summer): 373–393.

Harris, Mary. 1988. *Cholas: Latino Girls and Gangs.* New York: AMS Press.

Harrison, Faye, editor. 1991. *Decolonizing Anthropology: Moving Further Toward an Anthropology for Liberation.* Washington, D.C.: Association of Black Anthropologists, American Anthropological Association.

Harvey, David. 1980. *The Condition of Postmodernity.* Paperback ed. Cambridge, Mass.: Blackwell Publishers, 1990.

———. 1995. "Militant Particularism and Global Ambition: The Conceptual

Politics of Place, Space, and Environment in the Work of Raymond Williams." *Social Text* 46 (spring): 69–98.

Harvey, Penelope, and Peter Gow, editors. 1994. *Sex and Violence: Issues in Representation and Experience.* New York: Routledge.

Hastrup, Kirsten. 1992. "Writing Ethnography: State of the Art." In *Anthropology and Autobiography,* edited by Judith Okley and Helen Callaway, 116–133. New York: Routledge.

Hayes, Edward C. 1972. *Power Structure and Urban Policy: Who Rules in Oakland?* New York: McGraw-Hill.

Heath, Shirley Brice, and Milbrey W. McLaughlin. 1993. "Ethnicity and Gender in Theory and Practice: The Youth Perspective." In *Identity and Inner-city Youth: Beyond Ethnicity and Gender,* edited by Heath and McLaughlin, 13–35. New York: Teachers College Press.

Hebdige, Dick. 1979. *Subculture: The Meaning of Style.* Reprint, New York: Routledge, 1991.

Hess, Beth B., and Myra Marx Ferree, editors. 1987. *Analyzing Gender: A Handbook of Social Science Research.* Newbury Park, Calif.: Sage Publications.

Hinojosa, María. 1995. *Crews: Gang Members Talk to Maria Hinojosa.* New York: Harcourt Brace.

Hobson, Dorothy. 1982. *"Crossroads": The Drama of Soap Opera.* London: Methuen.

Hockings, Paul, editor. 1995. *Principles of Visual Anthropology.* 2d ed. New York: Mouton de Gruyter.

Hondagneu-Sotelo, Pierrette. 1997. "The History of Mexican Undocumented Settlement in the U.S." In *Challenging Fronteras: Structuring Latina and Latino Lives in the U.S.,* edited by Mary Romero, Pierrette Hondagneu-Sotelo, and Vilma Ortiz. New York: Routledge.

Horowitz, Ruth. 1983. *Honor and the American Dream: Culture and Identity in a Chicano Community.* New Brunswick, N.J.: Rutgers University Press.

Howell, Joseph T. 1973. *Hard Living on Clay Street: Portraits of Blue Collar Families.* Garden City, N.Y.: Anchor Press.

Huff, C. Ronald, editor. 1990. *Gangs in America.* Newbury Park, Calif.: Sage Publications.

Hymes, Dell, editor. 1972. *Reinventing Anthropology.* New York: Pantheon Books.

Jacobson, David. 1991. *Reading Ethnography.* Albany: State University of New York Press.

Jameson, Fredric. 1981. *The Political Unconscious: Narrative as a Socially Symbolic Act.* Ithaca, N.Y.: Cornell University Press.

Jankowski, Martin Sanchez. 1991. *Islands in the Street: Gangs and Urban Society.* Berkeley: University of California Press.

Johnson, Marilynn S. 1993. *The Second Gold Rush: Oakland and the East Bay in World War II.* Berkeley: University of California Press.

Jordan, Glenn H. 1991. "On Ethnography in an Intertexual Situation: Reading Narratives or Deconstructing Discourse?" In *Decolonizing Anthropology,* edited by Faye V. Harrison, 42–67. Washington, D.C.: Association of Black Anthropologists, American Anthropological Association.

Kaplan, Caren, and Inderpal Grewal. 1994. "Transnational Feminist Cultural Studies: Beyond the Marxism/Poststructuralism/Feminism Divides." *Positions* 2, no. 2 (fall): 430–445.

Kaplan, E. Ann. 1983. *Women and Film.* New York: Methuen.

———. 1987. *Rocking around the Clock: Music Television, Postmodernism, and Consumer Culture.* New York: Methuen.

———. 1988. "Theories and Strategies of the Feminist Documentary." In *New Challenges for Documentary,* edited by Alan Rosenthal, 78–102. Berkeley: University of California Press.

Katz, Jack. 1988. *Seductions of Crime: Moral and Sensual Attractions in Doing Evil.* New York: Harper, Basic Books.

Katz, Michael B. 1989. *The Undeserving Poor: From the War on Poverty to the War on Welfare.* New York: Pantheon Books.

———, editor. 1993. *The Underclass Debate: Views from History.* Princeton, N.J.: Princeton University Press.

Kingsolver, Anne. 1992. "Five Women Negotiating the Meaning of Negotiation." *Anthropological Quarterly* 65, no. 3 (July): 101–104.

Klein, Malcolm W. 1971. *Street Gangs and Street Workers.* Englewood Cliffs, N.J.: Prentice-Hall.

Knox, George W. 1991. *An Introduction to Gangs.* Barrien Springs, Mich.: Vande Vere Publishing.

Kondo, Dorinne K. 1990. *Crafting Selves: Power, Gender, and Discourses of Identity in a Japanese Workplace.* Chicago: University of Chicago Press.

Leach, Jerry W. 1988. "Structure and Message in Trobriand Cricket." In *Anthropological Filmmaking: Anthropological Perspectives on the Production of Film and Video for General Public Audiences,* edited by J. R. Rollwagen. Philadelphia: Harwood Academic Publishers.

Lefebvre, Henri. 1974. *The Production of Space,* translated by Donald Nicholoson-Smith. 4th ed. Cambridge, Mass.: Blackwell Publishers, 1994.

Lévi-Strauss, Claude. 1949. *The Elementary Structures of Kinship.* Rev. ed. Boston: Beacon Press, 1969.

Lewis, Lisa A. 1990. *Gender Politics and MTV: Voicing the Difference.* Philadelphia: Temple University Press.

Limon, José E. 1991. "Representation, Ethnicity, and the Precursory Ethnography: Notes of a Native Anthropologist." In *Recapturing Anthropology: Working in the Present,* edited by Richard Fox. Santa Fe, N.M.: School of American Research.

———. 1994. *Dancing with the Devil: Society and Cultural Poetics in Mexican American South Texas.* Madison: University of Wisconsin Press.

Lin, Paul Ming-Chang. 1963. "Voluntary Kinship and Voluntary Association in a Mexican-American Community." Master's thesis, University of Kansas.

Llewelyn-Davies, Melissa. 1981. "Women, Warriors, and Patriarchs." In *Sexual Meanings, the Cultural Construction of Gender and Sexuality,* edited by Sherry B. Ortner and Harriet Whitehead, 330–358. Cambridge and New York: Cambridge University Press.

Lopez, José. 1988–1990. "The Gangs of Orange County: A Critique and Synthesis of Social Policy." *Aztlán* 19, no. 1 (spring): 125–146.

————. 1991. "Profiles of Vengeance: In Search of the Chicano Gang World-view." *Mexican Studies/Estudios Mexicanos* 7, no. 2 (summer): 319–329.

Lopez, José, and Alfredo Mirandé. 1992. "Chicano Urban Youth Gangs: A Critical Analysis of a Social Problem." *Latino Studies Journal* 3, no. 3 (September): 15–28.

Lubiano, Wahneema. 1998. "Black Nationalism and Black Common Sense: Policing Ourselves and Others." In *The House that Race Built: Original Essays by Toni Morrison, Angela Y. Davis, Cornel West, and Others on Black Americans and Politics in America Today,* edited and with introduction by Wahneema Lubiano, 232–252. New York: Vintage.

Lujan, Lori. 1995. "A Short History of the Mexican-American Presence in Oakland." In *Chicano/Mexicano Traditional and Contemporary Arts and Folklife in Oakland,* edited by Willie R. Collins. Oakland, Calif.: Cultural Arts Division, City of Oakland.

Lutz, Catherine, and Jane Collins. 1994. "The Photograph as an Intersection of Gazes: The Example of *National Geographic.*" In *Visualizing Theory,* edited by Lucien Taylor, 363–384. New York: Routledge.

Maanen, John Van. 1988. *Tales of the Field: On Writing Ethnography.* Chicago: University of Chicago Press.

MacDougall, David. 1994. "Whose Story Is It?" In *Visualizing Theory,* edited by Lucien Taylor, 27–36. New York: Routledge.

MacLeod, Jay. 1987. *Ain't No Makin' It: Leveled Aspirations in a Low-Income Neighborhood.* Boulder, Colo.: Westview Press.

Madrid, Arturo. 1973. "In Search of the Authentic Pachuco: An Interpretive Essay." *Aztlán* 4, no. 1: 31–60.

Maher, Lisa, and Richard Curtis. 1992. "In Search of the Female Urban Gangsta: Change, Culture, and Crack Cocaine." In *The Criminal Justice System and Women: Offenders, Victims, and Workers,* edited by Barbara Raffel-Price and J. Sokoloff, 2d ed., 32–67. New York: McGraw-Hill, 1995.

Mallon, Florencia E. 1994. "The Promise and Dilemma of Subaltern Studies: Perspectives from Latin American History." *American Historical Review* 99, no. 5 (December): 1491–1515.

Manis, Jerome G., and Bernard N. Meltzer. 1978. *Symbolic Interaction: A Reader in Social Psychology.* 3d ed. Boston: Allyn and Bacon.

Marazzi, Antonio. 1988. "Ethnological and Anthropological Film: Production, Distribution and Consumption." In *Cinematographic Theory and New Dimensions in Ethnographic Film,* edited by Paul Hockings and Yasuhiro Omori, 111–134. Senri Ethnological Studies, no. 24. Osaka, Japan: National Museum of Ethnology.

Marcus, George, and Michael Fischer. 1986. *Anthropology as Cultural Critique: An Experimental Moment in the Human Sciences.* Chicago: University of Chicago Press.

Martin, Luther H., Huck Gutman, and Patrick H. Hutton, editors. 1988. *Technologies of the Self: A Seminar with Michel Foucault.* Amherst: University of Massachusetts Press.

Martinez, Joe L. Jr., and Richard H. Mendoza, editors. 1984. *Chicano Psychology.* 2d ed. New York: Academic Press.

Mazón, Mauricio. 1984. *The Zoot-Suit Riots: The Psychology of Symbolic Annihilation.* Austin: University of Texas Press.

McCorkle, Richard, and Terance D. Miethe. 2002. *Panic: The Social Construction of the Street Gang Problem.* Upper Saddle River, N.J.: Prentice-Hall.

McLaughlin, Lisa. 1993. "Feminism, the Public Sphere, Media, and Democracy." *Media, Culture, and Society* 15, no. 4 (October): 599–620. http://search.epnet.com/direct.asp?an=9402181057&db=aph

McRobbie, Angela. 1984. "Dance and Social Fantasy." In *Gender and Generation,* edited by Angela McRobbie and Mica Nava. London: Macmillan.

———. 1991. *Feminism and Youth Culture: From Jackie to Just Seventeen.* Boston: Unwin Hyman.

———. 1994. *Postmodernism and Popular Culture.* New York: Routledge.

McWilliams, Carey. 1949. *North from Mexico: The Spanish-Speaking People of the United States.* Reprint, New York: Greenwood Press, 1968.

Mead, Margaret. 1974. "Visual Anthropology in a Discipline of Words." In *Principles of Visual Anthropology,* edited by Paul Hockings. 2d ed. New York: Mouton de Gruyter, 1995.

Meehan, Johanna. 1995. "Autonomy, Recognition, and Respect." In *Feminists Read Habermas: Gendering the Subject of Discourse,* edited by Johanna Meehan, 231–246. New York: Routledge.

Mendoza, Richard H. 1984. "Acculturation and Sociocultural Variability." In *Chicano Psychology,* edited by Joe L. Martínez Jr. and Richard H. Mendoza. New York: Academic Press.

Mendoza-Denton, Norma. 1994. "Intraethnic and Interlinguistic Rivalries: Language Attitudes by Chicana High School Students." Panel presentation at the National Association for Chicano/Chicana Studies California FOCO regional conference, University of California at Santa Cruz, April.

———. 1999. "Fighting Words: Latina Girls, Gangs, and Language Attitudes." In *Speaking Chicana: Voice, Power and Identity,* edited by D. Letticia Galindo and María Dolores González. Tucson: University of Arizona Press.

Mercer, Kobena. 1994. *Welcome to the Jungle: New Positions in Black Cultural Studies.* New York: Routledge.

Merton, Robert K. 1963. *Social Theory and Social Structure.* Rev. ed. Glencoe, Ill.: Free Press.

———. 1974. "Insiders and Outsiders: A Chapter in the Sociology of Knowledge." *American Journal of Sociology* 78 (July): 9–48.

Milner, Andrew. 1994. *Contemporary Cultural Theory.* London: University College London.

Mirandé, Alfredo. 1985. *The Chicano Experience: An Alternative Perspective.* Notre Dame, Ind.: University of Notre Dame Press.

Mohanty, Chandra. 1991. "Under Western Eyes: Feminist Scholarship and Colonial Discourses." In *Third World Women and the Politics of Feminism,* edited by C. Mohanty, Ann Russo, and Lourdes Torres, 51–80. Bloomington: Indiana University Press.

Molina, Papusa. 1990. "Recognizing, Accepting, and Celebrating Our Differences." In *Making Face, Making Soul = Haciendo Caras: Creative and Critical Perspectives by Women of Color,* edited by Gloria Anzaldúa, 326–331. San Francisco: Aunt Lute Foundation Book.

Monroy, Douglas. 1990. "They Didn't Call Them 'Padre' for Nothing: Patriarchy in Hispanic California." In *Between Borders: Essays on Mexicana/Chicana History,* edited by Adelaida del Castillo. Encino, Calif.: Floricanto Press.

Moore, Joan. 1978. *Homeboys: Gangs, Drugs, and Prison in the Barrios of Los Angeles.* Philadelphia: Temple University Press.

———. 1990. "Hispanic/Latino: Imposed Label or Real Identity?" *Latino Studies Journal* 1, no. 2 (May): 33–47.

———. 1991. *Going Down to the Barrio: Homeboys and Homegirls in Change.* Philadelphia: Temple University Press.

———. 1994. "The Chola Life Course: Chicana Heroin Users and the Barrio Gang." *International Journal of Addictions* 29, no. 9: 1115–1126.

Moore, Joan, and John Hagedorn. 2001. "Female Gangs: A Focus on Research." March. Washington, D.C.: U.S. Department of Justice, Office of Justice Programs, Office of Juvenile Justice and Delinquency Prevention. http://www.ncjrs.org/pdffiles1/gangs.

Moore, Joan, and Raquel Pinderhughes, editors. 1993. *In the Barrios: Latinos and the Underclass Debate.* New York: Russell Sage Publication.

Moore, Joan, and James Diego Vigil. 1987. "Chicano Gangs: Group Norms and Individual Factors Related to Adult Criminality." *Aztlán* 18, no. 2 (fall): 27–44.

———. 1993. "Barrios in Transition." In *In the Barrios: Latinos and the Underclass Debate,* edited by Joan Moore and Raquel Pinderhughes, 27–50. New York: Russell Sage Publication.

Moore, Joan, James Diego Vigil, and Robert Garcia. 1983. "Residence and Territoriality in Chicano Gangs." *Social Problems* 31, no. 2 (December): 182–194.

Moore, Rachel. 1994. "Marketing Alterity." In *Visualizing Theory: Selected Essay from V.A.R.,* edited by Lucien Taylor. New York: Routledge.

Mujeres en Marcha. 1983. *Chicanas in the 80s: Unsettled Issues.* Proceedings of the National Association for Chicano Studies 11th annual conference, Tempe, Arizona, 1982. Berkeley: University of California, Chicano Studies Library Publication Unit.

Mulvey, Laura. 1989. *Visual and Other Pleasures.* Bloomington: Indiana University Press.

Muñoz, Carlos Jr. 1989. *Youth, Identity, Power: The Chicano Movement.* New York: Verso.

Murray, Yxta Maya. 1997. *Locas.* New York: Grove Press.

Nájera-Ramírez, Olga, 1993. "Engendering Nationalism: Identity, Discourse, and the Mexican Charro." Working Paper Series, no. 3. Chicano Latino Research Center, University of California at Santa Cruz.

———. "Personal Encounters: Performance and Positionality in Ethnographic Practice." Forthcoming.

Narayan, Kirin. 1993. "How Native Is a 'Native' Anthropologist?" *American Anthropologist* 95, no. 3 (September): 19–34.

Nathanson, Constance A. 1991. *Dangerous Passage: The Social Control of Sexuality in Women's Adolescence.* Health, Society, and Policy Series. Philadelphia: Temple University Press.

Negt, Oskar, and Alexander Kluge. 1993. *Public Sphere and Experience: Toward an Analysis of the Bourgeois and Proletarian Public Sphere,* with foreword by Miriam Hansen and translated by Peter Labanyi and Jamie Owen Daniel. Minneapolis: University of Minnesota Press.

Newcomb, Horace. 1988. "Critical Response." *Critical Studies in Mass Communication* 242 (September): 34–50.

Nicols, Bill. 1994. "The Ethnographer's Tale." In *Visualizing Theory,* edited by Lucien Taylor, 60–83. New York: Routledge.

Nutini, Hugo G. 1984. *Ritual Kinship: Ideological and Structural Integration of the Compadrazgo System in Rural Tlaxcala.* Vol. 2. Princeton, N.J.: Princeton University Press.

Nutini, Hugo G., and Betty Bell. 1980. *Ritual Kinship: The Structure and Historical Development of the Compadrazgo System in Rural Tlaxcala.* Vol. 1. Princeton, N.J.: Princeton University Press.

Nutini, Hugo G., Pedro Carrasco, and James M. Taggart, editors. 1976. *Essays on Mexican Kinship.* Pittsburgh, Pa.: University of Pittsburgh Press.

Oakland Crack Task Force (OCTF). 1994. *Umoja Project. After School Enrichment Program Proposal: Video Project for Public Service Announcements on Community Cable Television.* Manuscript. Narcotics Education League (NEL) Centro de Juventud, Oakland, Calif.

Oden, Robert Stanley. 1999. "Power Shift: A Sociological Study of the Political Incorporation of People of Color in Oakland, California, 1966–1996." Ph.D. diss., University of California at Santa Cruz.

Ortner, Sherry B. 1996. *Making Gender: The Politics and Erotics of Culture.* Boston: Beacon Press.

Ortner, Sherry B., and Harriet Whitehead, editors. 1981. *Sexual Meanings, the Cultural Construction of Gender and Sexuality.* Cambridge and New York: Cambridge University Press.

Paine, Robert. 1974. "An Exploratory Analysis in 'Middle Class' Culture." In *The Compact: Selected Dimensions of Friendship,* edited by E. Leyton. Newfoundland Social and Economic Papers, no. 3. St. John's, Newfoundland: Memorial University of Newfoundland, Institute of Social and Economic Research.

Panourgiá, Neni. 1995. *Fragments of Death, Fables of Identity: An Athenian Anthropology.* Madison: University of Wisconsin Press.

Paredes, Américo. 1977. "On Ethnographic Work Among Minority Groups: A Folklorist's Perspective." *New Scholar* 6, no. 1/2: 1–32.

Parker, H. Jane. 1992. "Engendering Identity(s) in a Rural Arkansas Ozark Community." *Anthropological Quarterly* 65, no. 3 (July): 148–155.

Paz, Octavio. 1960. *The Labyrinth of Solitude and Other Writings,* translated by Lysander Kemp, Yara Milos, and Rachel Phillips Belash. New York: Grove Press, 1985.

Pérez, Domino Renee. 2002. "Caminando con La Llorona: Traditional and Contemporary Narratives." In *Chicana Traditions: Continuity and Change,* edited by Norma E. Cantú and Olga Nájera-Ramírez. Chicago: University of Illinois Press.

Pérez, Emma. 1999. *The Decolonial Imaginary: Writing Chicanas into History.* Bloomington: Indiana University Press.

Pinney, Chris. 1992. "The Parallel Histories of Anthropology and Photography: Or the Impossibility of Photography." In *Anthropology and Photography, 1860–1920,* edited by E. Edwards, 35–55. New Haven, Conn.: Yale University Press.

Piven, Frances Fox, and Richard A. Cloward. 1982. *The New Class War: Reagan's Attack on the Welfare State and Its Consequences.* New York: Pantheon Books.

Plascencia, Luis F. B. 1983. "Lowriding in the Southwest: Cultural Symbols in the Mexican Community." In *History, Culture and Society: Chicano Studies in the 1980s,* edited by Mario T. Garcia et al. Ypsilanti, Mich.: Bilingual Review.

Pressman, Jeffrey L. 1975. *Federal Programs and City Politics: The Dynamics of the Aid Process in Oakland.* Berkeley: University of California Press.

Pressman, Jeffrey L., and Aaron Wildavsky. 1973. *Implementation: How Great Expectations in Washington Are Dashed in Oakland; Or, Why It's Amazing That Federal Programs Work at All, This Being a Saga of the Economic Development Administration as Told by Two Sympathetic Observers Who Seek to Build Morals on a Foundation of Ruined Hopes.* 3d ed. Berkeley: University of California Press, 1984.

Quintana, Alvina. 1996. *Home Girls: Chicana Literary Voices.* Philadelphia: Temple University Press.

Rabiger, Michael. 1987. *Directing the Documentary.* Boston: Focal Press.

Rabinow, Paul, editor. 1984. *Foucault Reader.* New York: Pantheon Books.

Radway, Janice. 1984. *Reading the Romance: Women, Patriarchy, and Popular Literature.* Chapel Hill: University of North Carolina Press.

Reiman, Richard A. 1992. *The New Deal and American Youth: Ideas and Ideals in a Depression Decade.* Athens: University of Georgia Press.

Reinharz, Shulamit. 1983. "Experiential Analysis: A Contribution to Feminist Research." In *Theories of Women's Studies,* edited by Gloria Bowles and Renate Duelli Klein, 162–191. Boston: Routledge and Kegan Paul.

———. 1993. "Neglected Voices and Excessive Demands in Feminist Research." *Qualitative Sociology* 16, no. 1: 69–76.

Rich, Adrienne. 1986. *Blood, Bread, and Poetry: Selected Prose 1979–1985.* New York: Norton.

Rodriguez, Luis J. 1993. *Always Running/La Vida Loca: Gang Days in L.A.* Willimantic, Conn.: Curbstone Press.

Rojas, James Thomas. 1995. "The Latino Landscape of East Los Angeles." *NACLA Report on the Americas* 28, no. 4 (January–February): 32–34.

Rollwagen, Jack R., editor. 1988. *Anthropological Filmmaking: Anthropological Perspectives on the Production of Film and Video for General Public Audiences.* Philadelphia: Harwood Academic Publishers.

Rosaldo, Renato. 1989. *Culture and Truth: The Remaking of Social Analysis.* Boston: Beacon Press.

Rose, Tricia. 1994. *Black Noise: Rap Music and Black Culture in Contemporary America.* Hanover, N.H.: Wesleyan University Press.

Rosen, Lawrence. 1984. *Bargaining For Reality: The Construction of Social Relations in a Muslim Community.* Chicago: University of Chicago Press.

Rosenthal, Alan, editor. 1988. *New Challenges for Documentary.* Berkeley: University of California Press.

Ross, William T. 1953. "Social Functions of the Mexican American Godparent System in Tucson." Ph.D. diss.

Rouch, Jean. 1974. "The Camera and Man." In *Principles of Visual Anthropology,* edited by Paul Hockings. 2d ed. New York: Mouton de Gruyter, 1995.

Rubin, Gayle. 1975. "The Traffic in Women: Notes on the 'Political Economy' of Sex." In *Toward an Anthropology of Women,* edited by R. R. Reiter, 157–210. New York: Monthly Review Press.

———. 1996. "The Traffic in Women: Notes on the 'Political Economy' of Sex." In *Feminism and History,* edited by Joan Wallach Scott, 105–151. New York: Oxford University Press.

Ruiz, Vicki L. 1998. *From Out of the Shadows: Mexican Women in Twentieth-Century America.* New York: Oxford University Press.

Ruoff, Jeffrey K. 1998. " 'A Bastard Union of Several Forms:' Style and Narrative in An American Family." In *Documenting the Documentary: Close Readings of Documentary Film and Video,* edited by Barry Keith Grant and Jeannette Sloniowski, 286–301. Detroit: Wayne State University Press.

Said, Edward W. 1979. *Orientalism.* New York: Vintage Books, 1979.

Saldívar-Hull, Sonia. 1990. "Feminism on the Border: From Gender Politics to Geopolitics." In *Criticism in the Borderlands: Studies in Chicano Literature, Culture, and Ideology,* edited by Hector Calderón and José David Saldívar, 203–220. Durham, N.C.: Duke University Press.

Salgado de Snyder, V. Nelly. 1987. "Mexican Immigration: Relationships of Ethnic Loyalty and Social Support to Acculturative Stress and Depressive Symptomology." DSW diss., University of California at Los Angeles.

Sanchez, George J. 1993. *Becoming Mexican American: Ethnicity, Culture, and Identity in Chicano Los Angeles, 1900–1945.* New York: Oxford University Press.

Sanchez-Tranquilino, Marcos, and John Tagg. 1992. "The Pachuco's Flayed Hide." In *Cultural Studies,* edited by Lawrence Grossberg, Cary Nelson, and Paula A. Treichler. New York: Routledge.

Sandoval, Chéla. 1991. "Feminist Theory under Postmodern Conditions: Toward a Theory of Oppositional Consciousness." In *Sub/versions: Feminist Studies, Work in Progress.* University of California, Santa Cruz.

———. 2000. *Methodology of the Oppressed.* Theory out of Bounds series, vol. 18. Minneapolis: University of Minnesota Press.

Sarris, Greg. 1993. *Keeping Slugwoman Alive: A Holistic Approach to American Indian Texts.* Berkeley: University of California Press.

Scott, Gillian. 1998. " 'As a War-horse to the Beat of Drums': Representations of Working-class Femininity in the Women's Co-operative Guild, 1880s to the Second World War." In *Radical Femininity: Women's Self-representation in the Public Sphere,* edited by Eileen Janes Yeo, 196–219. Manchester, England: Manchester University Press.

Scott, James C. 1990. *Domination and the Arts of Resistance: Hidden Transcripts.* New Haven, Conn.: Yale University Press.

Scott, Joan Wallach, editor. 1996. *Feminism and History.* New York: Oxford University Press.

Sedgwick, Eve Kosofsky. 1985. *Between Men: English Literature and Male Homosocial Desire*. New York: Columbia University Press.

Shelden, Randall G., Sharon K. Tracy, and William B. Brown. 1997. *Youth Gangs in America*. Belmont, Calif.: Wadsworth Publishing.

Shuman, Amy. 1986. *Storytelling Rights: The Uses Of Oral and Written Texts by Urban Adolescents*. Cambridge Studies in Oral and Literate Culture. New York: Cambridge University Press.

Siltanen, Janet, and Michelle Stanworth, editors. 1984. *Women and the Public Sphere*. New York: St. Martin's Press.

Sluka, Jeffrey A. 1992. "The Politics of Painting: Political Murals in Northern Ireland." In *The Paths to Domination, Resistance, and Terror*, edited by Carolyn Nordstrom and JoAnn Martin, 190–216. Berkeley: University of California Press.

Smith, Michael Peter. 2001. *Transnational Urbanism: Locating Globalization*. Malden, Mass.: Blackwell Publishers.

Smith Rosenberg, Carroll. 1996. "The Female World of Love and Ritual." In *Feminism and History*, edited by Joan Wallach Scott. New York: Oxford University Press.

Spector, Malcolm, and John I. Kitsuse. 1977. *Constructing Social Problems*. Menlo Park, Calif.: Cummings Publishing.

Spivak, Guyatri Chakravortsy. 1988. "Can the Subaltern Speak?" In *Selected Subaltern Studies*, edited by Ranajit Guha and Guyatri Spivak, 271–313. New York: Oxford University Press.

———. 1990. *The Post-colonial Critic: Interviews, Strategies, Dialogues*, edited by Sarah Harasym. London: Routledge.

Squires, Catherine. 1999. "The Black Public Sphere." Presentation at the Women's Center, University of California at Santa Barbara. May 16.

Stacey, Judith. 1988. "Can There be a Feminist Ethnography?" *Women's Studies International Quarterly Forum* 11, no. 1: 21–27.

Stack, Carol B. 1975. *All Our Kin: Strategies for Survival in a Black Community*. New York: Harper Paperback.

Starling, Jay D. 1986. *Municipal Coping Strategies: "As Soon as the Dust Settles."* Organization Studies and Decision-Making Series. Beverly Hills: Sage Publications.

Steward, Samuel M. 1990. *Bad Boys and Tough Tattoos: A Social History of the Tattoo with Gangs, Sailors, and Street Corner Punks, 1950–1965*. New York: Harrington Park Press.

Strathern, Marilyn. 1987. "An Awkward Relationship: The Case of Feminism and Anthropology." *Signs* 12, no. 2: 276–292.

———, editor. 1995. *Shifting Contexts: Transformations in Anthropological Knowledge*. New York: Routledge.

Tate, Will D. 1976. *The New Black Urban Elites*. San Francisco: R and E Research Associates.

Taylor, Carl S. 1993. *Girls, Gangs, Women, and Drugs*. East Lansing: Michigan State University Press.

Taylor, Lucien, editor. 1994. *Visualizing Theory: Selected Essays from V.A.R.* New York: Routledge.

Thompson, E. P. 1960. "The Long Revolution." *New Left Review* nos. 9 and 10.

Thornton Dill, Bonnie. 1994. "Fictive Kin, Paper Sons, and Compadrazgo: Women of Color and the Struggle for Family Survival." In *Women of Color in U.S. Society,* edited by Maxine Baca-Zinn and Bonnie Thornton Dill, 149–170. Philadelphia: Temple University Press.

———. 1996. "The Dialectics of Black Womanhood." *Feminism and History,* edited by Joan Wallach Scott, 34–47. New York: Oxford University Press.

Thrasher, Frederic M. 1927. *The Gang: A Study of 1,313 Gangs in Chicago.* Chicago: University of Chicago Press.

Trin, T. Minh-Ha. 1989. *Woman, Native, Other: Writing Post-coloniality and Feminism.* Bloomington: Indiana University Press.

Tsing, Ana Lowenhaupt. 1993. *In the Realm of the Diamond Queen: Marginality in an Out-of-the-Way Place.* Princeton, N.J.: Princeton University Press.

U.S. Bureau of the Census. 1974. *Low-income Neighborhoods in Large Cities, 1970: San Francisco and Oakland, California.* Series 1970 Census of Population Supplementary Report PC(S1)–101. Prepared by Donald G. Fowles, Poverty Statistics Program, Population Division. Washington, D.C.

Valenzuela, Angela. 1999. *Subtractive Schooling: U.S.–Mexican Youth and the Politics of Caring.* Albany: State University of New York Press.

Van Maanen, John. 1988. *Tales of the Field: On Writing Ethnography.* Chicago: University of Chicago Press.

Venkatesh, Sudhir Alladi. 1998. "Gender and Outlaw Capitalism: A Historical Account of the Black Sisters United 'Girl Gang.'" *Signs* 23, no. 3 (spring): 683–709.

Vigil, James Diego. 1983. "Chicano Gangs: One Response to Mexican Urban Adaptation in the Los Angeles Area." *Urban Anthropology* 12, no. 6 (spring): 45–75.

———. 1988. *Barrio Gangs: Street Life and Identity in Southern California.* Austin: University of Texas Press.

Visweswaran, Kamala. 1994. *Fictions of Feminist Ethnography.* Minneapolis: University of Minnesota Press.

Way, Niobe. 1997. "Using Feminist Research Methods to Understand the Friendships of Adolescent Boys." *Journal of Social Issues* 53, no. 4 (winter): 703–724. http://search.epnet.com/direct.asp?an=825809&db=aph

Weintraub, Jeff. 1997. "The Theory and Politics of the Public/Private Distinction." In *Public And Private In Thought And Practice: Perspectives On A Grand Dichotomy,* edited by Jeff Weintraub and Krishan Kumar. Chicago: University of Chicago Press.

Wellman, David. 1994. "Constituting Ethnographic Authority: The Work Process of Field Research, an Ethnographic Account." *Cultural Studies* 8, no. 3 (October): 569–583.

Whatley, Marianne H. 1994. "Keeping Adolescents in the Picture: Construction of Adolescent Sexuality in Textbook Images and Popular Films." In *Sexual Cultures and the Construction of Adolescent Identities,* edited by Janice M. Irvine, 183–205. Philadelphia: Temple University Press.

Wheatley, Elizabeth. 1994. "How Can We Engender Ethnography with a Feminist Imagination? A Rejoinder to Judith Stacey." *Women's Studies International Quarterly Forum* 17, no. 4: 403–423.

Whitaker, Mark P. 1996. "Ethnography as Learning: A Wittgensteinian Approach to Writing Ethnographic Accounts." *Anthropological Quarterly* 69, no. 1 (January): 1–13.

Whitney, Helen. 1980. "Youth Terror: The View from Behind the Gun." In *The Documentary Conscience: A Casebook in Film Making*, edited by Alan Rosenthal, 193–201. Berkeley: University of California Press.

Whyte, W. F. 1955. *Street Corner Society*. Chicago: Chicago University Press.

Williams, Raymond. 1977. *Marxism and Literature*. New York: Oxford University Press.

Willis, Paul. 1977. *Learning to Labor: How Working Class Kids Get Working Class Jobs*. New York: Columbia University Press, Morning Side, 1981.

Wilson, William Julius. 1987. *The Truly Disadvantaged: The Inner City, the Underclass, and Public Policy*. Chicago: University of Chicago Press.

Wolf, Diane L., editor. 1996. *Feminist Dilemmas in Fieldwork*. Boulder, Colo.: Westview Press.

Worth, Sol. 1981. *Studying Visual Communication*, edited by Larry Gross. Philadelphia: University of Pennsylvania Press.

Worth, Sol, and John Adair. 1975. *Through Navajo Eyes: An Exploration in Film Communication and Anthropology*. Bloomington: Indiana University Press.

Yablonsky, Lewis. 1962. *The Violent Gang*. New York: Macmillan.

Ybarra-Frausto, Tomás. 1989. "Rasquachismo: A Chicano Sensibility." In *Chicano Art: Resistance and Affirmation, 1965–1985*, edited by Richard Griswold del Castillo, Teresa McKenna, and Yvonne Yarbro-Bejarano. Los Angeles: Regents of University of California.

Yeo, Eileen Janes, editor. 1998. *Radical Femininity: Women's Self-representation in the Public Sphere*. Manchester, England: Manchester University Press.

Younis, Mona. 1998. "Fruitvale and San Antonio." *Cityscape, A Journal of Policy Development and Research* 4, no. 2: 221–244. U.S. Department of Housing and Urban Development, Office of Policy Development and Research Publication. http://www.huduser.org/periodicOakland.

Yúdice, George. 1993. "For a Practical Aesthetics." In *The Phantom Public Sphere*, edited by Bruce Robbins. Minneapolis: University of Minnesota Press.

Zavella, Patricia. 1991. "Mujeres in Factories: Race and Class Perspectives on Women, Work, and Family." In *Gender at the Crossroads of Knowledge: Feminist Anthropology in the Postmodern Era*, edited by Micaela di Leonardo, 312–336. Berkeley: University of California Press.

———. 1994. "Feminist Insider Dilemmas: Constructing Ethnic Identity with Chicana Informants." In *Feminist Dilemmas in Fieldwork*, edited by Diane Wolf. Boulder, Colo.: Westview Press.

Photography

Boyd, Anne. 1996. Photos of girls displaying tattoos at Narcotics Education League Centro de Juventud in Oakland, California.

Quiroga, Bibi, Beatriz Martínez, and Claudia Heredia. 1994. "Our Lives." Slide presentation at the National Association for Chicano/Chicana Studies California FOCO regional conference, University of California at Santa Cruz, April.

Sunshine, Alice. 2002. Photos of Fruitvale streets in Oakland, Calif.

Videography

It's a Homie Thang! 1994. Videotape. Narcotics Education League Centro de Juventud. Oakland Crack Task Force, Umoja Project After School Enrichment Program.

INDEX